Peasants,
Politics, and
Revolution

Joel S. Migdal

PEASANTS, POLITICS, AND REVOLUTION

Pressures toward Political
and Social Change in
the Third World

PRINCETON UNIVERSITY PRESS

LCC 74-2972
ISBN 0-691-02177-5 (paperback edn.)
ISBN 0-691-07567-0 (hardcover edn.)

Printed in the United States of America
First PRINCETON PAPERBACK Printing, 1977

To my parents, Benjamin *and* Rebecca Migdal

CONTENTS

ACKNOWLEDGMENTS

Far too many people had a hand in the ideas presented in this book for me to acknowledge them all adequately. Most likely, I am not even aware of the source of many of the concepts. I have attempted in the footnotes to show to where I turned when dealing with particular aspects of the problem. However, I would like to single out several people.

Professor Samuel P. Huntington gave freely of his time from the inception of this project through its completion. I want to thank him for his unfailing support, as well as his useful comments. I am also grateful to Samuel L. Popkin who made incisive criticisms throughout. My interest in the plight of peasants was in part sparked by his commitment to the subject. Robert I. Rhodes gave me a long list of useful comments which I have used throughout.

Also, I would like to express my appreciation to John Duncan Powell, Frances R. Hill, Jeffrey Race, Jorge Dominguez, Shimshon Zelniker, Everett E. Hagen, Penina M. Glazer, Myron Glazer, and Barbara Kreiger. They all read earlier versions of various parts of the book and gave useful (and used) criticisms. The members of the Ford Foundation office in New Delhi helped make my stay in India, and particularly in Uttar Pradesh, enjoyable and productive. I particularly want to thank Dr. Johnson and Mr. Shri Nath Singh of the Agricultural Division.

A special "thank you" goes to my wife Marcy. She was

chief critic, interpreter, interviewer of peasant women, traveling companion, and editorial associate. Finally, I have dedicated this work to my parents, who lit in me the spark of the quest for knowledge and wisdom.

J. S. M.

Peasants,
Politics, and
Revolution

CHAPTER I

Introduction: Why Peasants Change

OXEN lie listlessly in the dung and mud, and tall stalks of corn stand in the fields of Coyotopec, probably much as they grew years before. Only the occasional passing of a car on the highway dissecting the village or a radio blaring in the distance makes the bustle of far-off Mexico City seem real. The state of Oaxaca has not shared in much of the phenomenal economic growth that Mexico City and northwestern Mexico have undergone; the contrast is stark, and life in a Oaxacan village seems, on the surface, relatively undisturbed from that of centuries past.

Coyotopec never was an entirely isolated, self-sufficient village. It has long been involved in an intricate peasant marketing system that has had its focus in the nearby capital city of Oaxaca, to which, on Saturdays, the characteristic black pottery of the village has been brought, along with any corn and garden vegetables left over after subsistence needs have been met. And with the small cash earnings, minor purchases of goods from other villages or of manufactured products have been made. Some Coyotopec peasants have also traveled to other less important markets to sell or buy goods on other days of the week. The women have been the merchants, and it has been they who have set up the blanket with the family-produced goods to be sold. To the increasing number of tourists who buy at the famous Saturday market, the world of the

3

Oaxacan peasant seems far removed from the twentieth century. Yet it is these very tourists who have ensured a certain limited degree of prosperity for the artisans of the village by buying their black pottery for decorative purposes at a time when imported manufactured goods are replacing pottery for daily use in the area.

Peasant farmers in Coyotopec feel the changes of the century. The electric light bulb hanging in their one-room houses does not always bring light because of the difficulty of keeping up with the costs, but it is as important a part of the house as the altar on the wall or the rolled-up straw mats used for sleeping. Large containers of purified water also demand an extra outlay of cash, but they have become a recognized necessity of life.

Although their farming methods do not differ significantly from those of their forefathers, Coyotopec's peasants are very much aware of new methods being used. Tractors are not a part of their personal experience; yet, they know that *campesinos* (peasants) in the North are able to increase their yields significantly with the machines from the United States. No longer do Coyotopec's peasants talk of the future as if it will bring an indefinite extension of the past. Change has become the norm.

Peasant farmers in Coyotopec are deeply concerned with the river that cuts through the village fields. At most times it is nothing more than a lazy stream which winds through the *milpa*, but during the rainy season it spills over its banks and rages downstream. Flooding can damage some of the nearby crops. More importantly when the river swells to unusual dimensions, those with fields on the other side cannot cross it to tend their crops. If such conditions last long enough, as they did prior to the previous harvest, much of the corn is ruined.

The peasants of Coyotopec have long depended upon the movements of the river. Yet they no longer view this situation

4

as unalterable. They now believe that man can overcome the limitations of his physical environment. Man-made improvements can do away with the uncertainties of flooding. Their idea is simple: to build a footbridge over the river. They know, however, that such an undertaking is beyond the financial capabilities and engineering skills of them and their neighbors. In 1970, after much discussion, the peasants with fields across the river organized and selected a spokesman. He went to the city of Oaxaca and there submitted an official request to the government for the public construction of a footbridge. To date, all requests have resulted only in negative responses from the government.

Coyotopec's residents are certainly not the only peasants in recent years who have engaged in new kinds of political action in attempts to mold their environment. Peasants in many parts of the third world[1] have begun to join organizations and political parties and to participate in rallies and demonstrations. Implicit in these acts is the goal of somehow changing their physical and social environment through politics, through their efforts, and through the efforts of others. No longer do most peasants' political sights stop at the village border or at the local marketing town or at the doorstep of the local landlords. Peasants are increasingly participating in a new political world. The expansion of political ties outside the village has come in the wake of a tremendous increase in economic relations with outsiders. Paul Stirling describes some of these changes for two Turkish villages.

> . . . In general, the main change is the multiplication, for most adult villagers, of a new set of more or less impersonal social relations with employers, fellow-workers, officials, and buyers and sellers, different for each individual, all leading out of the village into national society. A gen-

---

[1] "Third world" is used in this study as a descriptive term to denote the countries of Latin America, Africa, and Asia, excluding the Soviet Union and Japan.

5

eration ago, such external relations were the prerogative of village leaders, and even for them were far fewer and less impersonal.[2]

These political and social changes in peasant life have occurred where Chinese or Bengali or Spanish is spoken; they have occurred in temperate areas and tropical areas; they have occurred among Buddhists and Christians and Muslims; they have occurred among Ceylon's Sinhalese and Mexico's Zapotec Indians. The subject of this book is when, why, and how peasants in Asia and Latin America have sought links to a new world whose boundaries are far wider than those of the village's bamboo hedge.

The question of under which conditions peasants change from a subsistence-oriented, village-based life to one involving sustained participation in outside institutions is crucial to the study of modernization.[3] Various models have been developed by social scientists to explore this question. Yet there is a common core to much of this literature: exposure to the modern—what we shall call "culture contact"[4]—leads people

[2] *Turkish Village* (London: Weidenfeld and Nicholson, 1965), p. 82.

[3] There is not a total consensus on the meaning of modernization. For a general and widely accepted definition of modernization, we can use that of David E. Apter, which refers to the rapid increase of roles in a society which are functionally linked in a setting marked by rational, hierarchical organizations (*The Politics of Modernization* [Chicago: University of Chicago Press, 1965], p. v). Generally, the term suffers from lack of precision, and, as we shall see later in this chapter, is often indiscriminately used to include processes such as social mobilization. For that reason, the remaining chapters will use other, more precise terms to describe processes of change.

[4] Culture contact has long been in use as a term in anthropology and, according to the author who is using it, has taken on various connotations. The emphasis here will be on the contact between traditional, village-based patterns and those patterns associated with more urban styles. More specifically, we are talking of the contact by traditional villages with the patterns and values characteristic of modern societies. For a brief discussion on the various uses of the term, see Raphael Patai, "On Culture Contact and Its Working in

to abandon their old patterns and adopt these modern ways. Contact between the old and the new leads to the triumph of the new patterns. In recent years there has arisen a growing body of literature pointing to weaknesses in this explanation, but there has not yet been developed an inclusive explanation which overcomes these weaknesses.

This book offers a theoretical alternative to the question of why peasants abandon their old patterns. Before outlining this theoretical alternative, let us first examine an explanation of culture contact and show some of the difficulties in analysis which it raises. This chapter argues that although culture contact may be a necessary condition for change, it is far from sufficient.

CULTURE CONTACT: AN EXPLANATION

The explanation or assumption that exposure and contact are the causes of change has three components: (1) The benefits of the modern far outweigh the benefits of the traditional.[5] (2) The individual is free from severe institutional restraints which would prevent his making an unimpeded decision. (3) Those individuals who select the new are rational and are optimizers, and those individuals who do not accept the modern fail to do so because of "wrong" or nonrational values. These components can be traced back to the early part of the century in social science literature, particularly in anthropology.[6] In 1934, Robert Redfield wrote that local differences in

---

Modern Palestine," *American Anthropologist*, n.s. 49 (October 1947), no. 67 in the Memoir Series of the American Anthropological Association.

[5] A. Irving Hallowell felt that acculturation is basically a learning process and that European culture has spread so rapidly because the rewards outweigh the punishments for the individual. "Sociopsychological Aspects of Acculturation," in *The Science of Man in the World Crises*, ed. Ralph Linton (New York: Columbia University Press, 1945), pp. 171-200.

[6] Malinowski was the preeminent scholar associated with this view in respect to tribal peoples. He wrote that change in Africa is

Yucatan villages can be attributed to differences in degree of exposure to "civilization"—schools, roads, and economic exploitation.[7] Almost thirty years after the writing of Redfield and Villa's study of Chan Kom, George M. Foster restated this theme, suggesting that the degree of contact with urban centers is the greatest determinant of change among peasants.[8]

Other branches of social science have subsequently adopted the culture contact mode of analysis. In his study of traditional society, the sociologist Daniel Lerner explicated the most complete and sophisticated model of culture contact. He attempted to go beyond the mere assertion that contact leads to change, by focusing on *why* such change occurs. His model begins with the person who accepts change and becomes modernized, whom he calls the mobile personality. Such a person is one who has a high capacity for identification with new aspects of his environment.[9] The question Lerner poses is how a society is able to produce many mobile personalities, the key ingredients in a modern society.[10]

Lerner states that the answer lies in an expansion of human communication. First, this expansion of communication came through an increase in travel, but the media now obviate the need for the physical displacement associated with travel. The media accent "the psychic displacement of vicarious ex-

"the result of an impact of a higher, active culture upon a simpler, more passive one." B. Malinowski, *The Dynamics of Culture Change: An Inquiry into Race Relations in Africa* (New Haven: Yale University Press, 1945), p. 15.

[7] Robert Redfield and Alfonso Villa Rojas, *Chan Kom: A Maya Village*, Phoenix Books (Chicago: University of Chicago Press, 1962), p. IX.

[8] *Traditional Cultures: and the Impact of Technological Change* (New York: Harper, 1962), pp. 25, 30. Foster writes, "The greater the range of novelty to which people are exposed, the greater the likelihood that they will adopt new forms. Contact between societies is the single greatest determinate of culture change" (p. 25).

[9] Daniel Lerner, *The Passing of Traditional Society: Modernizing the Middle East* (New York: The Free Press, 1958), p. 49.

[10] *Ibid.*, p. 50.

perience" and are, in fact, even better than travel, for exposure to them gives the person a more ordered sense of the whole.[11] After reaching a certain threshold of urbanization, literacy, mass media, and institutions of participation, a society can provide large numbers of people in its traditional sector with exposure and contact with the new, thus converting them into mobile personalities.

This assumption that increased contact with and exposure to new patterns will lead not only to increased knowledge but also to new behavior is found in other theories as well. In political science, for example, F. Lamond Tullis has used Frank Young's information-processing theory to build a paradigm of political and social change in Peru.[12] Tullis states that there is a direct link between the capacity of individuals to process complex information and modernization. A peasant who goes regularly to the city, he claims, probably would develop a higher "information-processing capacity" and would more quickly adopt modern ways than one who stays home.

The emphasis on culture contact as the major cause of individual and social change is probably most obvious in the large and growing body of "diffusion of innovation" literature.[13] The underlying ingredients of modernization in this literature do not differ significantly from those of Lerner's model. Communication is the key element, and the process of change is basically one without severe discontinuities, as the term "diffusion" itself connotes: the more that differing sectors come into contact with one another, the more individuals will gain the attributes associated with change.

In short, change is most often seen in terms of incentives for the *individual* to adopt the new over the old. Culture con-

[11] *Ibid.*, p. 53.

[12] *Lord and Peasant in Peru: A Paradigm of Political and Social Change* (Cambridge, Mass.: Harvard University Press, 1970), esp. ch. 1.

[13] See for example, Everett M. Rogers, *Modernization Among Peasants: The Impact of Communication* (New York: Holt, Rinehart, 1969), p. 292.

tact, either personally or through media exposure, presents the individual with the ability, the empathy, the information-processing capacity, or whatever to relate personally to the alternative life-styles. He then can weigh his present patterns and commitments against the modern, and there is little doubt among most authors that he will accept the modern. The barriers to change are seen as internal to the individual—his personal orientation—and little note is given to the strength of the traditional, parochial institutions to affect radically the individual's choice.

DIFFICULTIES IN THE CONCEPT OF CULTURE CONTACT

Two interesting monographs are representative of numerous documented cases where there has been very high cultural contact but little abandonment of the old patterns. In the Peruvian village of Hualcan, numerous men left the village each year for temporary work outside. A large proportion of these men went to work in modern agricultural-industrial plantations on the coast of Peru, far from their Andean village. These plantations presented a world culturally distinct to these men, and some worked there for up to two months at a time. Yet, according to William W. Stein, these contacts were "acculturationally irrelevant." This is not to say that no changes in village life resulted from the plantation work. Men returned with impressive sums of cash which affected the social stratification of Hualcan. Yet, interestingly, the men did not adopt the patterns they encountered. Their clothes changed little. Their money was invested in land and fiestas, the long-accepted way to dispose of surplus.[14]

Much the same set of events occurred among the men of

[14] William W. Stein, *Hualcan: Life in the Highlands of Peru* (Ithaca, N.Y.: Cornell University Press, 1961). Also his "Outside Contact and Cultural Stability in a Peruvian Highland Village," in *Cultural Stability and Cultural Change*, ed. Verne F. Ray, Proceedings of the 1957 Annual Spring Meeting of the American Ethnological Society (Seattle: American Ethnological Society, 1957), pp. 15-16.

Buarij, Lebanon. There, almost all the adult males left the mountainous village during the slack winter season to work elsewhere. Many of their jobs put them into contact with very different and very modern sectors in Lebanon. Although, once again, changes in village life occurred, the striking factor Anne H. Fuller discovered was the stability of attitudes, institutions, and behavior despite these early forays.[15]

Adherents of the culture-contact explanation have often attributed such lack of change in specific instances to the people's particular values or ethos.[16] Serious doubts must be raised about such undifferentiated concepts. For example, very near the Peruvian village of Hualcan is another Indian village called Recuayhuanca. There, too, peasants left the village during the off-season to take jobs on agricultural-industrial plantations on the coast. The results of their experience were much different from those of Hualcan's peasants, however. The young people adopted Western dress, and education went up in value. Some villagers followed their work on the plantations with temporary jobs in Lima, and almost all joined labor unions between 1945 and 1948. Many opted for permanent migration from the village, and others, while not yet able to migrate, held the goal of eventually living in Lima.[17] If values or ethos alone explain why some reject change and others accept it, how do we account for peasants in two such similar villages (both were freeholding[18] villages,

[15] *Buarij: Portrait of a Lebanese Muslim Village* (Cambridge, Mass.: Harvard University Press, 1961), p. 97.

[16] See, for example, Edward C. Banfield, *The Moral Basis of a Backward Society* (New York: The Free Press, 1958).

[17] Joan Snyder, "The Changing Context of an Andean Community," in *Cultural Stability and Cultural Change*, ed. Ray, pp. 20-29.

[18] The term "freeholding" is used throughout this study. It refers to those villages with no lords standing directly over the peasants limiting their outside contacts. Freeholding villages could consist totally of small farmers on private or communal lands but also could be villages in which only a portion had control of or access to cultivable land. In any case, however, no one person or several people in a freeholding village had the extensive control of a lord who could enforce restricted outside relations. This is not to say that

as opposed to the nearby *hacienda* of Vicos) who reacted so differently to culture contact? Can we assume that value structures are so different for the two?

A further problem in regard to the reliance on the culture-contact explanation stems from the numerous cases in which individuals change some patterns and commitments and not others.[19] Here, too, a rather extensive literature is growing which documents such cases of syncretic change and points to the weakness of the culture-contact explanation.[20] Most notably, C. S. Whitaker has challenged the underlying hypothesis of today's student of modernization: that ultimately all non-Western peoples will either accept or reject, more or less wholesale, the kind of institutions yielded by change in the West.[21]

An example of partial, or what Whitaker calls "dysrhythmic" change is found in the Jaunpur district of Uttar Pradesh, India, where university-educated sons still have their marriages arranged by their parents, and many return to live in the joint household. Others commute to the city to work as doctors or government clerks while their wives and children remain in the village and the joint household. In Latin America, social scientists have also noted the persistence of village-

---

power was distributed completely equally in these villages, for there were occupational and land pattern differentiations which gave some peasants more power than others.

[19] Gusfield, Whitaker, and others have begun to argue that modernity and traditionalism are not mutually exclusive. But they have not provided an alternative theory to explain why men accept some changes and not others. See Joseph R. Gusfield, "Tradition and Modernity: Misplaced Polarities in the Study of Social Change," *American Journal of Sociology* 72 (January 1967), 351-362; and C. S. Whitaker, "A Dysrhythmic Process of Political Change," *World Politics* 19 (January 1967), 198-201.

[20] Whitaker, cites Bendix, Black, Deutsch, Eisenstadt, Hoselitz, La Palombara, W. Moore, Pye, Sanger, and Ward and Rustow. Malinowski himself recognized the problem of syncretic change: "Can we analyze more fully the problem why certain elements survive and others disappear . . . ?" *The Dynamics of Culture Change*, p. 39.

[21] "A Dysrhythmic Process of Political Change," p. 191.

based patterns of behavior, both socially and politically, among people who have left the village to live in *barrios* surrounding the city.

Are these people innovators? Do they or do they not have empathy? Do they have high information-processing capacity or not? Why have they rejected many of the modern patterns they have witnessed? The questions become even sharper when we consider those (in India I interviewed several) who travel to Europe or the United States to study, yet maintain many of their old patterns and commitments.

Finally, culture contact as an explanation of change fails to take account of the differentiation between two distinct concepts in social science, social mobilization and modernization. Social mobilization is the breaking down of old social, economic, and psychological commitments;[22] modernization is the actual adoption of new commitments and patterns, resulting in use of new levels of technology and in structural differentiation. Given the assumption that culture contact causes change, it is easy to see why this merging of the two concepts should occur, for why abandon the old (social mobilization) if not simultaneously to adopt the new?

If one relies on the culture-contact explanation, he faces a difficulty in understanding the numerous cases in which there has been a process of abandonment of traditional patterns and commitments (social mobilization), but this has not *necessarily* led to the adoption of the ways and processes associated with modernization.[23] S. N. Eisenstadt has spoken of the "post-traditional" society, one in which long-held prac-

[22] Karl Deutsch, "Social Mobilization and Political Development," *American Political Science Review* 55 (September 1961), 493-514.

[23] Even Deutsch's measures of social mobilization, for example, highlight not only the erosion and breakdown of the old but such changes as urbanization, growth of the nonagricultural sector, increases in literacy, and growth in GNP, all of which reflect an adoption, by large numbers, of new patterns associated with modernization. In such cases, it is difficult to differentiate social mobilization from modernization itself. The two seem to be so closely tied that the existence of one presupposes the existence of the other.

tices and beliefs are discarded, but one in which new roles are not characterized by specificity in a setting marked by rational hierarchical organization nor by adoption of new levels of technology. The growth of certain millenarian movements may be an example of such social mobilization without modernization.[24]

OUTLINE OF AN ALTERNATIVE THEORETICAL EXPLANATION

Many of the difficulties of the culture-contact explanation stem from the static, ahistorical nature of much of current social science. Often the methodological base of studies is a "snapshot" of the constellations of structures and of the individual's values and beliefs at a particular moment. The resultant works fail to show that the village historically has been the focal point for a dynamic tension of forces. Just as there have been forces throughout history attracting particular peasants to the world and ways outside the little community, so too have there been opposing forces restraining their movement. Local social institutions in peasant societies have been a conservative factor, placing limits on contacts and interaction outside the village in various historical periods. To comprehend the process of change, one must first understand when and why these conservative (inward-oriented) forces were effective, for they kept individuals from a "free-state" condition in which only their values and beliefs would determine whether they would be attracted to new patterns and processes. Only when one comes to an understanding of the forces operative in the past can one turn to the uniqueness of the

---

[24] "The persistent vitality of groups that are neither traditional nor modern nor transitional poses one of the most stubborn conceptual and practical problems of political development" (Frances R. Hill, "Millenarian Machines in South Vietnam," *Comparative Studies in Society and History* 13 [July 1971], 325). Mrs. Hill goes on to say that tribes, castes, or millenarian movements cannot simply be considered aberrant vestiges.

present era: a period in which the dynamic historical factors led to the triumph of outward-oriented forces (those directed toward participation in institutions outside the village) over the inward-oriented forces.

To understand the situation in which inward-oriented forces have been effective, one must perceive the interplay between village-based behavior and those pressures from the world outside which have been applied by classes above the peasantry. Too often social science has viewed the individual or the community as though existing in a vacuum, divorced from the social classes pressing down. The theory developed here highlights this interplay between the peasant village and its social and political environment. The theory understands village-based behavior and institutions, at least in part, as adaptive responses to the severe pressures from outside.

Peasants have always been subordinate to others in their societies.[25] Whether these others have been local lords or the rulers of powerful centralized states, they have controlled resources essential to peasants' lives. Owing to their relative powerlessness in their societies, peasants have, as much as possible, shunned participation in unstable societal institutions in which they could suffer from the exploitation[26] of those above them on the social ladder. Peasants could never avoid outside contacts entirely, as they were always somewhat involved in and dependent on institutions such as the market. Yet it is striking how unstable local conditions and exploitative institutions precipitated a withdrawal by peasants from as much outside contact as possible.[27] Redfield character-

[25] Eric R. Wolf, *Peasants* (Englewood Cliffs, N.J.: Prentice-Hall, 1966), p. 11.

[26] I use the term "exploitation" much as it is used in Barrington Moore, Jr., *Social Origins of Dictatorship and Democracy: Lord and Peasant in the Making of the Modern World* (Boston: Beacon Press, 1966), pp. 453-483.

[27] See, for example, G. William Skinner, "Chinese Peasants and the Closed Community: An Open and Shut Case," *Comparative Studies in Society and History* 13 (July 1971), pp. 270-281.

ized this phenomenon as keeping the market at arm's length.[28] It is a major assumption in this book that as a result of this fear of dependency on outsiders, local social and political institutions, as we shall see in Part One, developed to satisfy needs and to shield the peasant from these outside forces. Although the historical evidence for such a view is still lacking, the universality of certain types of institutions, given specific conditions peasants faced, lends weight to the perspective of an historical development of these institutions to cope with particular problems.

Economically, withdrawal inward meant that peasants produced as many needs as possible themselves—from tools to food—without becoming dependent on outsiders. Subsistence agriculture was their primary means of livelihood—they produced their own consumption needs, some surplus to trade for such items as kerosene or salt, and a large share for the rents and taxes to the lord or to the state.

The withdrawal inward—the minimization of outside ties, the self-sufficiency of the family, the subsistence orientation— was never accepted by all villagers equally cheerfully. The peasant village historically was a place that harbored suppressed minority feelings.[29] Those peasants who were able to accumulate sufficient resources often wished to use those resources outside the village in order to solidify their high status position or to win prestige from a wider reference group. They felt such resources gave them the wherewithal to operate successfully in the larger economic and status system.

Strong lords saw such aspirations as threatening their power monopoly and applied sanctions against peasants with such ambitions. In villages without strong lords, the peasants

[28] Robert Redfield, *Peasant Society and Culture*, Phoenix Books (Chicago: The University of Chicago Press, 1960), p. 29.

[29] Guy Hunter, *Modernizing Peasant Societies: A Comparative Study in Asia and Africa* (New York: Oxford University Press, 1969), p. 31; also, see Mehmet Beqiraj, *Peasantry in Revolution*, Center for International Studies, Cornell University, Cornell Research Papers in International Studies, vol. v (1966).

themselves saw such actions as a danger to their self-insulation. They developed mechanisms to consume such surpluses within the local community. Crucial resources were thus taken from the hands of the wealthier peasants, preventing them from forging ties with outside institutions. Sanctions were applied against those who deviated.

In some instances, peasants were able to establish new roles and ties despite these barriers. Once they fortified their strength through ties to outsiders, the richer peasants could use their wealth as a means to dominate and exploit their fellow villagers. In other cases, outside institutions became stable enough to allow a portion of the community to increase its outside relations.

Most frequently in history, however, local lords and the community *did* function as effective restraints against individual mobility into alien patterns and value systems. The success of these local forces and institutions frequently created in villages an underlying tension stemming from the fact that there were those who, given the chance, would have opted for the connection and values of the outside. The local institutions and forces, then, repressed as well as protected, restrained as well as sheltered. And there were always those waiting for the opportunity to resolve the tension between inward- and outward-oriented forces in favor of the latter. It was finally a series of *economic crises* which tipped the balance in their favor. And these economic crises, too, resulted from the bearing down of outside factors on village life.

Peasants' lack of access to new technology prevented many of them from responding with sufficient increases in production to meet new situations or demands. Their inability to increase production significantly created crises throughout history as famines occurred or lords increased rents or taxes. In scattered areas such conditions led to impoverishment, enslavement, and starvation. The last two centuries, however, were extraordinary in that they witnessed such crises in unparalleled scope. The crises were not scattered by village or region but were worldwide. There were several causes for

17

the scope and depth of these crises among peasant families in Asia and Latin America, arising primarily from the changes wrought by the spread of worldwide imperialism in the eighteenth and nineteenth centuries. Chapter v will discuss the various processes, precipitated by imperialism, which caused an increased demand on peasant family incomes. What is important to note in this overview is that imperialism's integration of formerly fairly autonomous political and economic units around the globe also precipitated severe economic crises which were keenly, but differentially, felt by peasant families. Families varied widely in their capabilities: some were better suited than others to withstand the new conditions. Not every family owned or had direct access to farming land. The land was not distributed equally, nor was it of equal productive quality.

Those better-off families, often the same ones who had previously bristled under the sanctions against increased outside ties, now found that they could often take advantage of the crises of other families to further enrich themselves. They could buy land or earn interest on loans, for example, from those who were desperate for cash. And this frequently intensified the crises of the others in the long run, as one household's control of a large percentage of fertile village land meant that the pressure on all the rest was proportionately more severe.

Previously, status differences among the peasants were often not great enough for the wealthier members to risk violating community norms and incurring sanctions. Now, the increasing status (and power) differences caused by the differential impact of crisis on the community's families enabled the richer to forge their ties with the outside. And this further increased status and power differences, as these families acquired new tools and methods to increase even more their wealth—and the gap between themselves and the poor. Also, the challenge to local lords' primacy by the centralized, imperial institutions meant that lords' sanctions were also weakened considerably. In short, the economic crises that

18

struck families differentially paved the way for the triumph of the outward-oriented forces over inward-oriented ones by giving wealthier families both the resources and opportunity to operate in the outside economy. This growing income gap has precipitated the historical weakening of those institutions which had been able to suppress the feelings of peasants oriented toward outside mobility.

Unlike the wealthier peasants who abandoned the inward-orientation in order to achieve recognition and success in a wider system, poorer peasants had a second set of reasons for abandoning the old. They had relied on the functioning of the traditional institutions to protect and serve them, and they lacked the resources to advance in the wider status system. After the land consolidation and the economic centralization of the fortunate few, or after the termination of the lord's services, they were left not only without resources but without the community's or lord's protection. The sanctions and customs which provided for redistribution within the village were no longer operative. The barriers against outside alliances which could lead to increased economic exploitation fell, but their skills for advancement in the wider system were negligible.

These are the landless laborers who make up an increasing portion of rural society, and many of them are part of the vast worldwide migration from countryside to cities and towns. They have undergone social mobilization, but they were not prepared for this abandonment of their long-held patterns. They have neither the resources nor orientation to change. Social mobilization has not at all been coincidental with modernization for them. When they are able, they utilize aspects of the modern world. Some learn the rules of the game and adapt their economic behavior to the realities they face. For them, however, the world outside the village remains a hostile arena. They feel weak and vulnerable and therefore maintain as many of their old institutions as they can to protect them. Despite the end of the corporate village's and

19

lord's protection, many peasants continue to use smaller kin-ship and neighborhood groups as a means to protect the in-dividual against outside exploitation and as a corporate means to move upward socially in the wider status system. Simple exposure to the modern is not a sufficient condition of culture change.[30] In the peasant villages of Asia and Latin America, it has only been when economic crises have hit dif-ferentially that the old institutions have weakened sufficiently to allow the outward-oriented forces to triumph. Once that point is reached, the response of villagers is very dependent on their economic position within the village.

The focus in social science on the individual in the process of change, rather than on traditional institutions and people's relation to them, has led to a tendency to over-aggregate in studies of change. In fact, the dynamics of change can be understood only when one differentiates the village popula-

[30] Based on the explanation presented in this chapter, one can speculate on the different reactions of the peasants of Hualcan and Recuayhuanca to their working experience on Peru's agricultural-industrial plantations. For those with resources to make outside alliances, we have emphasized that there must have been a lessening of internal restraints as well as a sufficiently secure outside in which to risk participation. Two elements seem to be important in these cases. First, Recuayhuanca was a much poorer community than Hualcan, lacking highland grazing pastures. Second, Peru has had a caste system which has made upward mobility for Indians into creole or even mestizo society very difficult. Thus, in Hualcan, even with high culture contact, those with sufficient resources did not find a sufficient-ly hospitable and secure outside environment in which to invest and make alliances. The continuing viability of the Hualcan economy and prestige system may have made that the best place for an Indian to invest for prestige. Recuayhuanca's poverty, however, may have been so severe as to make investment there for prestige even less inviting than trying to break the larger societal caste barrier. There are in-teresting stories of how Indians in such cases adopt a mestizo self-identity, dress, etc. but are still considered lower caste Indians by the mestizos themselves. Severe poverty and a lack of viability of community institutions stemming from that poverty may make even an inhospitable environment more attractive for those with resources to invest.

tion according to each family's economic position as crisis struck. Social scientists have generally failed to differentiate those who profit in the process from those who suffer. For the latter, change is a tragic process. It is they who are most affected by the breakdown of people's commitment to each other as people, and the tendency toward relations based on specialized, organizational criteria. Their refusal to let go easily of these precious commitments sets the background for the pitched battles of social forces which characterize the process of societal change.

Peasants' participation in politics beyond the confines of the village can be understood only against the backdrop of this interpretation of why people change. The basic question of *why* peasants participate in national politics is all but neglected in the recent body of literature on peasant syndicates, unions, etc. Why should peasants participate politically? After all, they are generally extremely poor with little time for after-work activities and, also based on past experience, they are quite pessimistic about their abilities to manipulate the social and political environment to their advantage. This question is even more striking in the case of organized participation in revolutions, where peasants have incurred very substantial risks with even the most passive type of aid. The answer offered in Chapters ix and x spurns use of concepts such as ideological motivations or motivations oriented toward collective goals. Such concepts have entered political science literature on peasants as a result of a fundamental lack of understanding of why peasants expanded their social worlds and a failure to see the nature of the continuing weakness they suffer. This book argues that peasant participation in complex political organizations is realized in return for the material inducements that are offered to individuals or families seeking to solve their economic crises. The peasant sees politics as part of the large outside world into which he has been thrust. Here too he must learn the rules and minimize his vulnerability vis-à-vis those above him. His political

21

goals are limited and oriented to the administrative solution of his family's mundane problems rather than directed to the policy level of politics.

To close this section, I would like to digress for a moment and speculate on why the culture-contact explanation has persisted so long, despite the development of a literature attacking some of its basic assumptions. Why has it taken until now to introduce an explanation of peasant change which takes account of the historical forces restricting peasant choice and the causes of the triumph of the outward-oriented forces over the inward-oriented ones?[31] Why have politics and revolution often been analyzed outside the context of the specific pressures peasants face in their relations with other classes?

I believe two reasons account for the persistence of the culture-contact explanation. First has been the eagerness of Western social scientists to dismiss Marx. This has led them to relegate the role of economic constraints and class pressures to a secondary place in favor of an approach emphasizing the importance of culture, values, and norms.[32] This orientation was fortified by methodological breakthroughs. The ease with which a survey, highlighting individuals' values and norms, can now be administered makes it an inviting research tool. Although survey research is certainly an important aspect of social science, we may be witnessing a period in which method dictates not only the questions social science asks but the answers it refuses to consider.

A second reason stems more from anthropology than from

[31] One of the first serious steps in recent years to identify the interaction between outside forces and peasant change came from Eric R. Wolf. See, for example, his conclusion of *Peasant Wars of the Twentieth Century* (New York: Harper and Row, 1969).

[32] This argument has been developed by Robert I. Rhodes, "The Disguised Conservatism in Evolutionary Development Theory," *Science and Society* 32 (Fall 1968), 388. Also see Alvin W. Gouldner, *The Coming Crisis of Western Sociology* (New York: Basic Books, 1970).

sociology. This study relies heavily on anthropological literature and part of its purpose is to introduce this literature,
after much too long a hiatus, into political science. This literature, however, also has a weakness, and much of the anthropological data used here has therefore been reworked. Many
of the tools and orientations of anthropological research were
developed when the "primitive" tribe was the main object
of study. When applied to peasants who were long part of a
literate tradition and of a large marketing system, the tendency to "isolate" the unit being studied distorted reality.
Anthropologists have been much too prone to study the
internal dynamics of "their" villages without reference to
external political and social forces. Of course, there are exceptions (F. G. Bailey, T. S. Epstein, Eric R. Wolf, Jack M.
Potter, Bernard Gallin, and others), but the inclination all too
often has been to assume previous isolation and then "measure" the impact of "new" ideas from the outside.

Again, the methodological element plays a crucial role. In
anthropology, there has been an emphasis on village studies,
and the result is a compilation of numerous empirical studies,
with little theoretical connection to institutions and processes
studied by other disciplines in social science. Theory does
not simply arise by amassing descriptive atheoretical case
studies. All too little effort has been made in anthropology
to analyze changes in single peasant villages in terms of the
economic pressures generated by larger international and
national forces. It is to these weaknesses in sociological and
anthropological literature that the theory in this book addresses itself.

SOME FINAL COMMENTS

One of the ceaseless and futile debates of anthropology has
focused on the definition of peasant. Foster has stated that
Redfield's study of Chan Kom was really not of peasants,
since there was an insufficient degree of contact with an urban

area.[33] Oscar Lewis promptly replied that Foster's own study of Tzintzuntzan was the one that was not of peasants, since only one-third of the village inhabitants were primarily farmers.[34] And I am certain that someone could turn on Lewis and say that Tepoztlán was too large and complex by the time of his stay there in the 1950s for it to be considered a village any longer. As a town its inhabitants might not be considered peasants but rather townspeople. For the political scientist to enter this foray would be foolhardy.

In summarizing studies of peasants, Clifford Geertz has enumerated three criteria—economic, political, and cultural—which are most commonly used to assess who is a peasant.[35] The economic standard is that peasants are at least somewhat involved in both cash and market relations. Politically, they are subordinate in a hierarchical, relatively centralized state. This involves being subject to the demands and sanctions of powerholders outside the peasant class, and paying some percentage of income to them. And culturally, peasants are part of a society with a literate tradition which has critical and systematic religious and philosophical thought. Through their Little Tradition, they participate in what Redfield calls a Great Tradition.[36] Another element generally agreed upon is the centrality of land and agriculture to peasant societies.[37] Land is not something which is so much thought of in terms of price, as in terms of security and a way of life. Peasants

[33] George M. Foster, "Interpersonal Relations in Peasant Society," *Human Organization* 19 (Winter 1960-1961), 175.

[34] "Some of My Best Friends are Peasants," in *ibid.*, p. 180.

[35] "Studies in Peasant Life: Community and Society," in *Biennial Review of Anthropology, 1961*, ed. Bernard J. Siegel (Stanford: Stanford University Press, 1962), p. 5.

[36] Robert Redfield, "The Social Organization of Tradition," *The Far Eastern Quarterly* 15 (November 1955), 13-14.

[37] R. N. Henry, "Participation and Initiative of the Local People," in *Social Research and Problems of Rural Development in South-East Asia*, ed. Vu Quôc Thuc (UNESCO, 1963), p. 199. Also for a moving account of the peasant's relationship to the land, see William H. and Charlotte Viall Wiser, *Behind Mud Walls 1930-1960* (Berkeley: University of California Press, 1964), pp. 154-155.

24

survive by working the land directly or providing services for those who work the land.[38] This distinguishes them from lords who live off rents and interest, having no need to work the land personally.

This study focuses on peasant villages in Asia and Latin America.[39] I have included all working villagers even if they are not directly involved with agriculture. In India particularly this facilitates the inclusion of people involved in caste services but who neither own nor work land.[40] The limitation is that the community, to be considered a peasant village, must have agriculture as its primary source of income.[41] The study emphasizes the striking similarities of many peasant community patterns and processes in Asia and Latin America regardless of the particular national or cultural characteristics. As Raymond Firth wrote years ago, there is a characteristic shape to life in peasant communities.[42]

In order to analyze some of the key social and political changes that various peasant communities and their members

[38] In many cases, artisan tasks were part-time endeavors to the main activity of farming. In other cases, artisans became an extension of the concept underlying the division of labor within a household and, in fact, were often tied in their duties to specific households. The artisan thus guaranteed himself access to the fruits of the land by performing services for a fixed group which worked the land.

[39] Cases of Japanese and Russian peasantry were omitted. For a full discussion on this point, see Joel S. Migdal, "Peasants in a Shrinking World: The Socio-Economic Basis of Political Change," Harvard University, Ph.D. diss., p. 16.

[40] See Robert T. Anderson, "Studies in Peasant Life," in *Biennial Review of Anthropology, 1965*, ed. Bernard J. Siegel (Stanford: Stanford University Press, 1966), p. 176. Also see Raymond Firth, "Capital, Saving and Credit in Peasant Societies: A Viewpoint from Economic Anthropology," in *Capital, Saving and Credit in Peasant Societies: Studies from Asia, Oceania, the Caribbean and Middle America*, ed. Firth and B. S. Yamey (Chicago: Aldine, 1964), p. 18.

[41] Cases of plantations were omitted because of the wholly different forms of plantation economic organization.

[42] *Elements of Social Organization* (3d ed., Boston: Beacon Press, 1963), p. 88.

have been undergoing, peasant communities have been differentiated on the basis of the degree of their members' external relations.[43] Communities high on the scale of external relations (which, for style's sake, we shall refer to as outward-oriented) are ones in which peasants are tied to others outside the village in a variety of ways, not only in primary and secondary interactions, but also through other indirect, mediated connections. Peasants in such villages are involved in processes of social exchange and interaction with many people they never even see.

Communities low on the scale of external relations (inward-oriented villages), on the other hand, are ones in which there are more limited interactions by members with outsiders, these being chiefly in face-to-face, primary encounters. John T. McAlister, Jr. and Paul Mus beautifully portray such a village in Vietnam prior to French colonialism.

> The typical village of Viet Nam is enclosed within a thick wall of bamboo and thorny plants; the villagers used to live behind a kind of screen of bamboo, or perhaps it was more like living within the magic ring of a fairy tale. Supplying their needs from the surrounding fields, they kept to themselves behind their common protection, away from strangers, away, even, from the state. For instance, when it came to taxes (there, as elsewhere, the state's chief concern) they still presented a united front. They paid their taxes as a group, and the community was responsible. The villages dominated the landscape; they were the backbone

[43] Anthropologists have continually attempted to classify types of peasants and peasant communities in order to help explain the variety of life patterns they have found. See, for example, *The Peasant: A Symposium Concerning the Peasant Way and View of Life*, ed. F. G. Friedmann, no. 6 (February 1956), mimeo, pp. 3-5; Eric R. Wolf, "Types of Latin American Peasantry: A Preliminary Discussion, *"American Anthropologist"* 57 (June 1955); Charles Wagley, "The Peasant," in *Continuity and Change in Latin America*, ed. John J. Johnson (Stanford: Stanford University Press, 1964), pp. 22-23. My own study of change among peasants has been helped greatly by these typologies.

26

of the nation. Yet each preserved an internal autonomy, and autarchy, with an economy based on local consumption.[44]

The differentiation of villages on the scale of external relations can be done by specifying three factors which indicate, to some extent, the degree of the members' outside participation: external wage labor, commodity marketing mechanisms, and involvement with cash.[45] Each of these is a primary avenue along which villagers can increase their network of external interactions substantially, extending vastly their mediated, indirect bonds. The degree of their outside relations increase precipitously when they become involved with "multiplier" institutions, such as cash or external labor. The exact criteria used to classify communities on the scale can be found in Appendix A. Briefly, a village low on the scale is more likely to have members who use cash only infrequently; who engage in little or no external wage labor (except perhaps for certain agricultural labor during the off-seasons); and who use primarily local peasant markets or local traders to sell any surplus and buy any goods.[46] Villages high on the scale are more prone to include peasants who use cash almost daily; who engage in significant external wage labor (including nonagricultural jobs on a regular basis); and who market their surplus through wholesalers, cooperatives, or organizations whose primary task it is to distribute these products nationally or to export them.

The scale of external relations is a continuum[47] along

[44] *The Vietnamese and Their Revolution*, Harper Torchbooks (New York: Harper and Row, 1970), p. 31.

[45] Kunkel first enumerated these three criteria. John H. Kunkel, "Economic Autonomy and Social Change in Mexican Villages," *Economic Development and Cultural Change* 10 (October 1961), 51. He has used five variables to dichotomize villages. I found his categories difficult to use with certain non-Mexican cases.

[46] Peasant markets usually involve the sale of small amounts of goods directly (or at most with one or two intermediaries) from producer to consumer. They will be discussed more fully in ch. III.

[47] F. G. Bailey has expressed the idea of a continuum of cases in

27

which, at any point, one can find a variety of types of villages. We will be pointing time and again to the diversity and complexity and to the various limiting conditions of the cases on either end of the scale of external relations. There have always been peasant communities on both ends, and there has been movement of villages from one end to the other. G. William Skinner has described such changes in dynastic China. "The intriguing aspect of the Chinese case," he writes, "is the recurrent cyclical trend whereby peasant communities changed from relatively open to relatively closed and back again."[48] Besides this cyclical type of movement of which Skinner speaks, there has been a linear historical trend as well. Prior to the rise of the modern nation-state, most communities clustered on the low end of the scale. The nineteenth and twentieth centuries have been periods of a universal, vast increase in peasants' external relations. Thus, there has been a worldwide movement of peasant communities toward the high end of the scale. The primary focus of this study is on this linear historical trend: the movement of peasant community members from restricted to expanded external relations, from an inward- to an outward-orientation.

At this point, the conclusions in this book must remain hypothetical in large part. Enough historical data simply do not exist to verify the explanations set forth. The purpose of the study is to present an argument with supporting evidence. However, the references and cases that are presented must be seen primarily as illustrative material which "fit" the various hypotheses.[49] Much more work is needed in specific areas to test the theoretical assertions generated here.

---

discussing the economic aspects of the range of social interaction. He calls this continuum the "economic frontier." *Caste and the Economic Frontier: A Village in Highland Orissa* (Manchester: Manchester University Press, 1957), p. 5.

[48] "Chinese Peasants and the Closed Community," p. 271.

[49] On issues of method in comparative politics, see Arend Lijphart, "Comparative Politics and the Comparative Method," *American Political Science Review* 65 (September 1971), 682-693. At a time

The data from which the hypotheses grew were garnered from three main sources. First, fifty-one community studies on peasants in Asia and Latin American were utilized. (See Appendix B for a full listing and the ranking of each village on the scale of external relations.) These cases have helped fulfill one of the goals of this study, to relate and integrate into the political science literature some of the important social scientific work that ethnographers have been doing on peasant communities during the last forty years. A content analysis was carried out on the various ethnographic monographs and this material was incorporated into my analysis. Although the book is not a comparative study of these fifty-one cases, they are used as a basis to illustrate the arguments. Second, two summers of field work including observation and interviewing were carried out in Mexico (Morelos and Oaxaca) and India (Delhi State and Uttar Pradesh). Finally, a wide variety of secondary historical sources were used.[50]

The book is divided into four parts. Part One elaborates the historical circumstances of peasant villages. The analysis focuses on the inward-oriented forces and the conditions under which they succeeded in suppressing those who desired outside contact. Part Two is the pivotal section of the book, dealing with the change in outside forces which led to the move away from the village's inward-orientation. In Part Three, the social and economic changes in internal power, social structure, and social stratification which occurred with the triumph of the outward-oriented forces are analyzed. Finally, these social and economic changes are integrated into a theory of peasant participation in politics and revolution in Part Four.

---

of fascination with statistical method and validation, Lijphart wisely restates the importance of studies involving only a few cases or only a single case.

[50] For a more complete discussion of methodology, see Migdal, "Peasants in a Shrinking World," ch. 1 and Appendix B.

PART ONE

The Historical Domination of Inward-Oriented Forces

CHAPTER II

Lord and Peasant

INTRODUCTION

PEASANTS have long been subservient to other social classes in society, and their relationship to these classes has often impelled peasants to limit their participation outside the village. At times, these classes have been composed of rural lords who have governed the day-in and day-out activities of peasants.[1] Communities where lords exercised such power were most commonly found in political systems in which the power was dispersed[2]—usually referred to as feudal states[3] or patrimonial domains.[4]

In other instances there were no strong local lords in control. Rather, peasants had to adapt their behavior to powerful persons far removed from the village. In such cases barriers against outside involvement were often posed by the peasant community itself, stemming from its relationship to

[1] I am combining two types of class relationships according to Arthur L. Stinchcombe's classification: the manor type and the tenant type. His distinction is an important one, but many of the pressures in the two types are very similar. "Agricultural Enterprise and Rural Class Relations," *The American Journal of Sociology* 67 (September 1961), 165-176.

[2] See Samuel P. Huntington, *Political Order in Changing Societies* (New Haven: Yale University Press, 1968), p. 148.

[3] See Gaetano Mosca, *The Ruling Class* (New York: McGraw-Hill, 1939), pp. 80ff.

[4] See Eric R. Wolf, *Peasants* (Englewood Cliffs, N.J.: Prentice-Hall, 1966), p. 50.

the state and the insecurity it experienced in outside market participation. Freeholding communities posing such barriers were more often found in power-concentrated political systems (bureaucratic states or prebendal domains), but they could also exist in power-dispersed systems on marginal lands beyond the lord's control.

Part One investigates these two sets of forces to which peasants and peasant communities have had to adapt in the past—forces which determined the degree of the peasants' external relations and their types of social organization. This chapter analyzes the first set of reasons, the relationship of lord and peasant.[5]

THE LORD'S BASIS OF POWER

Where lords were powerful and controlled vital resources, it was they who enforced the peasants' inward-orientation, because it was outside the community that peasants might have found alternatives to the services they provided. For their part, peasants in such villages simply could not risk overinvolving themselves with outsiders for fear of losing what the lord supplied.[6] What determined the extent of the lord's control? Why were some lords better able to enforce such restrictions than others?

The degree to which a lord could keep peasants inward-oriented seems to have been dependent upon three interrelated factors. First was the *scope* of the lord's services. The more scarce the resources that a lord controlled, the more difficult was it for peasants to risk seeking alternative means to secure those resources. Second was the *primacy* of the

[5] Everett E. Hagen states that the core of the elite groups above peasants was typically an economically and politically strong class of landlords. *On the Theory of Social Change: How Economic Growth Begins* (Homewood, Ill.: The Dorsey Press, 1962), p. 59.

[6] On dependency relationships, see Peter M. Blau, *Exchange and Power in Social Life* (New York: John Wiley and Sons, 1964), p. 116.

services the lord performed: how important the elements that the lord controlled were to the peasant and his family. The more essential for survival—both objectively and subjectively determined—the resources he controlled, the more difficult was it for peasants to risk seeking alternatives.[7]

Third, was the *degree of monopoly* that the lord had over the services he provided. The fewer the available alternatives open to the peasant, the more likely was the lord to continue in firm control. These three factors—scope, primacy, and degree of monopoly—determine, then, the degree to which a lord could enforce restrictions on peasants' outside relations. At the same time, of course, these factors also determined the likelihood of the peasants' breaking from the relationship in order to establish ties with more specific outside groups which could perform the various services.

The Latin American *hacienda* or *latifundio* historically presented the most extreme cases of powerful lords placing effective restrictions on peasants' outside participation. Variations of these forms were found outside Latin America in Asia as well. In effect, the lord of a hacienda controlled his own little society in which he defined and enforced the rights and duties of the households. "The hacienda," Frank Tannenbaum wrote, "is not just an agricultural property owned by an individual. The hacienda is a society, under private auspices. It is an entire social system and governs the life of those attached to it from the cradle to the grave."[8]

The lord, however, could and did participate in social interactions and economic dealings with people outside the hacienda. Most importantly, he could call upon the force of his peers or superior lords to impose his will upon the peasants under him whenever necessary. The peasants in this

[7] For a distinction on types of resources, see Jeremy Boissevain's classification discussed in Rene Lemarchand and Keith Legg, "Political Clientilism and Development: A Preliminary Analysis," *Comparative Politics* 4 (January 1972), 155. Of course, the primacy of a particular resource could vary for peasants within the village.

[8] Frank Tannenbaum, *Ten Keys to Latin America* (New York: Alfred A. Knopf, 1962), p. 80.

closed society, on the other hand, had only one significant strand connecting them to the outside—the lord himself.[9]

By attempting to place himself as the source of fulfillment for all the peasants' needs, the *hacendado* (lord) also succeeded in discouraging his subjects from seeking each other out for help. The lord further played upon the weakness of the peasants, through his exploitative demands, thereby continually preventing the creation of a marketable surplus by them.[10] Peasants, owing to their lack of sufficient capital, constantly accumulated labor debts to the lord. They, of course, could not leave the hacienda until all such debts were paid off.[11]

In short, the lord's ability to keep the peasants inward-oriented came through the complete array of sanctions he was able to bring to bear on them, based upon his ties to other lords and his direct control of the most valuable economic resource—usually land. The power of the landlord manifested itself primarily in the reciprocity of rights and duties that characterized such a community. In Latin America, peasants were bound to give their lords loyalty and respect, service in the lord's armies, domestic service, and, above all, a certain number of work days each week on the hacendado's land.

In return, the peasants received a hut, a small piece of marginal land on which to grow subsistence needs, and advances for capital (such as seeds and tools). Also, the lord gave special favors such as fiestas, medical aid, etc. In other societies, rather than demanding work days, the lords ensured them-

---

[9] Whyte has termed this relationship the baseless triangle. See Susan C. Bourque, "Cholification and the Campesino: A Study of Three Peruvian Peasant Organizations in the Process of Societal Change," Latin American Studies Program, Dissertation Series, Cornell University (January 1971), pp. 55-56.

[10] Ernest Feder, "Societal Opposition to Peasant Movements and Its Effects on Farm People in Latin America," in *Latin American Peasant Movements*, ed. Henry A. Landsberger (Ithaca, New York: Cornell University Press, 1969), pp. 400-403, 428-429.

[11] Tannenbaum, *Ten Keys to Latin America*, p. 84.

selves of the surplus produced on small, peasant plots through the extraction of high rents and interest.

Whatever the exact mechanism of extraction (which could leave the peasants with less than subsistence needs), the key factor making the relationship one of unequal statuses was the control by the lord of the most important economic resource. The lord could legitimize his status by personalizing the reciprocal relationship with his peasants. In such cases, he became a patron for his lower-class clients.[12] In Vietnam, for example, landlords gave peasants money for the burial of kin and for the birth of a child, made loans in time of peasants' financial ruin, adjudicated disputes, and dispensed corporal punishment.[13] In India, "the landlord is a patron, a source of credit, a market, perhaps also a source of support in law-suits, and even a local police force for the small man."[14]

PATTERNS OF LORD-PEASANT RELATIONS

There were societies other than the hacienda where lords did not have such extensive control. At least three other patterns of lord-peasant relations can be identified. (1) There could be a single lord but with only some of the community's peasants falling under his domination, the rest having been independent smallholders or artisans. Even in such cases, those not directly beholden to the lord often had to tread lightly. For example, in relation to a *fazeda* (hacienda) owner in Brazil, "the small independent owners in the neighborhood had to

[12] On patronage, see Lemarchand and Legg, "Political Clientilism and Development," 151-152; also John Duncan Powell, "Peasant Society and Clientilist Politics," *American Political Science Review* 64 (June 1970), 413.

[13] Robert L. Sansom, *The Economics of Insurgency in the Mekong Delta of Vietnam* (Cambridge, Mass.: The M.I.T. Press, 1970), pp. 29-30. For India, see William H. and Charlotte Viall Wiser, *Behind Mud Walls 1930-1960* (Berkeley: University of California Press, 1964), pp. 14-15.

[14] Guy Hunter, *Modernizing Peasant Societies: A Comparative Study in Asia and Africa* (New York: Oxford University Press, 1969), p. 151.

keep on good terms with him, since they depended on him for occasional employment, a loan, an introduction to a bank, a favour. A conflict with him could cost them their land."[15] There were cases too, however, in which lords lacked the power to circumscribe the behavior of non-tenants. (2) There could be several lords controlling all the peasants of a community, with each lord having less than a complete monopoly over key resources. And (3) there could be several lords but with only a portion of the community coming under their control.

In these three patterns, the degree to which the lord could keep peasants inward-oriented was often much less than in the hacienda-type case. The lords in such cases had a lesser degree of monopoly and, often, control of a smaller scope of resources. Frequently, these lords could not call on outside forces so readily. In such villages, then, there were independent peasants or peasants who found the lord's control less extensive, and these were frequently somewhat more involved in the cash and market economies. In all these cases, the manner of restricting outside relations was similar. Peasants were getting tangible returns for their efforts (though undoubtedly not justly for the efforts expended) so that they simply could not choose, in most circumstances, to risk ignoring or flouting the one who supplied those necessities. Those who dared risk crossing the lord's will often found the additional element of outside forces used to suppress them.

The literature has emphasized the control of land by the lord a bit too much at the expense of control of other resources. The restrictions on increased outside involvement of many peasant communities were ensured, not by the mere fact that one person owned land and another was a tenant or agricultural laborer, but rather because the landlord controlled the vital *scarce resource* of cultivable land. It was the intensity of sanctions available to the landlord because of the primacy of land that was a key to his power.

[15] Benno Galjart, "Class and 'Following' in Rural Brazil," *América Latina* 7 (July-September 1964), 6.

In other words, lords could impose restrictions by controlling vital scarce resources other than land. In some cases land might not have been a vital scarce resource at all. In both Pul Eliya, Ceylon, and Sakaltutan, Turkey, there were landownertenant relationships which entirely lacked the landlord-tenant or landlord-laborer forms of reciprocity. There, labor rather than land, was often in short supply. A household might have owned land but lacked sufficient manpower to work all of it. In such cases, close kin became sharecroppers, often as much as a favor to the landowning household as to the sharecroppers themselves. At such times, of course, there were no overtones of patron-client relations, of paternalism, or of a lord restricting the relations of those below him, since there was no primacy to land ownership.[16] Only with the monopolization or scarcity of available land could a landlord enforce restrictions.

Other resources besides land, however, could have primacy and have been in short supply, and these also could serve as the basis for restricting peasant relations. Where capital and cash were scarce for example, as in nineteenth century Vietnam, lords could become entrenched by controlling moneylending. Note the description of the high status storeowners and the resources at their disposal in the village of Aritama in Colombia:

> These stores dictate the prices of cash crops and all locally
> manufactured goods. . . . The storeowner is a banker, phar
> macist, family counselor, accountant, public scribe, and a
> news service. . . . The storeowners can write to a govern
> ment agency and ask for new seeds; they can ask for loans
> in a lowland town; they know lawyers and judges and can
> carry on suits; they can travel to buy and sell their wares—
> all this because their educational level enables them.[17]

[16] E. R. Leach, *Pul Eliya, A Village in Ceylon, A Study in Land Tenure and Kinship* (Cambridge: Cambridge University Press, 1961); and Paul Stirling, *Turkish Village* (London: Weidenfeld and Nicholson, 1965).

[17] Gerardo and Alicia Reichel-Dolmatoff, *The People of Aritama:*

Again, it was the array of services which the storeowners directly controlled and their oligopoly over scarce skills that gave them their power. Because there were no alternative sources of fulfillment of this impressive list of available services to the mestizos and especially to the Indians, the storeowners enjoyed a significant degree of power and influence.[18]

James C. Scott has classified the possible resource bases of various patrons: they can have skill and knowledge (e.g., local military chief or guru); direct control over real property (landlords); or indirect office-based property (e.g., a chief who distributes communal land).[19] Similarly, Sansom mentions land tenure and control of money, product, and factor markets as the basic constraints peasants have faced.[20] Land, then, was the most important, though not the only, resource used by lords to make severe demands upon weak peasants.

The persistence of the lord's control lay in the lack of viable alternatives open to peasants. States did not exist as bases of resources for those at the bottom of the social order. Governments were often unable or unwilling to penetrate a lord's domain with their bureaucratic apparatus. The state's leaders, in such cases, often formed an implicit or explicit alliance with the most powerful lords and nobles. They could agree to allow a monopolistic niche in which the war lord, gentry, or noble could operate relatively unhampered. In return, these state leaders received a sufficient production of goods from the countryside to ensure their continued survival and even, perhaps, prosperity. As late as the sixteenth and seventeenth centuries in England, for example, there was little

---

The Cultural Personality of a Colombian Mestizo Village (London: Routledge and Kegan Paul, 1961), p. 459.

[18] See F. G. Bailey's description of a chief's basis of power in India: "The Peasant View of the Bad Life," *The Advancement of Science* 23 (December 1966), 402-403.

[19] James C. Scott, "Patron-Client Politics and Political Change" (paper presented at the American Political Science Association meetings, Los Angeles, Calif., September 8-12, 1970), pp. 11-13.

[20] Sansom, *The Economics of Insurgency*, pp. 3-4.

central or local government control of lords' domains. Queen Elizabeth was only able to prevent aristocratic disorder of feuding lords by playing one off against the other.[21]

Within each major lord's domain, there was often a hierarchy of lords and peasants below, and the lord within a village therefore often had to serve or obey another even more powerful lord. In China, there were clear distinctions among levels of gentry. European feudalism also was an expression of such a pyramid, with the gentry, for example, waiting on the nobility.[22] Besides these layers of lords, there were also layers of peasants in some instances. Thus, within the peasant community itself, there were differentiations in access to resources which enabled some peasants to restrict the external relationships of other peasants. Again, control of land was most often the key resource. In India, a single caste often controlled access to the land, and as M. N. Srinivas put it, had to "carry" the other castes through its payment of grain or small pieces of land.[23] One low-caste peasant in the Indian village of Sirkanda said, "You can't go against the wishes of high-caste people and get away with it around here."[24]

Each peasant, then, felt the cumulative effect of all the layers on top of him, because in the system of reciprocity, each layer could often call on the layer above to help maintain the status quo through the application of sanctions. The key to the power of lords on every level lay in their degree of monopoly over essential rural resources and the external forces they could call in to protect that monopoly.

Any threats to the preeminence of a lord came not from specific groups and organizations attempting to fulfill partic-

[21] Lawrence Stone, *The Crisis of the Aristocracy, 1558-1641* (Oxford: Clarendon Press, 1965), pp. 231-233.

[22] In England, the gentry waited on the nobility in personal service until the seventeenth century (*ibid.*, p. 213).

[23] M. N. Srinivas, "The Social System of a Mysore Village," in *Village India: Studies in the Little Community*, ed. McKim Marriott (Chicago: University of Chicago Press, 1955), p. 16.

[24] Quoted in Gerald D. Berreman, *Hindus of the Himalayas* (Berkeley: University of California Press, 1963), p. 246.

ular services but from fate or by other lords from below, from above, or from the same level. Inheritance patterns which divided land among one's heirs could be disastrous for a large family of minor lords (or powerful peasants), for this resulted in a reduced degree of monopoly or reduced scope for any one of them once the household divided. In fact, fate could transform the heirs into men who controlled barely enough land to support themselves.[25] Thus, the line between powerful peasants and minor lords was not impenetrable, and historically there was often significant movement of families from one category to the other.

PEASANT SOCIAL ORGANIZATION

Peasants under vigilant and strong lords had types of social organization which reflected the limitations the lord put on them. The most striking characteristic was the atomization of the community into individual households. In the extreme cases of haciendas, for example, lords attempted to make themselves the suppliers of all peasant needs. The hacendado sought to direct as many of the peasants' contacts as possible into dyadic relations with him, undercutting the need for dependence of the peasants on one another and thus undermining any possible basis of association that might challenge the lord.[26]

A community social and political organization able to make demands upon peasants also had to fulfill their needs to create loyalty to it and dependence upon it. The more the lord fulfilled those needs, the less area was there for community institutions to create bonds of dependency. In short, there was an inversely proportional relationship between the development

[25] See Gouranga Chattopadhyay, *Ranjana, A Village in West Bengal* (Calcutta: Bookland Private, 1964).

[26] For a discussion of various types of dyadic relations in a Tarascan village, see George M. Foster, *Tzintzuntzan: Mexican Peasants in a Changing World* (Boston: Little, Brown, 1967), pp. 212-243.

of a strong, effective village social and political organization, on the one hand, and the power of local lords, on the other. The greater the scope of resources controlled, the primacy of those resources, and the degree of monopoly of the lord (e.g., the hacienda), the less likely was it for a village to create mechanisms to spread risks, perform collective tasks, and ensure compliance. The weaker the lord's control, on the other hand, the stronger was the social and political organization, which provided services to and made demands upon the villager.

Atomization by the lord was not of individuals but of households. The homogeneity of these peasant households—each producing pretty much the same things on small plots of land—further inhibited interdependence and stable associations on an interhousehold level. Moreover, with protection already supplied by the lord, there was little reason to look to one's fellow peasants in that realm either.

Cooperation and division of labor in communities with strong overlords, however, was fostered within the individual households. A hacendado's demands, for example, were usually made to heads of households rather than on an individual basis. Many times the workdays on the hacendado's land could be fulfilled by any adult male of the household. Domestic service was demanded by the hacendado of the peasant women. More importantly, because access to outside markets and technology was denied to the peasants by overlords fearful of peasants' finding alternatives to their services, greater labor intensiveness was the only way for these peasants to increase production. In some cases, increased manpower might only have resulted in bringing production on the marginal bit of land to a level high enough to avoid starvation.

It was the household which allowed for a division of labor and an intensive exploitation of the soil. The way to guarantee maximum utilization of scarce land, given a constant level of technology, was to employ the combined labor of the household, both children and adults, in tasks ranging from the sowing of seeds to the cooking of meals. In societies in which

43

labor-intensive crops, such as wet rice, were grown, the marginal product of added labor was relatively high. It was therefore within the household that the individual found ways to spread the risks of survival created by the scarcity of productive land and by the demands put forth by the lord.

Summary

The ability of lords to restrict the degree of external involvement of their peasants depended upon the primacy of the resources they controlled, the scope of those resources, and their degree of monopoly. Where there was high covariation of these three factors in the hands of one lord and where there was an operative hierarchy in which minor lords could call upon the support of lords above, peasants were highly circumscribed in their ability to make individual contacts and connections with anyone but their lords. Through their control of land, contacts to the outside, credit, supplies, or the marketing mechanism for peasant products—or control of all of these—the lords acted as suppliers of many diffuse services to dependent peasants. They cut the peasants off from the multiplier institutions which could vastly increase indirect, mediated bonds for fear that interaction within those institutions could result in a challenge to their monopoly. The lords feared opening new lines of social exchange which could result in alternative flows of services in which peasants could build new dependencies and interdependencies.

Peasants, subject to overlords' controlling access to vital scarce resources, had social structures stemming largely from the demands and restraints put on them by lords. Dyadic relationships existed principally between the lord and the individual peasant households. As a result, such peasants actually lacked the very interaction and communication that normally define "communities." The lord, in extreme cases, such as that of the hacienda, reduced his subjects (as do all tyrants) to a mere administered entity. With an array of sanctions at his disposal, the lord prevented deviance and fostered a social

44

structure of atomized households in order to maintain complete peasant dependency. Politics was stripped from the peasants, and decision-making by peasants was confined in the most limited way to the affairs of the household—to a subcommunity level.

CHAPTER III

The Freeholding Village

INTRODUCTION

EVEN WHEN there were no lords in the village or when the lords were weak, there often still was only very limited outside involvement by peasants. Freeholding villages often had very little interchange of goods and services and manpower with the larger society. The food and handicrafts consumed in the village were produced by the consumers themselves or by other nearby villagers. Goods produced in the countryside, in many cases, reached centers only through the single strand of the tax collector.

Such villages, frequently existing on land marginal in both quality and location,[1] did not experience the same types of barriers found in lord-peasant relationships. The question that arises, then, is why freeholding villages (and villages with weak lords), free of the severe sanctions that powerful lords could apply, were so often inward-oriented.

Once again, the answer lies in the peasants' relations to other classes in the society. The fact that peasants in freeholding communities did not have another class directly over them with which they had frequent contact does not mean that they lived in a classless, homogeneous society. Even peasants in freeholding villages were part of the larger society, and they

---

[1] Andrew Pearse, "Metropolis and Peasant: The Expansion of the Urban-Industrial Complex and the Changing Rural Structure," in *Peasants and Peasant Societies: Selected Readings*, ed. Teodor Shanin (Baltimore: Penguin Books, 1971), p. 69.

46

sharply felt the pressures other classes generated. Their inward-orientation can be understood, in great part, as an adaptative response to their relationship with these socially and spatially removed classes which controlled the state, and to the insecurities of outside market participation.

PEASANTS' RELATIONS TO OTHER CLASSES: THE ROLE OF THE POWERLESS

The traditional state often had neither the bureaucratic capabilities nor the will to perform a variety of services within villages, especially when communities were far from the centers of the society. Unlike instances where the lord was the single strand connecting villagers to the outside, the link in freeholding communities was through the state's representative, the tax collector. "Diagrammatically the villages are small circles," Bailey wrote, "representing organic and functioning communities. The State is in the centre, linked to each village by a line representing *imperium*."[2] The two regular relationships between the central government and the villages were economic exploitation through taxation and the maintenance of external law and order by the government so that agriculture could proceed routinely.

This narrowly based village-state relationship was often an inimical one. Unlike the villagers who received many small benefits from their overlords, the freeholding peasants viewed the state as almost entirely exploitative. "It is in part this imbalance between what the state takes from the peasantry and the little that the peasantry gets in return," Befu noted, "that creates the hostility toward ruling elites that is so common among peasants of the classical state."[3] These peasants saw themselves as part of a periphery which somehow had to

[2] F. G. Bailey, *Caste and the Economic Frontier: A Village in Highland Orissa* (Manchester: Manchester University Press, 1957), p. 255.

[3] Harumi Befu, "The Political Relation of the Village to the State," *World Politics* 19 (July 1967), 609.

keep the state at bay. Berreman wrote of a village in the Indian Himalayas:

> In Sirkanda the unfamiliar, be it a person or a program of change, is regarded with suspicion. The reasons are readily apparent. Contacts with outsiders have been limited largely to contacts with policemen and tax collectors—two of the most unpopular forms of life in the Pahari taxonomy. Such officials are despised and feared, not only because they make trouble for villagers in the line of duty but also because they extort bribes on the threat of causing further trouble and often seem to take advantage of their official position to vent their aggressions on these vulnerable people.[4]

Peasants were at the mercy of the state. After tax collection they could be left with barely enough to survive. Although the form of economic exploitation differed from villages with strong lords, the effects were much the same: peasants produced the vast bulk of the economic value in the society, but much of that value was extracted for use by others.

The experience of exploitation and the strength of the state vis-à-vis each village led peasants to withdraw from any more outside participation than necessary, even though shunning such participation for subsistence-oriented agriculture effectively cut the peasants off from potential alliances that might have lessened their powerlessness. Peasants thus had no outside allies who could have influenced state policy on their behalf in order, for example, to lessen tax burdens.

The problem of peasant powerlessness extended beyond the absence of substantial economic or political connections with other classes in the society. Relative powerlessness in the state stemmed also from the nature of the peasants' relationship to each other. They were marked by a greater degree of

---

[4] Gerald Berreman, *Hindus of the Himalayas* (Berkeley: University of California Press, 1963), p. 322.

homogeneity than were those in other classes.[5] Along with the subsistence agriculture and low technology characteristic of peasant villages came a particular type of production. On small plots of land, households were ensuring their survival in very similar ways. One farming household performed much the same tasks as any other. Each head of the household had similar roles as other heads, and the same was true for other corresponding members. In other words, villages were marked by a relatively low degree of role differentiation and specialization of tasks.

Of course, some degree of differentiation often did exist. Artisan peasants, for example, differed from farming peasants. These forms of occupational specialization, however, must not be confused with the extent of role differentiation in more modern societies or even with the differentiation among other classes in the society. There was a lack of enduring interaction among peasants in performing tasks. The failure of a peasant cultivator had little effect on other peasant farmers in the village.

A lack of social differentiation meant that peasants found it relatively more difficult than others to build formal, complex organizations.[6] Inability to create and participate in enduring, complex, and formal organizations further led to powerlessness in the state compared to those in other classes. Peasants confronted their common problems and needs with

[5] Homogeneity was so marked in freeholding villages that Stirling goes so far as to reject the terms "stratification" and "social class" as applicable to the internal analysis of the peasant villages he studied. Paul Stirling, *Turkish Village* (London: Weidenfeld and Nicholson, 1965), p. 222.

[6] "The absence of diversified functions results in a dearth of secondary organizations, voluntary or otherwise. . . . The lines of possible organization are limited to those bases of loyalty already existing within the unspecialized frame of social and economic life." Melvin M. Tumin, *Caste in a Peasant Society: A Case Study in the Dynamics of Caste* (Princeton, N.J.: Princeton University Press, 1952), p. 156. Also see Bryce Ryan, *Sinhalese Village* (Coral Gables, Fla.: University of Miami Press, 1958), pp. 151-152.

a local social and political organization that was neither consciously goal-oriented nor rationally coordinated. Over time, however, institutions and methods developed which shielded peasants from the direct onslaught of outside pressures, yet these lacked the power potential of a strong complex organization and left the peasantry with relatively little influence on state policy. They were forced to avoid confrontation rather than trying to influence state decisions and practices.

One of the ways communities minimized contacts with the state was by maintaining their own administration of internal affairs. This was often successful because traditional states frequently did little to interfere with the village's self-administration. Writing of India in 1832, Sir Charles Metcalfe stated:

> The village communities are little republics, having nearly everything they want within themselves, and almost independent of any foreign relations. They seem to last where nothing else lasts. Dynasty after dynasty tumbles down; revolution succeeds revolution . . . but the village community remains the same.[7]

Perhaps Sir Charles exaggerated a bit about the lack of "foreign relations," for there were generally marriage networks, exchanges of caste services among villages, and some market participation. Nevertheless, the traditional state most often did not have the goal or capabilities to administer villages directly. Villages had the latitude to handle most internal problems without the interference of outsiders.[8]

INSECURITIES OF MARKET PARTICIPATION

Besides their relationship to the state, a second factor in these peasants' inward-orientation was the insecurities involved in market participation outside the local area. There

[7] Quoted in Bailey, *Caste and the Economic Frontier*, pp. 3-4.

[8] The nearer the village to the state's center and the stronger the state's bureaucracy, the less latitude for self-administration of villages.

were at least two aspects to this insecurity. First was the purely economic, in which peasants found an incomplete market
infrastructure and unstable price conditions. Lack of transportation facilities, for example, made marketing costs in-
tolerably high.[9]

The second aspect of their insecurity in market participation, not independent of the first, involved social and political
factors. Monopolization of key components of the marketing
infrastructure by lords, moneylenders, large merchants resulted in the small producer finding no profit in production for
the market. Often there was no protection against bandits on
the highways to the market. In early nineteenth century Haiti,
for example, following the uprising against the French there,
the peasants found that the state's political instability led to
a deterioration of market conditions. The transport system
was neglected, and there was even governmental plundering of
farms. Any capital investment for market production of export crops would have been senseless.[10]

Insecurity of market participation was, then, another reason for a self-restriction of outside contact by freeholding
villages and by villages with weak overlords. Instead of widespread political, social, and economic interaction with other
classes, such peasants met as many needs as possible locally.
Although there was always at least a minimal degree of market
participation,[11] nevertheless, the dominant type of production
by peasants was subsistence production, which demanded
minimal interaction with outsiders. The more insecure market participation for the peasant, the more likely was the pro-

[9] Folke Dovring, "Peasantry, Land Use, and Change, A Review
Article," *Comparative Studies in Society and History* 4 (April 1962),
372.

[10] Robert I. Rotberg, *Haiti, The Politics of Squalor* (Boston:
Houghton Mifflin, 1971), pp. 97-98.

[11] Even the highly autonomous medieval European village produced
some goods for market. Eileen Power, *The Wool Trade in English
Medieval History* (New York: Oxford University Press, 1941), p. 3.

portion of his subsistence production to be considerably higher than the proportion of his production for market.

Numerous examples of the relationship of market insecurity to a relatively high percentage of subsistence production exist. In Mexico, in the midst of the Revolution in 1915, peasants from the state of Morelos returned to devastated villages. These peasants who had previously grown the cash crop of sugar cane reacted to the insecurity of the times by switching to subsistence vegetable crops.[12] C. K. Yang has told how in prerevolutionary China, peasants who had long been part of the monetary economy sought insulation from that period's price fluctuations by becoming as self-sufficient as possible. The monetary disorders of the first half of the twentieth century in China had resulted in peasants finding their hard-earned savings greatly depreciated or, at times, even worthless.[13]

The more peasants relied on the market, the more they were forced to depend upon events and upon others over whom they had no control. If transportation became impossible, if prices for cash crops fell, if prices for imported necessities rose, if middlemen were inconsistent in getting the produce to market at the proper time, peasants might be thrust into utter deprivation. Subsistence-oriented agriculture minimized the extent to which peasants put themselves at the mercy of forces and people beyond their control. Such subsistence production was encouraged and then reinforced by the inconsistency of the components of the market. When the market became more secure, conditions in the state were settled, and the government was less oppressive, peasants slowly responded with increased outside participation. But a deterioration of

[12] John Womack, Jr., *Zapata and the Mexican Revolution* (New York: Alfred A. Knopf, 1969), pp. 240-241.

[13] Ch'ing-K'un Yang, *A Chinese Village and Its Early Change Under Communism* (Cambridge, Mass.: Massachusetts Institute of Technology Center for International Studies, 1954), p. 127; also see p. 46. For Vietnam, see Robert L. Sansom, *The Economics of Insurgency in the Mekong Delta of Vietnam* (Cambridge, Mass.: The M.I.T. Press, 1970), p. 193.

conditions led to a withdrawal toward insulation and self-sufficiency.[14]

When involved in primarily subsistence agriculture, the main forces beyond their control that peasants had to confront, besides exploitation through tax collection, rent, etc., were those of nature. And even the vagaries of nature were minimized by them as much as possible. This does not refer to the countless beliefs and ceremonies associated with the agricultural cycle which served to lessen peasants' anxieties in dealing with nature. Rather, their seed varieties, though producing generally low yields, were often suited to produce at least *some* yield to get them through to the next harvest, even in times of excess (or insufficient) rain or sun. They were suspicious of new types of seed or new crops which offered higher yields under ideal conditions but had not been proven to the peasants as having the stamina to survive on their worn-out piece of land, in extreme weather conditions, or under a siege of local disease.[15]

In short, peasants followed a minimax strategy, maximizing control over their environment with a minimum of risk. Innovations were looked upon skeptically, for the peasant was aware that so-called advances could leave him worse off than before, and this could be an intolerable risk to those already hovering near the brink of survival.[16] The Crooks describe the insecurity involved with innovative ventures for peasants in a prerevolutionary Chinese village.

> Winter wheat had always been considered a risky proposition in the past, for it was absolutely dependent on the

[14] For China, see G. William Skinner, "Chinese Peasants and the Closed Community: An Open and Shut Case," *Comparative Studies in Society and History* 13 (July 1971), 270-281.

[15] Guy Hunter, *Modernizing Peasant Societies: A Comparative Study in Asia and Africa* (New York: Oxford University Press, 1969), p. 34.

[16] Andrew Pearse, "Agrarian Change Trends in Latin America," *Latin American Research Review* 1 (Summer 1966), 65. Also, see Joel M. Halpern, "The Rural Revolution," *Transactions of the New York Academy of Sciences*, ser. II, 28 (November 1965), 78.

weather. When taxes had been crushing and rents took 50 per cent or even more of the crop, few but the most prosperous could risk such a gamble. For the poor, who had to borrow seed, failure meant falling into the hands of usurers; success meant that the greater part of the crop was lost in rent or taxes.[17]

Peasants were always well aware that there were those at hand who would exploit them even more if they failed because of fluctuating prices or unsuccessful investments.

TYPES OF FREEHOLDING COMMUNITIES

Even though the dominant type of production was subsistence-oriented, there were differences among freeholding communities in the degree to which the peasants had face-to-face, primary contacts with other peasants in the local region. There were two main types of freeholding communities, the corporate village and the regional network village. Like the hacienda, the corporate village tended to be almost a society unto itself. In fact, Manning Nash goes so far as to call the corporate village in Mesoamerica a quasi-tribal system.[18] In many respects this is true. The village itself was a closed corporation, with land—the source of livelihood—available only to those born in the community. There was a differential allocation of power among all the households to make decisions concerning economic affairs, especially where land was scarce.[19] Often the land was communally owned. Almost all contacts with the representatives of the state and other outsiders were through the official representative (headman) of the village. Taxes were paid by the village as a unit. Even interaction with other peasant communities was minimal: local market relations were few and the villages were endogamous.

[17] Isabel and David Crook, *Revolution in a Chinese Village: Ten Mile Inn* (London: Routledge and Kegan Paul, 1959), pp. 161-162.

[18] Manning Nash, *Primitive and Peasant Economic Systems* (San Francisco: Chandler Publishing, 1966), p. 61.

[19] Befu, "The Political Relation of the Village to the State," p. 610.

Other types of freeholding communities (also of communities with weak lords), regional network villages, had the same limitations against expanding external relations through multiplier institutions and also buffered the individual against the state. In such villages, however, regional, face-to-face contacts were an essential part of the peasants' lives. Many of the peasants' needs in regional network villages were always met by local people or local goods from outside the immediate community.

Where the neighboring villages were not similar in economy and local services, the regional network was likely to be based on trade. Sol Tax's famous study, *Penny Capitalism*, describes such a system in Guatemala. The unusual ecological variation within the regional area allowed each community to specialize in particular crops. The Indians of Panajachel, for example, grew very few of the staple crops of corn and beans but rather produced primarily onions, garlic, fruits, and coffee. They used the cash they earned from these crops to buy the other foods grown in neighboring villages, necessary to round out their diet. Daily or weekly markets came in a regular sequence, each specializing in certain goods but also carrying a small supply of other products. These markets were characterized by the numerous small producers and small buyers (either consumers themselves or traders who took goods to another market to sell directly to consumers).[20]

Regional peasant markets often did not involve the same risks to small cultivators and the same insecurities as did larger, national markets.[21] First, when dealing in regional peasant markets, the cultivators were interacting with people roughly equal in status to them and thus people who were

[20] Sol Tax, *Penny Capitalism: A Guatemalan Indian Economy* (Chicago: The University of Chicago Press, 1963).

[21] For the distinction between regional peasant markets and larger marketing systems, see Cyril S. Belshaw, *Traditional Exchange and Modern Markets* (Englewood Cliffs, N.J.: Prentice-Hall, 1965), p. 69, and Eric R. Wolf, "Closed Corporate Peasant Communities in Mesoamerica and Central Java," *Southwestern Journal of Anthropology* 13 (Spring 1957), 4-5.

unable to bring to bear the types of pressures and monopolistic practices that more powerful people might have brought. Second, the face-to-face, habitual contact characteristic of such markets mitigated against inconsistent behavior by others. Third, peasant markets themselves helped spread risks. Because of the large number of peasant middlemen, the risks for each were minimized. Produce was spread so that no one peasant merchant had invested enough capital to incur substantial loss.[22] The numerous peasant middlemen with small stocks also made for a perfectly competitive situation. This shielded the other peasants from the types of abuses they suffered where there was monopolistic control over certain components of a larger market.

In different areas, regional networks were based on interaction that was not economic in nature. Lewis contrasted the intervillage network of two communities he studied on opposite ends of the world. Tepoztlán, Morelos, in Mexico had intercommunity ties that were almost purely trade-oriented. Rampur in Delhi State, India, on the other hand, was part of a complex intervillage system resulting primarily from kinship ties, secondarily from religious pilgrimages, and only lastly from trade.[23]

The importance of ritual interdependence and social interaction among local peasants was observed quite often in South and Southeast Asia. Rani Khera (Delhi State, India), for example, was within a multiple intervillage network in which it had ties with over 400 other villages,[24] yet all these ties were face-to-face. [25]

[22] Shepard Forman and Joyce F. Riegelhaupt, "Market Place and Marketing System: Toward a Theory of Peasant Economic Integration," *Comparative Studies in Society and History* 12 (April 1970), 202.

[23] Oscar Lewis, *Village Life in Northern India: Studies in a Delhi Village* (Urbana: University of Illinois Press, 1958), pp. 324-325.

[24] Oscar Lewis, "Peasant Culture in India and Mexico: A Comparative Analysis," in *Village India*, ed. McKim Marriott, p. 167.

[25] Sirkanda, India's, "culture-area" encompassed about sixty villages with about 5,000 people. Berreman, *Hindus of the Himalayas*, p. 295.

Non-trade type relations within a regional network have been described vividly in relation to Pelpola, a village in Ceylon.

> The village family dressed in its colorful best and bearing baskets of goodies on head or by hand is a familiar sight along the lanes and cart-tracks. Pelpola is deeply and intricately immersed in its own self-contained life but the ties to kin in surrounding villages are complex, close, and very nearly universal. These bonds are expressed mainly in family visiting and reciprocities, but sometimes in attendance at special religious observances in the neighboring village temples or other social events outside the immediate kinship sphere.[26]

Whatever the exact pattern of the relationships, the point to be emphasized is the regional system's geographic limitation. Moreover, relations remained primary and face-to-face. The networks, of course, expanded the number of face-to-face encounters compared to those of peasants in corporate villages, but still there were few secondary or indirect relationships. Peasants in regional network villages did not interact within multiplier institutions that related peasants to large numbers of others—others who might be quite different from themselves—whom they never saw.

The question that remains is why some inward-oriented villages were more involved in regional networks than others. To date, almost none of the literature has addressed itself to this question. It is hypothesized here that at least two factors determine whether an inward-oriented village employed institutionalized channels of contact on a regional basis. First is the ecology for diverse crop-growing in an area. If within a small region there was significant ecological variation, as in Panajachel's region in Guatemala, various villages could specialize offering supplements to each other's specialties. Where ecology for growing over an area was much the same, there was less reason for regional interaction of this kind.

[26] Bryce Ryan, *Sinhalese Village*, pp. 5-6.

Population density also seems to have had an effect on regional interaction. Where cultivable land was quite limited, villages widely scattered, and transportation poor, as in much of Latin America, one is likely to have found entities which were societies unto themselves, corporate villages. In South and Southeast Asia, however, the high population density in many areas, stemming from large tracts of cultivable land and the growing of an intensive crop such as wet rice (especially where shared irrigation systems were employed) resulted in various unavoidable contacts with a larger number of people over a wider area than just the village boundaries. Just as villages devised mechanisms to avoid disputes within their boundaries which would bring in outside forces or disrupt the village economy, so too did areas of habitual contact devise such mechanisms—marriage networks, ritual interdependence, etc.—even when the motivations for trade were low. It should be remembered that these mechanisms were not always successful, and peasant villages have been known to have engaged in destructive fighting against one another.[27]

SUMMARY

Lords saw peasant contacts with outsiders as a threat to their control and applied heavy sanctions against those who endangered the inward-orientation they worked to maintain. What is not as easily grasped is the fact that pressures from outside the village, from those classes above the peasantry, acted to produce inward-oriented communities even when lords were not present administering sanctions.

This chapter has identified two reasons why freeholding peasants historically limited their degree of external relations. First, peasants withdrew from significant participation with

[27] In my current research on Arabs of the West Bank of the Jordan River, I have found such warfare to be one of the causes for the depopulation of Palestine until the mid-nineteenth century. See A. Granott, *The Land System in Palestine: History and Structure* (London: Eyre and Spottiswoode, 1952), p. 73.

others because of their powerlessness to manipulate the outside world for their benefit. Exploitation by those classes controlling the state or their representatives was a continuing problem. There resulted an orientation toward minimization of outside dependencies in favor of supplying needs within the family and the local area.

The second reason freeholding peasants were inward-oriented is integrally related to the first. The insecurity of market participation discouraged peasants from raising cash crops and instead further encouraged primarily subsistence agriculture in which the peasants minimized reliance on people and events over which they had no control. Such insecurity stemmed from the gaps and inconsistencies in the market's components, as well as monopolization by powerful members of other classes. As a result of this paucity of economic interdependence, peasants lacked the types of interactions which could have served as bases for political alliances. Inadequate market institutions meant that peasants lacked the medium of exchange whereby they could have created economic interdependence between themselves and those from other classes, and this further accentuated their powerlessness.

CHAPTER IV

Mechanisms of Survival

INTRODUCTION

THE PREVIOUS CHAPTER, focusing on the economic and political relationship between the peasantry and the classes above them, analyzed the reasons *why* freeholding communities were inward-oriented. What still remains to be explained is *how* freeholding communities were able to enforce this minimization of outside ties, the inward-orientation. Unlike the situation in which a lord could call on outsiders or use his control of vital resources to apply sanctions, freeholding villages were composed of people much more equal in resources and power.

This chapter explores the question of how such communities were able to prevent specific peasants from using a momentary advantage in order to form outside alliances and then to dominate their neighbors. In addition, the chapter will analyze the ways in which peasants in freeholding communities managed to meet their needs despite their withdrawal from reliance on outsiders.

The precise forms of peasant social and political organization varied in different cultures but not so much so that they cannot be compared in terms of their similar effects on peasants' actions.[1] Certainly, village institutions in each culture evolved in unique ways because of a variety of complex rea-

---

[1] A similar point has been made in *The Peasant: A Symposium Concerning the Peasant Way and View of Life*, ed. F. G. Friedmann, no. 6 (February 1956), mimeo, p. 3.

sons. Topography, land fertility, climate, and numerous other factors made distinct demands upon peasant life. The argument developed here, however, is that there were common cross-cultural characteristics of social and political organization as well, which stemmed from peasants' subservience to other classes in the society and from the internal conditions such subservience produced.

Such an analysis views the community's social and political organization as putting restraints on individual behavior. This is not to say that there was an iron law within the village which was followed to the letter by all. There was often a high degree of dissatisfaction, and some members' behavior stretched the limits of the community's tolerance. Some secretly deviated from community norms, and peasants who had the resources to do so could even flout the village institutions openly. Yet, despite this element of choice of action, the community still was strong enough to act as an effective deterrent and was a guide for social behavior for the great majority of peasants.

This book rejects the point of view that poor motivation or traditional values of individual peasants caused peasant economic isolation (and related low productivity). Kalman Silvert in his discussion of traditional peoples suggests this latter method of analysis. In a traditional society, he states, "the motivation for decision is ritualistic. ('What was good enough for my father is good enough for me.')"[2]

This type of analysis which views people's outmoded opinions and values as preventing them from doing things the "better way" is especially prevalent among writers concerned specifically with peasants. One author, Bertram Hutchinson, writes that the chief obstacle to economic change among peasants was the social ethos that is inimical to it.[3] Edward Banfield has canonized this idea in his widely read *The Moral*

[2] Kalman H. Silvert, *Man's Power: A Biased Guide to Political Thought and Action* (New York: The Viking Press, 1970), p. 24.

[3] Bertram Hutchinson, "The Patron-Dependant Relationship in Brazil: A Preliminary Examination," *Sociologia Ruralis* 6 (1966), 3.

Basis of a Backward Society, which is about peasants in a southern Italian village.[4]

Focus on peasant values and motivation certainly offers insight into peasant life. Elevation of such findings to highly significant causal factors, rather than intervening variables, however, indicates an insufficient sensitivity to the broader physical, social, political, and economic realities to which peasants had to accommodate. The explanation here shows that certain types of social and political organization persisted as mechanisms that best coped with a hostile environment.

SUBCOMMUNITY LEVEL SURVIVAL MECHANISMS

In much the same way as peasants who were atomized by strong lords, peasants who did not experience such powerful or direct control placed great stress on the household as a mechanism to spread risks. The household ensured that responsibility for one's economic survival did not fall only on the individual. The following lengthy quotation of an Indian villager indicates the utter importance such domestic groups had in spreading risks and dividing labor.

> No villager thinks of himself apart from his family. He rises or falls with it. In the cities families are scattering. But we need the strength of the family to support us. We do not trust the outside world, and we are suspicious of each other. Our lives are oppressed by mean fears. We fear the rent collector, we fear the police watchman, we fear everyone who looks as though he might claim some authority over us, we fear our creditors, we fear our patrons, we fear too much rain, we fear locusts, we fear thieves, we fear the evil spirits which threaten our children and our animals, and we fear the strength of our neighbor. Do you wonder that we unite the strength of brothers and sons? That man is to be pitied who must stand alone against the dangers seen

[4] Edward C. Banfield, *The Moral Basis of a Backward Society* (New York: The Free Press, 1958).

62

and unseen, which beset him. Our families are our insurance. When a man falls ill, he knows that his family will care for him and his children until he is able to earn again. And he will be cared for without a word of reproach. If a man dies, his widow and children are sure of the protection of a home.[5]

Households adapted to their environment in order to maximize the chances of survival in an uncertain world. An inadequate labor force meant the household's land was underutilized, and an oversupply of labor also put great strains on the sources of income. Peasants facing scarcity seemed to have attempted to optimize household size at a number which brought the fullest return per capita.[6] This implies that there were mechanisms, either social or mechanical, for controlling the number of members of the household. Other things being equal, then, one would expect to find larger numbers in households (and ultimately, a higher birth rate) in areas of crops demanding more labor intensity (e.g., wet rice areas of dynastic China) than in areas with crops demanding low labor intensity (e.g., medieval Europe).

Methods to control household size often became institutionalized into the culture and were not necessarily purposeful on the part of individual peasants. For example, optimization of household size when there were too few members was often achieved when peasants had such practices as an

[5] Quoted in William H. and Charlotte Viall Wiser, *Behind Mud Walls 1930-1960* (Berkeley: University of California Press, 1964), pp. 122-123.

[6] More explicitly, we can hypothesize that peasants low on the scale of external relations, having a relatively unchanging level of technology and a fixed amount of land, attempted to optimize household size at the number at which the marginal product of an additional member equaled only the amount that member consumed. It should be added here that although peasants attempted to optimize their size, historically great surges or losses in size of populations were often caused by factors outside their control. As a result, they were faced with periods of large surpluses and with periods of excruciating shortages.

early marriage age, which served to keep the birth rate high. They also sometimes took outsiders into the household. Widows, orphans, poor children, and others[7] were incorporated into the household along with the members of the nuclear or extended family.[8]

Even the propensity in so many villages to take in elder parents and other old relatives can be understood in terms of these people's contribution to the overall production of the household. The old people's care of infants might have freed the wife to work in the fields, or their weaving might have brought in badly needed cash. Hopefully, this is not too mercenary a view of human nature. However, in a society where old people add almost nothing to the productive capacities of the living group, as in the current United States, countless numbers of them are forgotten and left in abject poverty relative to others in the society. In inward-oriented villages, where the household—not the individual—was the basic economic unit, pooling and dividing the work served as an insurance policy for the elderly even when their range of capabilities decreased.

Households were not always successful in adding members. At other times they grew beyond the optimal size. If the point

[7] Four of the fifteen monographs on villages low on the scale of external relations indicated the existence of such household compositions. Also see Gerald D. Berreman, *Hindus of the Himalayas* (Berkeley: University of California Press, 1963), p. 43; William W. Stein, *Hualcan: Life in the Highlands of Peru* (Ithaca, N.Y.: Cornell University Press, 1961); and Michael Moerman, *Agricultural Change and Peasant Choice in a Thai Village* (Berkeley: University of California Press, 1968).

[8] For the fifteen villages of limited outside participation in this study, the breakdown follows below. These figures are only suggestive since there is considerable variation in the degree to which the authors of the monographs described the composition of households.

5 all or almost all nuclear
3 mostly nuclear
3 fairly evenly split
2 mostly extended
2 all or almost all extended

of full utilization of land was already achieved or exceeded, households sought to limit their members or extend their landholding. Various forms of birth control[9] (e.g., delaying marriage, abstinence, etc.), infanticide,[10] and selling of children were used to ensure that the household was not too large when there was no access to additional land.

The household was much more than a purely economic unit: it was the primary social group within which most villagers interacted. It was built upon multiplex[11] ties of its members to ensure that seeds were planted, sexual pleasure was provided, crops were cared for and harvested, meals were prepared, children were born and raised, and other numerous functions were performed. Through reinforcement of ties, stemming from the household's function as the productive unit, beyond the economic realm into realms of kinship and religious obligation, peasants succeeded in creating some degree of economic and social stability in their very precarious circumstances.[12]

Most peasants did not limit themselves to only the household to spread the risks of survival.[13] The prevalence of the household, however, can be explained in part by the suit-

[9] Edwin D. Driver, *Differential Fertility in Central India* (Princeton, N.J.: Princeton University Press, 1963), pp. 12-13.

[10] Infanticide is not well documented, but it is striking in going through monographs on peasant villages how often there are more men than women in the village. Chinese poor families engaged in infanticide in times of desperation. For an interesting comment on a French case, see Emily R. Colemen, "Medieval Marriage Characteristics: A Neglected Factor in the History of Medieval Serfdom," *The Journal of Interdisciplinary History* 2 (Autumn 1971), 209-210.

[11] The term refers to relationships that were not specialized. See F. G. Bailey, "The Peasant View of the Bad Life," *The Advancement of Science* 23 (December 1966), 401.

[12] For a deviant case, see E. R. Leach, *Pul Eliya, A Village in Ceylon: A Study of Land Tenure and Kinship* (Cambridge: Cambridge University Press, 1961).

[13] See, for example, Melvin M. Tumin, *Caste in a Peasant Society: A Case Study in the Dynamics of Caste* (Princeton, N.J.: Princeton University Press, 1952); and Banfield, *The Moral Basis of a Backward Society*.

ability of its size and organization to the economy of subsistence production. Other institutions within which peasants sought insurance against their precariousness usually lacked the economic rationale of the household and served in addition to it, rather than instead of it.

Survival mechanisms, such as godparent relations, neighborhood groups, castes, and most importantly kinship groups, were thus additional means of maximizing stability for the individual through multiplex ties.[14] Without extensive economic role differentiation and specialization, peasants lacked the social experiences that would have enabled them to build complex, goal-oriented organizations. However, such alliances served to reduce the chances of internal conflict among those who had the most habitual contact. In case of intra-village quarrels, they provided support groups for the peasant, and they also presented the peasant with others on whom he could rely in his struggle against fate and exploitative outsiders.

COMMUNITY LEVEL SURVIVAL MECHANISMS

The strength of the community level institutions—the village social and political organization—varied with the degree to

[14] On neighborhood groups, see, for example, William F. and Corinne Nydegger, *Tarong: An Ilocos Barrio in the Philippines* (New York: John Wiley and Sons, 1966). On godparent relations, see Sidney W. Mintz and Eric R. Wolf, "An Analysis of Ritual Co-Parenthood (Compadrazgo)," in *Peasant Society: A Reader*, ed. Jack M. Potter, May N. Diaz, and George M. Foster (Boston: Little, Brown, 1966), pp. 174-199; and Francisco Rojas Gonzalez, "La Institución del Compadrazgo entre los Indios de México," *Revista Mexicana de Sociología* 5 (1943), 213. For a discussion of compadrazgo in the Philippines, see Mary R. Hollnsteiner, "Social Structure and Power in a Philippine Municipality," in *Peasant Society*, ed. Potter *et al.*, pp. 200-212. For poignant examples of the role of kinship and friendship groups, see the accounts in Zekiye Eglar, *A Punjabi Village in Pakistan* (New York: Columbia University Press, 1960); and Alan R. Beals, *Gopalpur, A South Indian Village* (New York: Holt, Rinehart, 1962).

66

which the peasants were free of lords' restraints. Perhaps the most typical experience of peasants was that of facing some restraints from a less than all-powerful lord and participating, as well, in a moderately strong village social and political organization.

This section will analyze the relationship between community level institutions and the threats to the peasants' survival—threats from outside the community, from within the community, and from fate. The social and political organization of inward-oriented villages had the effect of dealing with these threats in three ways: (1) it inhibited establishment of alliances between individual peasants and potentially disruptive (to other peasants) outside institutions; (2) it spread the risks associated with fate and scarcity; and (3) it maintained domestic tranquility. Again, the degree to which these three effects were actually achieved varied considerably and depended greatly on the strength of the village social and political organization.

1) *Inhibiting Outside Alliances and Limits on Upward Mobility*

Even though inward-oriented villages are often thought of as unchanging, in reality there was a considerable degree of both upward and downward social mobility within such communities.[15] In Sirkanda in the Indian Himalayas, for example, of the four wealthiest households (and wealth was a basis of high status there), two became so in the last generation. Several other households were not as wealthy as they had been, mostly because of insufficient labor to work the land.[16] In India, entire castes have moved upward through accumulation of wealth and subsequent changes in their ritual and social behavior ("sanskritization").[17]

---

[15] For example, in the cases used in this study, seven of the fifteen monographs on such villages, specifically mention the existence of downward mobility within the peasant communities.

[16] Berreman, *Hindus of the Himalayas.*

[17] Bailey wrote of one caste in Bisipara (Orissa, India), that "there

One of the interesting and crucial differences between such villages and other sectors of society was the absolute limits on upward and downward mobility often found in peasant villages. Unlimited upward mobility of a household presented a direct threat to the remainder of the community. Once one household accumulated sufficient wealth and power, it could form alliances with groups outside the community, becoming immune to other villagers' sanctions. A hole in the dike would threaten the weak—those who did not have the capabilities to withstand direct involvement of outsiders in the affairs of the village.

Outside involvement for such peasants might have meant increased exploitation rather than an alliance providing reciprocal benefits. Or services now provided free by other villagers might have been put beyond their grasp in an entirely cash economy. Therefore various social mechanisms developed which had the effect of preventing unlimited upward mobility. In general, the village's social mechanisms required consumption of wealth as a means of earning prestige within the community. Thus, if one strove to achieve prestige within the village, he found himself without the necessary resources to forge alliances and achieve social mobility in the larger society.[18] It should be mentioned that such mechanisms were never entirely successful and there were always cases of peasants accumulating sufficient wealth

---

is no doubt that the Distillers, from being just above the line of pollution, are now in the upper levels of Bisipara's caste ladder." F. G. Bailey, "Parapolitical Systems," in *Local-Level Politics: Social and Cultural Perspectives*, ed. Marc J. Swartz (Chicago: Aldine, 1968), p. 284.

[18] What were the bases for high status within inward-oriented communities? Although ascriptive criteria predominate, there is certainly no rigid exclusion of achievement criteria. In nine of fifteen villages low on the scale of external relations, some form of achievement, usually involving land and wealth accumulation, was mentioned as one component of status assignment. In only one of those villages, however, was it the sole determinant mentioned.

to move into the gentry and become exploiters of their former neighbors.

Within the village's closed status system, then, a prestige economy developed which either redistributed or consumed the surplus wealth of the richest. In Vietnam, parties, banquets, and subscriptions were ways of divesting the rich of some of their wealth and redistributing it among the rest of the community.[19] Wolf found that in both Mesoamerica and Central Java, the community motivated the expenditure of surpluses beyond subsistence needs on communal religious cults and allied religious activities.[20] Fiesta systems and other expensive ceremonial activities were popular methods of earning religious merit and prestige within these villages.[21] In Panachel, Guatemala, the wealthier members paid the high cost of liquor at public rituals.[22]

There was a recognition of status differences[23] in inward-oriented villages, but those with wealth were prevented from jeopardizing others by using their resources to create alliances outside the village. The prevalence of status differences indicates that even in such homogeneous, autonomous com-

[19] John T. McAlister, Jr. and Paul Mus, *The Vietnamese and Their Revolution*, Harper Torchbooks (New York; Harper and Row, 1970), p. 33.

[20] Eric R. Wolf, "Closed Corporate Peasant Communities in Mesoamerica and Central Java," *Southwestern Journal of Anthropology* 13 (Spring 1957), 4.

[21] For a note of caution on when fiestas, etc., actually consumed or redistributed wealth, see William F. Whyte and Lawrence K. Williams, *Towards an Integrated Theory of Development: Economic and Non-economic Variables in Rural Development* (Ithaca, N.Y.: New York State School of Industrial and Labor Relations, Cornell University, 1968), p. 18.

[22] Sol Tax, *Penny Capitalism: A Guatemalan Indian Economy* (Chicago: The University of Chicago Press, 1963).

[23] Only one of the monographs on villages low on the scale of external relations stated that there were no status differences to be found. W. R. Geddes, *Deuba: A Study of a Fijian Village* (Wellington, New Zealand: The Polynesian Society, 1945). All the others specifically pointed to some kind of stratification.

munities, there were differentiations of power. Although no one person or household had the power of a lord, the possession of certain resources or traits allowed some to make greater demands on others. Certain people could expect more deference than others.[24] Despite these power differences, community mechanisms in such villages had the effect of limiting the resource base of wealthier peasants.[25]

Besides redistributive mechanisms and activities consuming wealth, there was one more way of avoiding the problem of unlimited accumulation, one that has been largely misinterpreted. This factor is the limitation of work. There is a striking contrast among communities in the amount of work actually done by peasants. Cultivators in Mohana (India), a village which has recently begun to increase outside relations, worked "laboriously and incessantly," having little recreation besides several fiestas during the year.[26] On the other hand, peasants of Aritama in Colombia, a village at about the same point on the scale as Mohana, were very nonchalant about their agriculture, leisurely going out to their fields several days a week to collect food.[27]

Such differing cases should dispel either of the two conflicting stereotypes of the peasant as a lazy person or as someone working from sunrise to sunset stooped over a parched piece of earth. Where the soil barely produced enough for subsistence needs, hard work was demanded of peasants for survival. In other cases, where soil was fertile and plentiful, producing more than enough for subsistence and fiestas, inward-oriented peasants might have limited accumulation through an anti-Protestant Ethic.

[24] See Tumin, *Caste in a Peasant Society*, p. 14.

[25] Manning Nash, "Political Relations in Guatemala," *Social and Economic Studies* 7 (March 1958), 69.

[26] D. N. Majumdar, *Caste and Communication in an Indian Village* (Bombay: Asia Publishing House, 1958), p. 163.

[27] Gerardo and Alicia Reichel-Dolmatoff, *The People of Aritama: The Cultural Personality of a Colombian Mestizo Village* (London: Routledge and Kegan Paul, 1961).

More specifically, where scarcity of resources was not a problem, it is hypothesized that inward-oriented villages prevented private, unlimited accumulation through a credo in which people who accumulated significantly beyond their needs and the demands of the prestige economy were looked down upon. In the case of Aritama (Colombia), the prestige economy demanded food exchange, "a control system that tends to hinder the individual from achieving a higher status level from which recrimination might be directed against those who remained on a lower level."[28] Beyond production for food exchange and for subsistence in Aritama, peasants had to limit their labor so as not to be thought aggressive. "What the casual observer would simply call laziness, inertia or lack of responsibility must then be viewed rather as evidence of a very fine social balance which has to be maintained by a conscious effort to restrict one's personal ambitions and potential resources."[29]

The evidence presented here corroborates Cyril Belshaw's argument that extensive market involvement did not simply begin when peasants were able to create a surplus, as has been too often assumed.[30] There were limitations on market participation not because of a lack of surplus but because self-sufficiency was demanded by the insecurity of outside participation for most village peasants and by the powerlessness of peasants in respect to that world outside. To understand that there were forces within the village countering a wealthy minority's attraction to a national market and to the accompanying wider status system is a first step in recognizing the tension involved in the process of peasant economic and social change.

It is the argument of this book that peasant social institutions grew to ensure survival in an insecure world. To this end, they created a force against any person's showing eco-

[28] *Ibid.*, p. 254.   [29] *Ibid.*, p. 260.
[30] Cyril S. Belshaw, *Traditional Exchange and Modern Markets* (Englewood Cliffs, N.J.: Prentice-Hall, 1965), pp. 77-78.

nomic initiative.[31] Mere culture contact with a national marketing system or other modern institutions did not free the peasant from institutionalized procedures within the village which prevented outside participation.

2) *Spreading Risks and the Limits on Downward Mobility*

Because peasant villages were so often close to the line between famine and subsistence and because fate could be particularly harsh to even relatively prosperous peasants, there developed community mechanisms to maximize security for the household. The very precariousness of middle income and even wealthier peasants was such that they too had little margin for safety.[32] A fire in one's fields, the death of one's oxen, or numerous other contingencies could mean utter destitution. Village cooperation in assuming the responsibility that no one fell below the survival line was, then, simply a "shared risk insurance policy." Although such insurance policies in many cases failed to keep starving peasants alive, they did do the job many times in instances of less than community-wide disasters.

Access to the land or to the produce of the land for everyone was one of the primary characteristics of such an insurance policy. Hunter cites various landowning, tenancy, sharecropping, and bondsmen relationships which guaranteed access to food except in times of total crop failure. Also, craftsmen, priests, and servants with no access to land were paid with a share of the harvest.[33] Other villagers provided

[31] George M. Foster, "Peasant Society and the Image of Limited Good," *American Anthropologist* 67 (April 1965), 296-305, stresses the cognitive orientation of peasants which prevented change. Our analysis emphasizes, on the other hand, the very real social and economic conditions which have caused such an orientation.

[32] See, for example, Ch'ing-K'un Yang, *A Chinese Village and Its Early Change Under Communism* (Cambridge, Mass.: Massachusetts Institute of Technology Center for International Studies, 1954).

[33] Guy Hunter, *Modernizing Peasant Societies: A Comparative Study in Asia and Africa* (New York: Oxford University Press, 1969), pp. 32-33.

direct aid to those with whom fate dealt harshly. In Buarij, Lebanon, for example, if a man's crops were destroyed, the others replenished them. If there was a household without children, people gave a free day of plowing.[34]

Other means to implement a shared risk insurance policy involved the development of restrictions. Such a policy demanded that the village deny certain members the right to import "progressive methods" because of the detrimental effect they could have on the poorest. The lower limit on downward mobility was thus integrally related to the limit on upward mobility. Hunter expressed this idea well:

> Cow dung is used for fuel—the slow heat is just right for making curds—and for plastering walls and floors; a little milk from a starveling cow—there cannot be oxen without cows—makes a vast difference to diet, or perhaps a little cash by sale of ghee; how will a tractor replace the dung, the plaster and the milk? Weeds grow between the lines of grain—and are allowed to grow and are cut from time to time (not uprooted) to feed the cattle. Undigested grain is picked out from cattle-dung and eaten; rats, snakes, white ants, locust—all may be sources of food. It is not the bigger farmers who depend on such trifles. But a change of crop and system, enclosure, mechanization, clearance of the waste, almost any progressive action may be cutting away an element of livelihood from the poorest.[35]

The intrusion of outside forces could therefore be *differentially* unsettling. In Tepoztlán (Morelos, Mexico), for example, a government department took control of the wooded areas around the village and prohibited burning of wood in order to prevent soil erosion. This action was felt most acute-

[34] Anne H. Fuller, *Buarij: Portrait of a Lebanese Muslim Village* (Cambridge, Mass.: Harvard University Press, 1961).
[35] Hunter, *Modernizing Peasant Societies*, pp. 35-36.

73

ly by the very poorest because they had depended on wood burning for charcoal production as a source of income.[36]

There were, then, differentiations among peasants within inward-oriented, freeholding villages in wealth, power, and relation to community institutions. Some peasants owned and worked part of their land and rented out other parts if they had more than the household could cultivate; others were tenants; still others were artisans or agricultural laborers without any tenure rights to land. As in other sectors of society, the possession of resources by some at any moment was used as a basis of power within the village. Yet, such differences among peasants were often not long-lived. There was frequently a fluidity to the internal stratification of such villages. One Chinese proverb pointed to the fluid nature of the social structure: "Nobody stays rich for three generations; nobody stays poor for three generations."[37] What the poor were experiencing at any moment, the rich could have feared in the not distant future.[38]

3) *Maintaining Domestic Tranquility*

Limits on upward and downward mobility dealt with the two threats posed by possible alliances with outsiders and by natural disaster. A third threat to survival that peasants had to face was posed by internecine struggles within the village itself.

In their own village, peasants had to have habitual contact with the other inhabitants; they did not have such daily con-

---

[36] Oscar Lewis, *Tepoztlán, Village in Mexico* (New York: Holt, Rinehart and Winston, 1960), pp. 102-103.

[37] Quoted in McAlister and Mus, *The Vietnamese and Their Revolution*, p. 33.

[38] The "poor," "middle," and "rich" distinctions made in this chapter must be seen as relative in nature. The "poor" were not so destitute and powerless compared to the "rich" that they did not participate in and influence village political institutions and decisions, although they certainly felt the power of the wealthier peasants, and to an outsider who walked into such a village, everyone seemed poor.

74

tact with any people from outside the village. Walking to one's field might have taken a villager through the fields of others. One's cattle might have grazed with the animals of others in scarce pasture land. These numerous contacts among village residents demanded social patterns which would have minimized any sources of friction that could have threatened the agricultural cycle. Moreover, it was within the village that peasants searched for alliances and unions upon which they could have depended for support under varying circumstances. A village consisted first of households, but they were too small and weak to afford the kind of security a community as a whole could give. For example, more than one household was needed for security against bandits or marauders.[39]

Internal conflict within the village could undermine the cooperation necessary for everyday work, such as gaining access to one's fields through the fields of others. Conflict could also undermine the viability of social institutions which lessened the other threats to survival. Fear of internal conflict that might undermine daily cooperation and disrupt security mechanisms were all the more real since there were a number of sources of tension and strife in inward-oriented peasant villages.

First, as we have seen, the institutions limiting upward and downward mobility demanded disproportionately large contributions from the wealthier peasants. The differences in wealth in the village made surplus consumption and redistribution more burdensome to some than to others.[40] Second,

[39] The peasants of Buarij, Lebanon, for example, build their houses in a cluster as "a means of unified defense against the outer world and also to ensure all village persons having easy access to one another" (Fuller, *Buarij*, p. 8). For a first-hand account of village disputes in nineteenth century Palestine, see James Finn, *Stirring Times: Or Records from Jerusalem Consular Chronicles of 1853 to 1856* (London: Kegan Paul, 1878), II, 193-210.

[40] Mehmet Beqiraj, *Peasantry in Revolution*, Center for International Studies, Cornell University, Cornell Research Papers in International Studies, vol. V (1966).

sanctions within the village were another source of tension. These sanctions had the effect of guaranteeing fulfillment of established obligations and thwarting the development of new roles by the wealthier members that might have jeopardized the others through an expansion of outside involvement. Those who were more wealthy and powerful often bristled at the curbs against deviance and at the assumption that their deviance was a harbinger of social change that could have affected the others' chances for survival.

Sanctions, then, maintained conformity, but they simultaneously heightened tension.[41] Informal social controls, depending mostly on shaming the individual, were some of the most important sanctions.[42] In Mohla in Pakistan's Punjab, elder women openly criticized anyone who did not engage properly in the institutionalized gift giving. Also, gifts were rejected there if the recipient felt they were insufficient.[43] Both these procedures, of course, brought great shame to the gift giver. The means of creating shame were a bit more subtle in Deuba (Fiji Islands). There the sanction involved showing slightly less deference to deviants, which brought them a serious loss of face.[44]

Gossip,[45] slander, criticism, insult, and ridicule were several of the prime informal social controls which helped maintain a conformity to existing roles in such villages.[46] These sanctions, though often successful in preventing the development of new roles and alliances, had at the same time the pathological effect of heightening opportunities for personal en-

[41] F. G. Bailey, "The Peasant View of the Bad Life."

[42] Everett E. Hagen, *On the Theory of Social Change: How Economic Growth Begins* (Homewood, Ill.: The Dorsey Press, 1962), pp. 176-177.

[43] Eglar, *A Punjabi Village in Pakistan.*

[44] Geddes, *Deuba.*

[45] Tumin, *Caste in a Peasant Society*, p. 31, talks of the importance of slaughtering the reputations of others.

[46] In Panajachel, Guatemala, for example, all these methods were quite prevalent (Tax, *Penny Capitalism*).

mity to grow and for interpersonal friction to arise in every-day dealings.

Other types of sanctions put similar strains on interpersonal relations. Refusal of cooperation to any household in completing any of the few tasks that took a large amount of labor was a harsh but effective sanction.[47] The most severe (and rarely used) means on the hierarchy of sanctions were ostracism and banishment.[48] Alienation from the land and from the protection of the village was especially feared by those who knew the outside world to be anything but friendly. In some villages, actual physical coercion to ensure conformity took place. Peasants in Gopalpur, South India, for example, physically banded against any member of their jadi (caste) who succeeded in advancing himself economically.[49]

The important point to note here was the price paid for such control. It is ironic that in order to minimize the threats to survival posed by fate and outside forces, villages increased the third type of threat: internal tension and conflict. Suspicion, faction,[50] and distrust were thus characteristic of social relations of inward-oriented villages.

Cooperation went only so far as the formal mechanisms prescribed. Mutual suspicion limited any cooperation beyond that of honoring reciprocal obligations to the letter.[51] This lack of extensive economic interdependence, coupled with sanctions which could affect a man's standing among others in the village, led to a condition of envy and distrust.[52] Such

[47] Hagen, *On the Theory of Social Change*, p. 66.

[48] Hunter, *Modernizing Peasant Societies*, p. 40, also mentions witchcraft.

[49] Alan R. Beals, *Gopalpur, A South Indian Village*.

[50] For a discussion of factions, see Ralph W. Nicholas, "Factions: A Comparative Analysis," in *Political Systems and the Distribution of Power*, ed. Michael Banton (New York: Barnes and Noble, 1965), pp. 21-61.

[51] Foster, "Peasant Society and the Image of Limited Good," p. 308.

[52] See the statement by George M. Foster, *Traditional Cultures: and the Impact of Technological Change* (New York: Harper, 1962), p. 50.

lack of interpersonal trust in part stemmed from and, in turn, reinforced the familistic orientation of peasants. Such an orientation was already strong because of the organization of production along household lines.[53]

The third effect of village social institutions—besides the two of minimizing the threats of fate and a union of wealthy peasants with outside forces—was to maintain domestic tranquility, or at least stability, given such an atmosphere of familism and distrust. Because there was a paucity of regular economic interaction to help maintain some minimal solidarity, villages turned to other mechanisms to achieve this goal. (It should be noted that, as with the other two threats, there were numerous instances when the village's institutions failed in this respect. In such cases, villages split permanently or experienced open hostilities between factions.)

Fictive kinship for the entire village was one method of promoting tranquility and cohesion. In Pul Eliya, Ceylon, for example, the villagers maintained the fiction that the entire village was within one kinship group, even though when pressed they admitted that this was not true.[54] Endogamy, as in Demirciler in Turkey, was often combined with a myth of the founding of the village by a common ancestor.[55] Many Chinese villages were built by single lineages, another means of reinforcing solidarity.[56]

[53] See Banfield, *The Moral Basis of a Backward Society* for a discussion of what he calls amoral familism. Unfortunately, Banfield spends too little time identifying the basis of such an orientation, but he does show the effects it has on the ability to cooperate. Also, see Stein, *Hualcan.*

[54] E. R. Leach, *Pul Eliya.*

[55] Joe E. Pierce, *Life in a Turkish Village* (New York: Holt, Rinehart and Winston, 1964).

[56] This is often maintained even in outward-oriented villages. See Jack M. Potter, *Capitalism and the Chinese Peasant: Social and Economic Change in a Hong Kong Village* (Berkeley: University of California Press, 1968). In Taitou, Shantung Province, all refer to

In all these cases, peasants again maximized stability by building multiplex relations, reinforcing ties through fictional or real ascriptive associations when there was little economic bond to tie people together. This was supplemented by the existence of an accepted rating system which provided a stable basis for interaction among all villagers. For example, in Demirciler, Turkey, stratification was by age and sex. Every person knew exactly to whom he should show deference and respect (and how much) and from whom he could expect the same.[57]

Reciprocal gift giving (with no or little redistributive effect) was a prime procedure for maintaining domestic tranquility. Gift giving served as a means of building clear expectations of reciprocal obligations so that little margin for error was left in interpersonal relations which might have led to hostility.[58] Another example of establishing clear expectations of reciprocity was cooperative labor or mutual aid. The forms of cooperative labor were numerous. Deuba (Fiji Islands) demanded an extreme amount. Every Thursday, the men cleaned the village and repaired the latrines. Besides that, four months through the course of the year were spent on cooperative housebuilding.[59] In Tarong (Philippines), a cooperative work group was formed for big tasks. The man needing the work done supplied the materials and a large fiesta-like meal for those who showed up for work.[60] Societies with intensive wet rice agriculture used cooperative labor both as a means to create clear reciprocal social obligations, as well as to assure that big work groups were available for

each other by kinship terms. Martin C. Yang, *A Chinese Village: Taitou, Shantung Province* (New York: Columbia University Press, 1945).

[57] Pierce, *Life in a Turkish Village.*

[58] See Stein, *Hualcan*; and Hagen, *On the Theory of Social Change*, pp. 66-67.

[59] Geddes, *Deuba.*

[60] Nydegger, *Tarong.* There are also smaller mutual aid groups there.

some of the large-scale, short-term work associated with that type of cultivation.[61] Although there was some economic utility to such practices, they were also means of solidifying bonds in the village.

Besides reciprocal gift giving, cooperative labor, and mutual aid, the existence of a village political organization was another means of maintaining internal stability. To this end, the political organization of inward-oriented villages had three primary functions: (1) to ensure that all fulfilled their duties (specifically in regard to such things as cooperative labor) and that all received their rights; (2) to settle disputes and maintain internal law and order; and (3) to act as the negotiator with outside forces, preventing them from forming alliances with stronger segments of the village population and buffering the weaker segments from their impact.

Village political organizations varied in their ability to perform those functions. One of the strongest was the political structure of Chan Kom in the Yucatan Peninsula. Head of the political organization there was the *comisario* who was elected yearly by all the adult males. He was aided by a deliberative body of *sargentos* who usually were the most educated men in the village. Each sargento headed a team of four village men which served for a week as *policia* on a rotating basis. The labor performed in such teams was called *fagina* and consumed up to one-quarter of any villager's work time. Membership in the village was, in fact, conditional on participation in fagina, which amounted to cooperative labor on various public works. Failure to participate was punished by the political leaders, first in arrest and imprisonment and, if necessary, later in total banishment from the village. Such banishment was all the more severe because local villages had an agreement to ban anyone from the village who had

---

[61] In Ku Daeng (Thailand), for example, transplanting and rice cutting were done with one's friends. Also, maintenance of the public irrigation system was done communally. Konrad Kingshill, *Ku Daeng —The Red Tomb, A Village Study in Northern Thailand* (Chiangmai, Thailand: The Prince Royal's College, 1960).

failed to perform fagina in another village in which he had resided.[62]

Settlement of disputes played a large role in the political life of inward-oriented villages. In Tarong, in the Philippines, for example, there was a hierarchy of means to settle disputes, starting with the household and going to the barrio (village) level. At each level, there were appropriate sanctions and mechanisms for dealing with deviance and failure to accept arbitration.[63] Villages' political leaders were well aware that the hierarchy of groups dealing with conflict did not stop at the village level. Peasants, in many cases, could have taken their dispute to an outside court or administrator, yet there was a strong desire to maintain village mechanisms for handling disputes. In Tarong, only two cases in three years went to court. Confinement of disputes to the village minimized the involvement of outside institutions in purely internal affairs and thus maintained the relatively closed status system.[64]

The political structure itself was, in most cases, a reflection of the village's relatively closed status system. In Demirciler in Anatolia, for example, influence in the village's deliberative body varied directly with age, as age was the prime status determinant, and usually the eldest of the males was the Muhtar (headman).[65] In Guatemala's Panajachel, where wealth rather than age played the leading role in assigning high status, there were political and religious offices in a single hierarchy. It was the wealthy who could afford the great expenses associated with various offices on the ladder to the top, and thus it was they who moved up most rapidly.[66]

[62] Robert Redfield and Alfonso Villa Rojas, *Chan Kom, A Maya Village*, Phoenix Books (Chicago: University of Chicago Press, 1962).

[63] Nydegger, *Tarong*.

[64] See Bernard Gallin, "Conflict Resolution in Changing Chinese Society: A Taiwanese Study," in *Political Anthropology*, ed. Marc J. Swartz, Victor W. Turner, and Arthur Tuden (Chicago: Aldine, 1966), p. 268.

[65] Pierce, *Life in a Turkish Village*.

[66] Tax, *Penny Capitalism*. Also, see Nash, "Political Relations in Guatemala," 67-71; and, on Peru, Stein, *Hualcan*.

Politics in inward-oriented villages was a parochial affair. Peasants faced exploitation from other classes in society and insecurities at every turn at which they attempted to strengthen their power position. Over the years, structures developed in such villages which had the effect of preventing (as best they could) outside forces from dealing with specific segments of the population. For example, paying taxes in kind as an entire village aided, not the wealthy who could have paid their taxes on an individual basis just as easily, but the man who did poorly this harvest. The village political leadership could compensate for his inability to pay by making slightly higher demands on others. Formal political structures in such villages, then, reflected and reinforced the inward-looking orientation. These political structures had the effect of strengthening a social organization oriented toward self-sufficiency. Through the settling of disputes, the political institutions also helped preserve the stability necessary for completion of the agricultural cycle in communities which lacked clear differentiation of economic tasks and interests and which faced the distrust generated by its informal social sanctions.

As other village institutions, the political structures also failed in many villages. Politics, in those cases, became marked by dissension and faction. Sanctions were ignored. The ability to execute decisions, if any were made, declined. And the villagers were denied that element of protection against outside forces which the community could have provided.

SUMMARY

Part One of this book has focused on the inward-orientation of historical peasant villages. This inward-orientation was expressed in a high degree of economic self-sufficiency of households, familism, a low level of technological innovation, and a relatively closed status system. Whether the village was a freeholding community, or a manor under a lord's rule, there were forces which acted to prevent any peasant from forming alliances with powerful individuals or institutions outside the community. Lords feared that such alliances would challenge the monopoly of their power. They used their resources and ties to other lords to apply severe sanctions against serfs or tenants challenging their basis of control.

The inward-orientation of freeholding communities also stemmed from the peasants' relations to classes above. The peasantry often faced a powerful and exploitative state organization demanding high taxes to finance itself. At other times, freeholding peasants found themselves paying tribute to provincial warlords or powerful others. Lack of peasant economic innovation (more extensive market involvement for distribution of their goods and for procurement of items which could be used for a capital intensification of agriculture) stemmed from the nature of the world outside the village.

Insecurity of market participation and peasant powerlessness in respect to outsiders led to the development of a village social and political organization oriented to provide services within the community. In order to guarantee the survival of its mechanisms, the community attempted to block any member from gaining power through outside alliances which could place him in a position of not being dependent on those mechanisms.

Limiting the degree of external relations reduced dependence on a hostile outside. Sanctions ensured this limitation of outside involvement. These sanctions served as restraints against any attempts at undermining the degree of self-sufficiency, much as the sanctions of the lord (though different in kind) restricted the outside participation of peasants under him. In essence, this amounted to circumscribing interaction with multiplier institutions which could greatly expand one's indirect, mediated ties to others. It also had the effect of limiting direct contact with the state's administrative personnel by placing a buffer (village chief or other village official) between the individual peasant and the administrator. In many instances, these effects of sanctions and particular social obligations were not always clear to peasants, who did not always consciously relate them to the need for limiting outside involvement.

The success of the restrictions of lords and communities against outside involvement by peasants varied considerably. Less powerful lords did not have the success of those controlling a wide scope of crucial resources with a high degree of monopoly. Similarly, in communities with a weak social and political organization, stronger peasants ignored sanctions when these villagers felt secure in expanding their external participation at the expense of their neighbors. Yet the striking characteristic of the historical village is the degree to which the inward-oriented forces generally dominated.

The pivotal question is what tipped the balance? Why have the nineteenth and twentieth centuries been periods of such rapid expansion of external relations for third world peasants? Despite the existence of powerful sanctions from lords and peasant communities themselves, outward-oriented forces have become dominant. Part Two analyzes this shift in forces —the crucial change from the inward-oriented to the outward-oriented peasant community.

The Fulcrum Shifts: The Challenge of Outward-Oriented Forces

CHAPTER V

Villages Under Stress

INTRODUCTION

DESPITE the sanctions and other obstacles restricting outside involvement, there has been a worldwide movement of peasant communities in the last century and a half from the low to the high end of the scale of external relations. Peasants have been forging new, complex relationships with strangers outside the bounds of the village. Increasingly, peasants have become more involved with and dependent on the multiplier mechanisms: markets, cash, and wage labor. The changes have extended beyond the social and economic realm and have affected peasants' politics as well. To understand these social and economic changes and new political orientations among peasants, a sequential explanation is developed in this book which will help answer the following questions: Under which circumstances have villages increased their outside participation? Who within the village has initially been involved in the process and how have groups differed in their reaction to the new conditions? Which institutions within the village have taken on different structures and functions or have died altogether?

The sequential explanation has five basic components: (1) Within the inward-oriented village, aspirations to increase outside participation exist among those with sufficient resources to make outside alliances. These aspirations are thwarted by a combination of restrictions by lords and by villages' social and political organization. (2) These restric-

87

tions on outside participation and the insecurity of market participation lead to a rather fixed level of technology and thus to fairly constant income and expenditure levels for the village. (3) Sustained crisis strikes families in the village, resulting in a drop in the ratio of income to expenditure. The crisis is felt on a differential basis within the village. (4) Under the impact of the crisis or with some withdrawal of the lords' vigilance (often associated with the crisis), there is a decrease in the effectiveness of restraints against outside involvement. (5) Those *least* affected by the crisis, i.e., those with adequate resources, take advantage of this decrease in effectiveness to increase their power and establish new outside ties. This leads to new kinds of much more rigid patterns of peasant social stratification.

The first component was explored in Part One. This chapter will analyze the next two components of the historical process, that is, the constant levels of income and expenditures, and the crises that have affected such villages. It will explore under which conditions villages have been affected, by analyzing what have been the forces able to overcome the strong resistance of the village's social and political organization and able to undermine the powers of strong lords.

Balancing Accounts

Total income was severely limited for the vast majority of peasant households in inward-oriented villages by the scarcity of either fertile land or an adequate labor force. Household budgeting in such villages, then, consisted of a fine accounting balance. From its meager income the household had to provide itself with enough for subsistence food needs, for participation in the prestige economy, and for payment of often staggering amounts of rent, interest, and taxes. The following chart shows, on the one hand, most of the typical sources of income of such peasant households and, on the other hand, the items of consumption and expenditures which used up that income.[1]

[1] For an example of a specific account of peasants' income and

ITEMS OF CONSUMPTION AND EXPENDITURE	SOURCES OF INCOME
Household Consumption	*Agricultural Production*
Food	Crops
Clothes	Animal Husbandry
Tools	
	Artisan Services
Village Expenditures	
	Handicraft Production
Village Taxes	Barbers
Prestige Economy	Butchers
	Priests
Payments to Other Classes	Medicine Men, etc.
Rent	*Prestige Economy*
Interest	
Taxes	Gifts
	Dowries, etc.

The striking aspect of the debit side of the account is that, except for the amount expended on the prestige economy, peasants had very little flexibility in consumption and expenditure. Since they already generally lived with few frills in their lives, household consumption could have been cut for many households only at a cost to health or future productive capacities. And, of course, there was little control by peasants of the amount of payments to other classes.

On the income side of the ledger, there was only a bit more flexibility. Generally, the level of technology used in agriculture, the major source of productive income, and the level used in handicrafts were fairly constant. Historically, although there always were some technological innovations and setbacks that could have increased or decreased productive capabilities, these were relatively minor and came fairly infre-

---

expenditure, see I. Elazari-Volcani, *The Fellah's Farm* (Tel-Aviv: Jewish Agency for Palestine, 1930), p. 49.

quently.[2] Moreover, peasants' limited supplies of cash often precluded substantial investment in new products of technology even when they existed. The principal flexibility in agriculture in inward-oriented villages came in the amount of land cultivated and the labor expended. And where land was a scarce resource, even that degree of flexibility was eliminated.

For such peasants to have increased production in case of higher taxes, crop disease, or any other number of long- or short-term crises meant augmenting the amount of labor, that is, engaging in more labor-intensive agriculture. Yet, even additional hands may have afforded little help in increased net production. If we recall the hypothesis from Chapter IV, peasant institutions had the effect of attempting to optimize household size. If a household was already fully utilizing its land, given its relatively fixed level of technology, an additional worker would have cost more than he produced.[3]

The very limited response, then, that peasants with limited land and restricted external participation could have given to a crisis was what A. V. Chayanov called "self-exploitation."[4] This means simply that the same household members had to work harder and longer hours, yet, in instances where the peasant household already had to toil almost ceaselessly to eke out subsistence, its ability to increase production levels through much additional self-exploitation was quite small.

As a result of this relative inflexibility of debits and income, peasant accounts were generally quite stable. Of course, there

[2] There were some interesting changes, though relatively minor by today's standards. Folke Dovring, "Peasantry, Land Use, and Change, A Review Article," *Comparative Studies in Society and History* 4 (April 1962), 371.

[3] This statement should be qualified if certain new types of "work sharing" took place. See Warren C. Robinson, "The Economics of Work Sharing in Peasant Agriculture," *Economic Development and Cultural Change* 20 (October 1971), 139.

[4] A. V. Chayanov, "On the Theory of Non-Capitalist Economic Systems," in *A. V. Chayanov on The Theory of Peasant Economy*, ed. Daniel Thorner, Basile Kerbloy, and R.E.F. Smith (Homewood, Ill.: Richard D. Irwin, 1966), pp. 5-6.

was more flexibility for the wealthier members of the community but even theirs was highly limited. There was little margin for error or adaptation on either side of the accounting sheet. Miscalculation or sudden crisis could result in peasants tragically sinking below subsistence levels, at times to actual starvation.

Movement from an inward- to an outward-orientation was most likely to occur when there were forces at hand which *consistently* and *systematically* made it impossible for large numbers of the village's households to balance their accounts. Specifically, this movement arose when consumption and expenditure began *continually* to exceed the household's income, a condition of family economic crisis. The forces which precipitated such crises all over the world are the key to understanding why vast changes have shaken the largely rural societies of the world in the course of this century.

The central factor setting these forces in motion was the worldwide imperialism of the eighteenth and nineteenth centuries.[5] In Asia, the imperialist penetration struck long-established, highly complex peasant societies. Latin America, on the other hand, faced what amounted to a second wave of imperialism. The first wave had had severe repercussions on the Indian population. Spanish and Portuguese penetration of the varied and autonomous Indian cultures had resulted in the establishment of a settled peasantry on haciendas and in freeholding villages out of the reach of daily governmental con-

---

[5] Imperialism, as used here, is seen mainly as a dominance relationship resulting in the transfer of resources from peripheries to centers. This follows Johan Galtung's argument that imperialism is not merely an international relationship but a combination of intra- and inter-national relations. "A Structural Theory of Imperialism," *Journal of Peace Research* 8 (1971), 81-117. One can think of a case of such transfer from the peripheries to the center as being almost wholly internal (Japan) without the international element to fit it into the rubric of imperialism. Nevertheless, I have used the word imperialism because of its effect in uniting the various peripheries (albeit in what Galtung calls a feudal interaction) and causing such crises almost universally and simultaneously.

trol. The second wave of imperialism amounted to a challenge to even this relative autonomy.

What was in the nature of imperialism that had such drastic effects on peasant life? Imperialism caused a reorganization of societies' centers, enabling them to achieve new levels of efficiency in the transfer of wealth from the peripheries. Direct colonial rule or indirect imperial domination led to vast increases in the state's power through more effective administrative techniques. Bureaucracies became more complex and coherent and, as a result, were able to penetrate rural areas on a much broader spectrum than previously. The basic unit they dealt with devolved from the village or the lord's domain to the individual or the family.

Administrative reorganization was accompanied by a number of other changes prompted by the center. Communication and transportation facilities were greatly improved, thereby increasing the ability to rule and extract surpluses more effectively. The development and regulation of more complex markets came about as the peasants were incorporated into a process of industrial development centered in Europe and the United States.[6] The peasants' produce supplied investment capital, crucial raw materials for industrial development, and products for consumption in the industrial centers.

In essence, peasants were confronted with demands which resulted in continuous stress and desperation, demands which made the method of increased self-exploitation in response to past crises (such as famine, plague, or war) wholly insufficient in balancing the household's accounts.

FACTORS RESULTING IN STRESS

1) *Population Growth*

By far the most important and far-reaching of all the factors upsetting the peasants' balance sheets was the start of an

---

[6] Andre Gunder Frank, "The Development of Underdevelopment," in *Imperialism and Underdevelopment: A Reader*, ed. Robert I. Rhodes (New York: Monthly Review Press, 1970), p. 6.

incredible growth of population in inward-oriented villages. Despite the overwhelming proportions of the problem, relatively little research has been done on the effects such growth has had on the economy, social organization, etc. of individual communities.[7] Rather, the focus in studies dealing with the population explosion has been on macro-data from whole countries or regions which dramatize the proportions of the problem without analyzing its dimensions or components. Although the macro-economic and demographic facts are in themselves essential, much more analysis is needed to understand the relationship of the breaking of the dam to the tiny stream that suddenly overflowed its banks—of the mind-boggling multiplication of numbers of people to the actual households, communities, and resources that have born the effects.

Why have the rates of population growth increased so dramatically in peasant villages during the last two centuries? Why has the population growth been so much more rapid, sustained, and universal than in previous eras? The reasons are complex and more diverse than one might imagine. In Java, for example, the population grew from about 7 million in 1830 to 41.7 million a century later. In analyzing that growth, Geertz speculates that under Dutch rule the destruction of crops in internal wars was stopped. More importantly, the improvement of transportation meant that crop failures did not necessarily result in famine for those areas,[8] and consequently the death rate decreased appreciably.

A more prevalent reason for the growth in population in rural areas, it seems, has been a decrease in mortality rates—

[7] An exception is Mahmood Mamdani, *The Myth of Population Control: Family Caste, and Class in an Indian Village* (New York: Monthly Review Press, 1972). Also, see John H. Kunkel, "Economic Autonomy and Social Change in Mexican Villages," *Economic Development and Cultural Change* 10 (October 1961), 51-63.

[8] Clifford Geertz, *Agricultural Involution: The Process of Ecological Change in Indonesia* (Berkeley: University of California Press, 1966), p. 80n.

93

especially among infants—due to innovations in public health.[9] Of course, historically there also had been many swings in population in inward-oriented villages due to changes in the mortality rates. At times populations grew but at other times the large number of infant deaths combined with devastating epidemics to reduce numbers. The new pattern was one of consistency in which there was a much more steady decrease in the death rate.

Historically, Western countries also underwent a rapid increase in population that prompted Malthus' famous treatise,[10] yet there are several differences in kind between the Western experience and that of third world countries. In the West, technology developed almost simultaneously in two areas. Progress was made in public health so that there were decreased mortality rates. Somewhat before that, however, economic organization changed as industrialization proceeded rapidly. At first, there was an increase in birth rates as former serfs, freed from feudal restrictions, had more babies.[11] This combined with lower death rates somewhat later, adding up to a phenomenal growth in population size.

Because of the change in economic organization in the West, however, the desirability of large families gradually decreased. No longer did each member of the family contribute labor toward a single, integrated productive unit, the household. Wages in factories were paid to individuals for individual work. An additional child, then, was an economic liability until he or she could earn a wage. Birth rates began to fall dramatically just as mortality rates had done previously. And

[9] See Konrad Kingshill's account of the virtual disappearance of epidemics in the course of the century. *Ku Daeng—The Red Tomb, A Village Study in Northern Thailand* (Chiangmai, Thailand: The Prince Royal's College, 1960), p. 19.

[10] Thomas Malthus, "A Summary View of the Principle of Population," in *On Population, Three Essays: Thomas Malthus, Julian Huxley, Frederick Osborn* (New York: The New American Library, A Mentor Book, 1960).

[11] William L. Langer, "Europe's Initial Population Explosion," *The American Historical Review* 69 (October 1963), 1-17.

once child labor laws were enacted, children became economic liabilities until a relatively late age.[12]

Experience in the third world has been greatly affected by that of the West. The imperialist states introduced the two strands of technology of the West—public health and industrialization—differentially into these areas. Large-scale public health measures (which had *followed* slightly behind the process of industrialization of the West) were applied widely in the colonies. There was no need to go through the extended process of research to develop such measures. Smallpox, for example, was a disease that had struck almost everyone, killing approximately one-quarter of its victims. By the late 1700s, the research was completed which led to the almost universal control of the disease 170 years later. Moreover, application of many of the innovations, such as malarial control, demanded only minimal manpower and little immediate psychological or social adjustment on the part of the rural inhabitants.

On the other hand, the Latin American and Asian countries were tied to the industrialization process, chiefly as suppliers of raw materials. Most often, the commercial and industrial aspects of the process remained in the hands of the imperialists, and much of it in the imperialist country itself. In most of Latin America and Asia, agricultural production continued unmolested: the household remained the primary institution in the rural societies.[13] Even after the colonialists departed or

---

[12] Analyses of the interaction of recent changing economic conditions with fertility have been done in the West. See, for example, Richard A. Easterlin, "On the Relation of Economic Factors to Recent and Projected Fertility Changes," *Demography* 3 (1966), 131-153. Besides the importance of economic factors in drops in birth rates, Harold Frederiksen also stresses the centrality of a previous drop in death rates. "Dynamic Equilibrium of Economic and Demographic Transition," *Economic Development and Cultural Change* 14 (April 1966), 316-322.

[13] For cases where production modes *were* dramatically changed, see, for example, Geertz, *Agricultural Involution*, and Eric Williams, *Capitalism and Slavery* (London: Andre Deutsch, 1964).

in states which had not undergone direct colonial role, indigenous leaders found it far easier to apply public health measures than to spur industrialization, which made tremendous demands upon the people by changing the economic organization of the society away from household production. Since Independence in India, for example, despite a severely lagging process of industrialization, leaders have all but eliminated the great killers, smallpox, malaria, cholera, and bubonic plague.

As had occurred previously in the West, the new public health measures in the third world have resulted in a great drop in mortality rates, especially infant mortality rates. Yet, the lack of substantial organizational changes in the industrial-agricultural sphere meant that the economic individualism which resulted in an eventual drop in birth rates in the West did not appear extensively in the third world.[14] Household production continued to reign, and large families remained of primary value to peasants. The rate of natural increase in most Latin American and Asian countries is between 2.0 and 3.0 percent (the overall rate is about 2.6 percent),[15] while in Europe its growth hovered around one percent.[16]

We have hypothesized in Chapter IV that inward-oriented peasants tended to optimize household size, which would indicate that there would have been a limitation on family size in third world countries. In that case, why was there not a limitation of the rate of population increase even *with* the persistence of household production? Why did peasants not respond to the falling death rate by having fewer children? Again, this is a question whose answer demands evidence that is simply not available. Tentatively, however, several answers

[14] Where industrialization has proceeded most rapidly in Asia—Japan, Taiwan, and Korea—the fertility rates have decreased significantly, as well.

[15] United Nations, *Statistical Yearbook 1971* (New York: 1972), pp. 78-79.

[16] See James P. Grant, "Marginal Men: The Global Unemployment Crisis," *Foreign Affairs* 50 (October 1971), 114.

can be offered. The first is that peasants found themselves unprepared to curb the tremendous increases in population with their old methods of birth control. This was certainly true in areas in which the chronic problems were a shortage of manpower and underutilization of the land. In such cases, means of limiting family size had not been as important as means of increasing the number of people in the household.

Even peasants who had previously limited family size because of shortages of available fertile land found themselves unprepared for the new conditions. Many of their means of birth control, as mentioned in the previous chapter, were institutionalized social mechanisms which had the effect of limiting family size without demanding conscious efforts by the peasants.[17] Some examples are the custom of prolonged breast feeding and the abstinence demanded at certain times. High infant mortality rates and periodic epidemics often made conscious means of limiting family size unnecessary. These peasants were therefore unprepared in terms of conscious social and mechanical arrangements to deal with the unprecedented decline in mortality rates. Also, the fall in such rates was so rapid that there was insufficient time for social mechanisms to adjust.

Such unpreparedness characterized villages in the state of Uttar Pradesh, India. For generations, births had been limited by a unique system of living arrangements. Each joint family built two houses for itself, one for the men and another for the women. This served to limit the actual number of sexual encounters between husbands and wives. These arrangements were strengthened by the accepted value in the communities whose people looked down upon those who gave birth to a child within four years of the birth of their previous child. With the introduction of new public health measures, separate living quarters for women and men no longer had the effect

[17] Edwin D. Driver, *Differential Fertility in Central India* (Princeton, N.J.: Princeton University Press, 1963), p. 12, lists a number of factors which affected the frequency of a group's exposure to the risks of pregnancy.

of limiting the number of offspring. Even the limited encounters resulted in enough *surviving* children to send the population growth rate soaring. The value of looking down upon those who had two children within four years disappeared, as such families became increasingly common.

The argument of why peasants failed to limit family size sufficiently goes a step further than simple unpreparedness. It must be remembered, as discussed in Chapter IV, that the parents' security in their old age depended upon the continued functioning of the household as an economic unit. As they grew older, parents wanted to be as certain as possible of having a surviving son with whom they could have continued to live and to whom they could have offered their declining economic services. If this desire remains intact as a society experiences falling death rates, it can lead to a situation in which there are vast increases in population.

David M. Heer and Dean O. Smith devised a model which attempts to trace the effect of this desire to have a living son when the parents get old.[18] Their model estimates people's reproduction rates, given the assumption that parents continue to bear children until they can be 95 percent certain of having at least one son surviving to the father's 65th birthday. In a society with a high death rate (average life expectancy at birth of 20 years), women must bear an average of more than ten children to be 95 percent certain of having one son survive to the father's old age. In a society with such a high death rate, the second generation will have a bit more than one and a half times as many members as the first.

When the average life expectancy rises to 45 years, the second generation will have almost twice as many children as the first. A couple now need have, on an average, only five children to be 95 percent sure of having a surviving son. The important point is *they will have more surviving children bearing only five children than the couple in the society with the high death rate bearing ten children.* Only when the life

[18] David M. Heer and Dean O. Smith, "Mortality Level, Desired Family Size, and Population Increase," *Demography* 5 (1968).

expectancy rises all the way to 72 years (comparable to that of the current industrialized states of the West) do we reach a situation in which the second generation has only as many members as the first (see Table 1). All these figures, of course, are based on the hypothetical models.

TABLE 1
CHILDREN BORN TO PARENTS UNTIL PARENTS CAN BE 95 PERCENT CERTAIN THAT THEY WILL HAVE AT LEAST ONE SON SURVIVING TO FATHER'S 65TH BIRTHDAY

Life expectancy at birth	Percentage of wives who never bear needed number of sons	Average number of children born	Average number of children surviving[a]
20.0	38.9	10.40	3.25
32.5	6.4	7.86	4.10[b]
45.0	2.0	5.47	3.82
73.0	0.0	1.94	1.89

SOURCE: David M. Heer and Dean O. Smith, "Mortality Level, Desired Family Size, and Population Increase," *Demography* 5 (1968), 108.

[a] Two children means there are just as many in the second generation as the first.

[b] This is the largest average number of surviving children, meaning that the second generation will have more than twice as many members as the first.

Heer and Smith's model weighs only the factor of ensuring a surviving son in determining family size. Such a goal contradicts the attempt to optimize household size when there is a surplus of manpower. However, because the means to limit births in inward-oriented villages were usually not consciously directed to that goal, peasants historically did not have to face the contradiction directly. They simply had as many children as possible within the framework of practices whose latent function was to limit births. Only those families in the direst circumstances need have engaged in such practices as infanticide (especially girls) and selling of children (especially boys).

99

The contradiction of values became much more explicit when the social mechanisms for limiting births became inadequate. When the average life expectancy rose appreciably within a single generation, social customs and institutions did not adapt quickly enough to prevent severe overpopulation. As Table 1 demonstrates, even if peasants bore almost half as many children as life expectancy rose from 20 to 45 years, they still would have ended up with more surviving children. If they were to bring down the birth rate, peasants would have to decide to employ mechanical or other conscious means, rather than rely only on the effects of social mechanisms. They were now forced to face the conflicting goals of optimizing household size and of ensuring a son's survival. Peasants' behavior under such circumstances seems to have been ambivalent. There is evidence of a falling birthrate in several studies, but there are also indications of the continued importance of attempting to ensure the survival of a son.[19]

It is important to remember that children were still less of an economic liability in an inward-oriented peasant village than in a modern sector. Although additional children might not have produced what they consumed, they still did work at a young age and did help increase production somewhat. Also, some of the burdens associated with a young population in modern society, e.g., high costs of education, did not always apply in such peasant societies where education was of lower value and generally unavailable.

In short, the social mechanisms which had the effect of optimizing household size no longer accomplished this as life expectancy increased rapidly. Even when peasants significantly

[19] See, for example, H. Frederiksen, "Determinants and Consequences of Mortality Trends in Ceylon," *Public Health Reports* 76 (August 1961); also Driver, *Differential Fertility in Central India*, p. 4. Philip A. Neher, "Peasants, Procreation, and Pensions," *American Economic Review* 61 (June 1971), speaks of the pension motive. John B. Wyon and John E. Gordon, *The Khanna Study: Population Problems in the Rural Punjab* (Cambridge, Mass.: Harvard University Press, 1971), p. 170.

reduced the number of births, the lower rate of infant mortality often meant the community was still faced with a growing population and family economic crises. The desire to ensure a surviving son may have led some peasants to gamble with a somewhat lower income despite their precariousness. Each family's separate calculus of which values are most important in determining its size has resulted in an overall situation of a worldwide demographic crisis.

The effects of this growth on individual villages have been staggering. In Elbaşi, Turkey, one old man remembered a population of 450 people. In 1951 it stood at 1,200.[20] In Huecorio (Mexico) the population was 400 in 1930 and 844 in 1962,[21] and these rates do not include the numbers who emigrated from these villages. Table 2 shows only the numbers of births and deaths during a fourteen year period for an Indian village.[22] Note the decreasing number of deaths.

With production and income that could expand only slightly, the addition of each person who consumed more than he added to the household's production potential meant that per capita income fell where people might already have been living at subsistence levels. A crucial threshold seemed to be reached when the majority of an inward-oriented village household went from insufficient manpower—as was common, for example, in the village of Sirkanda, India[23]—to insufficient resources to support the available manpower.

The population density alone is not enough of an indicator to assess whether the majority of households was in the midst of an economic crisis. Instead, one wants to gauge how population growth progressively reduced allotment of the fruits of the land for the various households in the community. Mi-

[20] Paul Stirling, *Turkish Village* (London: Weidenfeld and Nicolson, 1965).

[21] Michael Belshaw, *A Village Economy: Land and People of Huecorio* (New York: Columbia University Press, 1967).

[22] Taken from D. N. Majumdar, *Caste and Communication in an Indian Village* (Bombay: Asia Publishing House, 1958), p. 10.

[23] Gerald D. Berreman, *Hindus of the Himalayas* (Berkeley: University of California Press, 1963), p. 55.

TABLE 2

NUMBER OF BIRTHS AND DEATHS IN
MOHANA (1941-1954)

Year	Number of births	Number of deaths
1941	22	15
1942	24	13
1943 1944	22	28
1945	21	not available
1946	17	15
1947	20	22
1948	20	19
1949	not available	not available
1950	19	16
1951	16	8
1952	26	10
1953	34	6
1954	18	4

chael Moerman suggests employing nutritional density by region or even community.[24] For example, one crop (rice) yields more nutritional content than another (wheat) and so can withstand a larger population in the same area. Even this kind of assessment, however, is insufficient in determining the pressure that has been applied by population increases.

It ignores the vast drainage of resources through taxes, interest, and rent, which varied widely from region to region or even among households within a village. Also, it ignores the fact that not all owned or had direct access to land, that land was not distributed equally, that land could vary greatly within a village in productive quality, and that households were not equal in size. One household's control of a large percentage of fertile village land meant that the pressure on all the rest was that much more severe. As a result, even compara-

[24] Michael Moerman, *Agricultural Change and Peasant Choice in a Thai Village* (Berkeley: University of California Press, 1968), p. 84.

tive nutritional density figures for individual communities are meaningless unless one knows household-by-household distribution of wealth producing resources.

Population growth has had a number of secondary effects on peasant communities. Village populations have become much younger, creating bottom-heavy labor forces.[25] Stable inheritance patterns have been upset as there are more children than adequate land (or occupational roles) than a father can bequeath. Village systems of justice have been strained as there are more claimants to traditional offices. Thus, although the most pressing effects of population growth were felt in the economic realm as balance sheets found consumption and expenditure outpacing income, there were other social effects which compounded the strain on such communities.

2) *Patron Withdrawal*

The population explosion was not the only result of imperialism which caused peasant economic crises. In many cases, it was powerful lords who undermined longstanding patterns and upset the peasants' economic situation. The relatively closed status system of which even the lord was a part was subjected to competition from a wider status system in which the lord could find new sources of prestige. With the imperialist penetrations, this outside status system began increasingly to encroach on the rural areas. It was the participation of lords in the wider status systems which was often the first step leading to the end of the inward-oriented community.[26]

For example, unrest grew among Brazilian peasants who had come to expect economic, political, social, and even medical services from their lords. These landlords began to show

[25] See Kingshill, *Ku Daeng*, p. 17.

[26] For example, on the breaking of the traditional marketing mechanism in Bolivia, see Andrew Pearse, "Peasants and Revolution: The Case of Bolivia: Part II," *Economy and Society* 1 (August 1972), 412.

a decreasing ability or will to provide those services.[27] Many fazeda (hacienda) owners left the land for the town or city and appointed overseers for the daily tasks. The result was that the lord-tenant bond remained, but the additional patronage the peasants had received was no longer available. Galjart wrote, "The more or less prolonged absence of the owner loosens considerably the bond between him and his peasants. The absent owner can not render assistance to a peasant at the moment it is needed."[28] In China in the early part of this century, similar withdrawals were accompanied by increased demands on peasants. The luxuries and comforts of the cities, which drew the lord from the rural hinterlands, demanded greater outlays by the lords. These were "met by raising their demands from the peasants in terms of rent, interest, or tax."[29]

As they became actively involved in an alternative status system, the interest of lords waned in providing the paternalistic types of services, such as fiestas, funerals, or marriages. It is not surprising that lords were the first to be drawn into the alternative status system since their role as brokers gave them the opportunity to operate in the world outside the village with other lords of equal and higher status. Yet, even after they ceased to provide paternalistic services, lords often continued to make the same work and rent demands on the peasants, and in some cases they augmented these demands by using peasant wives and daughters as domestics for their new homes in town, as well.[30] Supervision of work on an

[27] Bertram Hutchinson, "The Patron-Dependant Relationship in Brazil: A Preliminary Examination," *Sociologia Ruralis* 6 (1966), 16-17.

[28] Benno Galjart, "Class and 'Following' in Rural Brazil," *América Latina* 7 (July-September 1964), 9.

[29] Shu-ching Lee, "Agrarianism and Social Upheaval in China," *The American Journal of Sociology* 56 (May 1951), 518.

[30] See Barrington Moore, Jr., *Social Origins of Dictatorship and Democracy: Lord and Peasant in the Making of the Modern World* (Boston: Beacon Press, 1966), p. 460.

hacienda or collection of rents and interest in a village was frequently given over to a manager or foreman who little comprehended the odd basis of reciprocal obligations.

Although the incidental expenditures previously made by the lord for or to the peasants might have been small for him, they provided crucial supplements to the peasants' meager incomes. Withdrawal of patronage services meant that the peasant came up short on the income side of the ledger to satisfy his consumption and expenditure needs. Often "patron withdrawal" from a dominating role was not totally voluntary on the part of lords. There were also challenges to the degree of monopoly of any service provided by the lord and, ultimately, to the scope of the services he controlled. The traditional patron in Southeast Asia, Scott writes, began to face competing sources of patronage in the form of schools, agricultural services, regional banks, and public employment.[31] Through such competition, many of the barriers to a wider scope of external relations were removed, though so might certain sources of income that the lord had provided in a paternalistic fashion.

Governments in the third world have often been overstrained in their attempts to compete with numerous lords in the provision of services; others have lacked the will. Yet, the reorganization of centers set in motion by imperialism meant that some were able to break or modify their implicit alliance with the lords of the rural hinterlands.[32] City-based institutions and bureaucracies began to challenge the degree of monopoly and scope of the rural lords, undermining the local lords by providing numerous, *specific* services. Note Susan C. Bourque's description of the Peruvian situation.

[31] James C. Scott, "Patron-Client Politics and Political Change" (paper delivered at the Sixty-sixth Annual Meeting of the American Political Science Association, Los Angeles, Calif., September 8-12, 1970), p. 20.

[32] Samuel P. Huntington, *Political Order in Changing Societies* (New Haven: Yale University Press, 1968), p. 76, calls this the urban breakthrough.

The expansion of modern large scale enterprises to the sierra magnified the inefficiency of the *gamonals'* (landlords') *latifundia*. As the *gamonal* fell under increased financial pressure he tended to increase his exploitation of the peasants and consequently not only lost their tacit support for the system, but incurred their opposition in the process. The growth of commercial centers in the sierra was expanding the impact of coastal society and the opportunities of the campesino. All of these factors combined to weaken the control of the traditional authority structure, the closed system of the *gamonal*.[33]

3) *Increased Demands by the Center*

Government taxes were one of the key factors on the peasant household's accounting sheet. In cases where inward-oriented peasants were fully utilizing their resources, given their relatively fixed level of technology, and were already living at subsistence levels, any increase in taxes made their situation desperate. Increased extractive demands by governments did not take the form only of increased taxes; often taxes were demanded in cash instead of kind.[34] The effect of such a change on primarily subsistence-type farmers could be enormous. In Vietnam, for example, the scarcity of cash forced peasants to change their subsistence-oriented agriculture, and it opened the way for exploitative middlemen, who took advantage of their dire need for cash.[35]

[33] Susan C. Bourque, "Cholification and the Campesino: A Study of Three Peruvian Peasant Organizations in the Process of Societal Change," Latin American Studies Program, Dissertation Series, Cornell University (January 1971), pp. 34-35.

[34] N. G. Ranga, *Credo of World Peasantry* (Andhra, India: Indian Peasants' Institute, 1957).

[35] John T. McAlister, Jr. and Paul Mus, *The Vietnamese and Their Revolution*, Harper Torchbooks (New York: Harper and Row, 1970), pp. 36, 41, 73-74. For an example of the effects of demands for cash on peasants in China, see Hsiao-Tung Fei, *Peasant Life in China: A Field Study of Country Life in the Yangtze Valley* (London: Routledge and Kegan Paul, 1939), p. 260.

Demands for payment of taxes in money made peasants seek ways to transform their crops into cash and impelled them to move toward increased market involvement. Similarly, growing urban centers at times increased demands directly for rural products which also undermined the peasants' restrictions on outside involvement. In Brazil, this increased urban demand resulted in a change in the traditional peasant markets, the *feiras*. With the need to get larger amounts of rural goods to the city, wholesalers began to go directly to farms to buy produce in bulk. No longer did only a small proportion of the peasant produce filter up to the urban areas through the feiras. Now, instead of serving as starting points for the upward flow of goods to urban centers, the feiras became principally buyers' markets for manufactured goods that had filtered down. A secondary effect of the many wholesalers' participating was the drastic cut in the use of the numerous peasant middlemen, depriving them of their traditional source of income.[36]

4) *The Market's Impingement on Income*

Although the source of the overwhelming majority of productivity for most peasants was agriculture, in some societies their ability to survive often depended on supplemental sources of income: handicrafts and performance of special services. In certain other societies, services and handicrafts were means for those with little or no direct access to land to gain the fruits of agriculture from the farmers. In either the case of the full-time or part-time craftsmen, the actual productive value of crafts was usually small relative to that of agriculture, but the meager amounts of cash or grain they helped procure often kept the household at, or slightly above, the subsistence level.

Foreign and national manufactured goods as well as pro-

---

[36] Shepard Forman and Joyce F. Riegelhaupt, "Market Place and Marketing System: Toward a Theory of Peasant Economic Integration," *Comparative Studies in Society and History* 12 (April 1970), 202.

fessional services cut deeply into these sources of income in many peasant villages and were a further cause of economic crises. Hardest hit were those communities where people engaged full-time in craft production and provision of services. Mohla in Punjabi Pakistan is an example. There, the importation of goods from the city, especially by the agricultural castes, meant that many of the other traditional caste occupations became irrelevant.[37] In Gaon (India), castes that were involved in ropemaking found themselves without work, as such products could be bought more cheaply in town.[38] In many societies specialists, such as Shamans, suffered with the greater availability of modern medical services.[39]

Although less obvious in terms of immediate effect, the loss of income to cultivators who engaged in handicrafts part-time for supplemental income was also quite serious. In Jendram Hilir (Malaysia), for example, practically all the traditional handicrafts—weaving, carving, canoe-building—almost disappeared entirely as Chinese merchants imported inexpensive manufactured products.[40] Shu-ching Lee described the effect of the infusion of foreign manufactured goods into China.

The first effect of the introduction of Western civilization and a money economy into China is the substitution of

[37] Zekiye Eglar, *A Punjabi Village in Pakistan* (New York: Columbia University Press, 1960).

[38] Henry Orenstein, *Gaon: Conflict and Cohesion in an Indian Village* (Princeton, N.J.: Princeton University Press, 1965). Also, for a similar account on Samiala, see Tadashi Fukutake, Tsutomu Ōuchi, and Chie Nakane, *The Socio-Economic Structure of the Indian Village, Surveys of Villages in Gujarat and West Bengal* (Tokyo: The Institute of Asian Economic Affairs, 1964).

[39] See, for example, E. R. Leach, *Pul Eliya, A Village in Ceylon: A Study of Land Tenure and Kinship* (Cambridge: Cambridge University Press, 1961). On Mexico's *curanderos*, see Oscar Lewis, *Life in a Mexican Village: Tepoztlán Restudied* (Urbana: University of Illinois Press, 1963).

[40] Peter J. Wilson, *A Malay Village and Malaysia: Social Values and Rural Development* (New Haven: HRAF Press, 1967).

imported manufactured goods in great quantities for the homemade handicrafts. In this slow but steady process, the peasant's income has been lowered and rural economy drained, both of which bring forth a ruthless operation of usury, which, in turn, results inevitably in the peasant's loss of his farm.[41]

Some villages participated in market relations for years but primarily with their handicrafts, attempting to maintain sub-sistence agriculture as a form of self-protection. Often such villages depended on a particular rural industry for supple-mental income, and they were particularly vulnerable to the impingement of national market forces. In Kaihsienkung (East China), the village was supported primarily by agri-culture and secondarily by a domestic silk industry. Partly because of a long-term decline in world prices for silk, and partly because the village produced silk that was not fine enough for the new factory-machine weaving process, the income from silk dropped steadily. For more than a decade the peasants eliminated ceremonies, marriages, or recreation. Only the actions of a technical school which introduced a silk factory into the village saved the peasants from complete impoverishment.[42]

Besides craft income *per se*, many villagers experienced other less obvious forms of income loss. For example, when there had been limited market involvement, goods had been hauled to market on bullock carts. Motor buses or railways often made the market more demanding in getting the goods to urban centers quickly,[43] and the costs of motorized trans-port were more difficult to bear than those expended for bullock cart transport.[44]

[41] Shu-ching Lee, "Agrarianism and Social Upheaval in China," pp. 517-518.

[42] Fei, *Peasant Life in China.*

[43] Ranga, *Credo of World Peasantry*, p. 91.

[44] Only in rare cases did the national market affect traditional handicraft production favorably. In Coyotopec (Mexico), as we saw in ch. I, the peasants gained from the development of the Oaxaca market into a tourist attraction.

SUMMARY

In Chapter III, the point was made that peasants minimized external ties as a means of insulation against an exploitative outside. Yet, this was possible only as long as the state lacked the ability or will to administer the villages directly. As higher taxes were levied, handicraft production was damaged, and urban demand for rural products was increased, the threat to self-limited outside involvement grew. If a government wanted taxes in money, for example, this caused a crisis of adopting wholly new social patterns to gain the needed cash. Very frequently peasants' fears of the exploitative outside turned out to be justified as moneylenders took advantage of their need for cash and eventually laid claim to their land.

Behind the new demands on peasants' resources and energies was the force of imperialism and the active, extractive centers it created.

The universal threats to an inward-orientation stemmed from a convergence of the factors precipitated by the reorganized centers—severe population growth, patron withdrawal, new tax demanded by the center, and losses of craft income. All these were dynamic forces challenging the restraints on outside participation. They have been responsible for the rapidity and universality of movement from an inward- to an outward-orientation.

Transistor radios, paved roads, secure market investment opportunities have been only means to an outward-orientation. It has been the dynamic force of the factors thrusting peasants into economic crisis, particularly the force of the enormous growth in the rate of population increase, which has impelled peasants so dramatically within the last century to question whether relief is possible within the boundaries of the village.[45]

[45] "Railroads and truck routes lead the way only to limited change unless dynamic factors, 'pressure toward change,' are involved in the situation." William W. Stein, *Hualcan: Life in the Highlands of Peru* (Ithaca, N.Y.: Cornell University Press, 1961), pp. 8-9.

The means to gain income outside (roads, etc.) became important at a particular moment in the history of the village. That moment was when the economic crises of numerous families undermined the old social organization. William Hinton describes this moment for the Chinese village of Long Bow.

Weighed down by high interest rates, harassed by heavy taxes, caught in the snares of a rigged market, many landowning peasants went bankrupt, sold out their holdings strip by strip, and ended up with the yoke of rent around their necks, or left for the city hoping to find some work in industry or transport that would keep them alive. Others became soldiers in the armies of the warlords or joined local bandit gangs.[46]

[46] William Hinton, *Fanshen: A Documentary of Revolution in a Chinese Village* (New York: Monthly Review Press, 1966), p. 45.

111

CHAPTER VI

Relieving the Stress

INTRODUCTION

VILLAGES which had been controlled by strong and vigilant lords faced an uncharted course once the power of the lords eroded. The social organization of such villages had been built primarily on the separate dyadic ties between the lord and each of the peasant households. After patron withdrawal, the peasants were left without long-established and complex patterns of mutual interaction and cooperation to meet the needs that transcended the household level. These needs had previously been most often satisfied by the lord.

This lack of elaborate institutions and mechanisms among those peasants also meant that they did not experience community restraints on individuals' outside participation. If opportunities arose to alleviate the economic crisis through such means as the national market, there was little in the form of community resistance to stop them from participating extensively. For example, the decrease in vigilance among hacendados in the La Convención Valley of Peru resulted in a rapid conversion of peasants to farming the cash crop of coffee.[1] Unlike peasants under strong lords, freeholding peasants and peasants living under less powerful lords still faced obstacles to vastly increased outside participation even

---

[1] See Wesley W. Craig, "Peru: The Peasant Movement of La Convención," in *Latin American Peasant Movements*, ed. Henry A. Landsberger (Ithaca, N.Y.: Cornell University Press, 1969), pp. 293-294.

112

after economic crises struck. The very social and political organizations of their communities continued to have the effect of keeping them inward-oriented.

This chapter will analyze the ways in which these peasants tried to solve their economic crises without running headlong into these obstacles, in other words, while continuing to restrict relations with the outside world. It will then outline the paths of action these peasants have taken when such outlets no longer solved the problem.

BALANCING ACCOUNTS WHILE MAINTAINING AN INWARD-ORIENTATION

The first attempts by peasants to deal with their sustained economic crises were to take the paths of least resistance. This involved reestablishing (if possible) a balance in their accounts without confronting the social and political organization of the village. Three means were most commonly used: (1) conquering the frontier, (2) long-term out-migration, and (3) short-term out-migration.

1) Conquering the Frontier

Expanding the amount of land under cultivation, while keeping a constant level of technology was a means of alleviating economic pressure on households that had an oversupply of labor. This was done within the boundaries of the community or in virgin areas outside.[2] The effect was to increase net production per capita without the necessity of confronting the community's barriers against expanded outside relations. The area for house sites in Ku Daeng (Thailand), for example, was cut in half in less than a century, as peasants increased the amount of land for agriculture. In addition, some of the population purchased cheap land and

[2] Ester Boserup, *The Conditions of Agricultural Growth: The Economics of Agrarian Change under Population Pressure* (Chicago: Aldine, 1965), p. 13, talks of "frequency of cropping" which includes intensification, as well as expansion, of agriculture.

113

brought it under cultivation in the village of Myang Fa-ng, which became known as the "New Ku Daeng."[3]

In Sirkanda (India), population pressure resulted in an expansion of farming land to the surrounding hills. When the new fields became too far from the central village compound, people built semi-permanent homes in clusters in the outlying areas. At times, a cluster developed into an independent village. Others continued to identify Sirkanda as their village, but usually only about half the village population resided in the central compound at any one time. As a result, this central compound population of Sirkanda remained stable from 1815 to 1958 while the overall village population and the amount of land under cultivation doubled.[4]

Another interesting case is the village of Ban Ping, Thailand. It appeared to be adopting new agricultural techniques, as indicated by the use of tractors, in order to relieve its population crisis. A close look at the way the tractors were used, however, shows that in reality its peasants were attacking the problem by conquering the frontier and avoiding permanent incorporation of the outside technology.[5]

Although the population of Ban Ping was growing, it had not reached the crucial threshold where there were land shortages rather than labor shortages. In fact, the lack of sufficient labor to work the available land and optimize yields continued to plague many households. Close kinsmen donated labor to each other when one was busy and the other was not. Despite the labor shortages, productivity was relatively high. Even when there were crop failures in other nearby provinces, the fertile land in Ban Ping always produced sufficient rice yields for the peasants' consumption needs. The

[3] Konrad Kingshill, *Ku Daeng—The Red Tomb: A Village Study in Northern Thailand* (Chiangmai, Thailand: The Prince Royal's College, 1960), p. 16.

[4] Gerald D. Berreman, *Hindus of the Himalayas* (Berkeley: University of California Press, 1963).

[5] This account is taken from Michael Moerman, *Agricultural Change and Peasant Choice in a Thai Village* (Berkeley: University of California Press, 1968).

114

village was open to new settlers and almost everyone was able to become a landowner either by buying irrigated land or by clearing some of the frontier land.

When easily cleared frontier land diminished as population continued to grow, the tractor provided an easy means of clearing and plowing huge new tracts of virgin land that had been too difficult to clear with the old tools. The tractors enabled the peasants of Ban Ping to farm an additional 550 acres, more than doubling the amount of the village's cultivated land. The peasants simply went to town and hired the townsman and his tractor to help do what they had been doing themselves for many years without a tractor—conquering the frontier.

When the anthropologist Michael Moerman returned to Ban Ping for additional observation four years after his initial visit, he was surprised to see that the tractor was no longer in use. Moreover, the agricultural practices of the peasants had not changed significantly. Though they were aware of the benefits of new seed varieties, chemical fertilizers, and weed control, they did not employ any of them. Why? "One answer is that, even before the introduction of the tractor, the availability of land permitted farmers . . . to expand production at the expense of unit quality."[6]

Since they had not reached the point where population pressure was forcing new solutions upon them, they were not inclined to adopt methods that would threaten the village's political and social organization. Expansion of land under cultivation in order to increase yields was a path of lesser resistance than the adoption of new methods involving much more consistent market interaction. The tractor enabled them to increase their capabilities by further opening the frontier. Once that was accomplished, the dynamic force of population growth was neutralized for the time being and use of the tractor was abandoned.

This is not to say that no changes in social behavior resulted from use of the tractor. Cash gained in importance,

[6] *Ibid.*, p. 81.

and this stimulated increased production for the market (though subsistence needs were still grown first). Friends and neighbors became more reluctant to participate in cooperative labor in the distant fields which the tractor made available. *Any* new cultural artifact that is assimilated demands some changes in social behavior, and even the most inward-oriented villages were never entirely static.

Ban Ping was able to remain inward-oriented by clearing the frontier. Accounts were balanced because the frontier continued to allow each household member to produce at least the amount he consumed—and usually considerably more. The point is that mere contact with the products of modern technology was not alone sufficient to bring about sustained challenges to the village social and political organization. As long as the frontier was open, there were no dynamic forces making the old ways untenable, forces moving the peasants dramatically to an outward-orientation.[7]

2) *Long-term Out-migration*

If the means were available, migration by some village members to an urban area could diminish the pressure on the land. These migrants could also help their families meet the added demands from those in other classes by sending back money. Out-migration could be for as short a time as several weeks and as long a period as decades or the remainder of one's life. (Long-term migration refers here to a period greater than a single agricultural cycle.) And out-migration could be to places as near as a town within the province or as far as another continent.

Baytīn, in Jordan, is a village that suffered from severe overpopulation, and its inheritance system of dividing land plots among all the males resulted in extremely fragmented

---

[7] For another case of abandoning previously used modern methods once frontier land is settled, see Carlos Joaquim Saenz, "Population Growth, Economic Progress, and Opportunities on the Land: The Case of Costa Rica," R. P. no. 47, Land Tenure Center, University of Wisconsin, Madison (June 1972), pp. 68-69.

holdings. The average per capita landholding was one-half acre, but it is estimated that 2.5 acres were needed per person merely for subsistence. Everything that was produced in the village was consumed there, but that still left most needs unmet. With the emigration of a substantial number of men to the United States, some pressure was alleviated, though not enough to serve as a permanent solution to the problem of overpopulation.[8] Those who emigrated from Baytīn, however, maintained their ties with their families and planned to return after several years. While abroad, they earned money and sent some back to the village. The additional income was at first used to purchase more land (the amount of village land tripled). This solidified the households of the emigrants at the top of the village status hierarchy, since land was a major determinant of prestige.

Saucío, an endogamous *vereda* (village) in Colombia, had a fantastically high rate of natural increase. The average number of surviving children per couple was 6.5. Yet, the low productivity of the land resulted in an actual decrease in population size. Two out of three children left the parental home to live in other parts of Colombia, and two-thirds of those emigrating were women, as there was a great demand in Bogotá for women domestic servants. Saucío is a good example of the spur given to out-migration by readily accessible means for travel once the pressure from economic crises sets in. The completion by 1931 of a major highway and a railroad line near the village enabled villagers to journey to Bogotá easily and relieve, at least temporarily, the economic pressures.[9]

[8] Abdulla M. Lutfiyya, *Baytīn, A Jordanian Village: A Study of Social Institutions and Social Change in a Folk Community* (London: Mouton, 1966).

[9] Orlando Fals-Borda, *Peasant Society in the Colombian Andes: A Sociological Study of Saucío* (Gainesville: University of Florida Press, 1955), pp. 23-59. Villages successfully using long-term migration to keep an inward-orientation are reported in W. R. Geddes, *Deuba: A Study of a Fijian Village* (Wellington, New Zealand: The

Many peasants in inward-oriented villages were reluctant to abandon permanently the security of the land to gamble on outside opportunities. Frequently, they left kin in the village working the land as best as possible or rented their holdings out to others and became absentee landowners in an attempt to retain a foothold in the security offered by subsistence agriculture. In turn, any success on the outside was not a private one but was shared with those left at "home." As a result, urbanization in such cases was much less the social equivalent to cutting the umbilical cord than a total uprooting of entire kin groups would have been.

3) *Short-term Out-migration*

Short-term out-migration was different from long-term out-migration in that the peasants left the village for less than a complete agricultural cycle. In other words, they still remained peasants, since they migrated for several months, at most, and they then returned for their agricultural or service work at home. Also, short-term out-migrants differed from daily commuters to outside wage labor whose life no longer centered around family production. The short-term migrants' outside work was seasonal, and they perceived their primary work still to be that within the village.

While working on the Peruvian coast for periods ranging from a week to two months, the peasants of Hualcan insulated themselves from others. (See Chapter I.) Their life and community were in the highlands. With the money earned on the coast they could solve the problem of overpopulation without drastically changing the social and political organization of the village. They relieved the stress, while maintaining the security of subsistence agriculture.[10] Certainly, changes in

Polynesian Society, 1945); and Emilio Willems, *Buzios Island: A Caiçara Community in Southern Brazil* (Locust Valley, N.Y.: J. J. Augustin, 1952).

[10] William W. Stein, "Outside Contact and Cultural Stability in a Peruvian Highland Village," in *Cultural Stability and Cultural Change*, ed. Verne F. Ray, Proceedings of the 1957 Annual Spring

social behavior and in village institutions resulted from such short-term out-migration by a significant number of villagers. Even with insulation against adoption of outside habits and against permanent institutionalization of relationships with outside organizations, many things could not remain the same once migrants returned to the village. Use of cash became more prevalent. The basis of status may have been more easily achieved by those who returned—they could buy land or give bigger fiestas. Yet, even given such changes, the striking aspects of villages such as Hualcan or Buarij, Lebanon, are how much did remain the same. The villages were still inward-oriented. The peasants did not take permanent wage-earning jobs. And they did not use their new resources or knowledge to adopt the technology or techniques of the outside to gain greater productivity from their main economic activity, agriculture.

One additional way besides frontiers and migration that pressure could be relieved historically was through action on the part of one segment of the village against the other. If one group was successful, it could eliminate the other from the village, being left with the additional resources. There is little available evidence about such conflicts,[11] but the partition of India at the time of independence may be one example of that occurring on a widespread basis. The religious strife enabled Hindus, in some cases, to kill Moslems and

---

Meeting of the American Ethnological Society (Seattle: American Ethnological Society, 1957), pp. 15-16. Also see Isabel and David Crook, *Revolution in a Chinese Village: Ten Mile Inn* (London: Routledge and Kegan Paul, 1959), p. 4.

[11] "Thus was expressed, in violent form, that endless struggle among the Maya settlements: a factional dispute within a settlement is resolved by the victory of one party; those of the defeated party take refuge and establish residence in some neighboring village . . ." (Robert Redfield, *A Village that Chose Progress*, Phoenix Books [Chicago: The University of Chicago Press, 1962]), p. 11. On Palestine see Y. Ben-Zvi, *Ochlusaynu Ba'aretz* [*Our Population in the Land*] (Warsaw: Brit Ha'noar, 1932), Part B, pp. 52-54 (Hebrew).

drive others from the village. The opposite occurred in the Pakistani sector. The burden of these driven-out people then shifted from individual villages to refugee centers like Karachi or Calcutta.

By the mid-twentieth century, the factors outlined above were fast disappearing as solutions to crises. Frontiers and both long- and short-term out-migration proved insufficient to the economic conditions that peasants faced. Diminishing frontiers continue to be conquered at growing costs, but even this is not enough. In Latin America, the area devoted to major crops increased between 1948-1952 and 1962-1963 by one-third.[12] But still rural population densities continue to rise in this region having the world's highest population growth rate. Out-migration continues as a major outlet, but it too is not a total solution. For example, it is estimated that one million people sleep each night on the streets of Calcutta —refugees of the phenomenal growth of population in the countryside—and still rural Bengali villages continue to grow in population. There are rare exceptions which continue to be inward-oriented and have been able to avoid the forces of the nineteenth and twentieth centuries by making use of one or more of the three outlets: frontier, short-term out-migration, and long-term out-migration. The chart on p. 121 indicates the solutions used by the fifteen inward-oriented villages in this study.

BALANCING ACCOUNTS: INCREASING OUTSIDE INVOLVEMENT

With the waning of possibilities of solving economic crises without a great increase in outside relations, two powerful forces came into direct opposition. On the one hand was the social and political organization of those peasant villages which had strong sanctions against accepting daily wage labor

[12] Alfonso Gonzaléz, "Some Effects of Population Growth on Latin America's Economy," in *Population Geography: A Reader*, ed. George J. Demko, Harold M. Rose, and George A. Schnell (N.Y.: McGraw-Hill, 1970), p. 508.

Frontier	*Short-term out-migration*
Sirkanda (India)	Hualcan (Peru)
Ban Ping (Thailand)	Buarij (Lebanon)
Chan Kom (Mexico)	
Ku Daeng (Thailand)	

Long-term out-migration	*Population Growing but have not reached limit of resources*
Deuba (Fiji Islands)	
Panajachel (Guatemala)	Demirciler (Turkey)
Buzios Island (Brazil)	Pul Eliya (Ceylon)
Ku Daeng (Thailand)	Gopalpur (India)
Mohla (West Pakistan)	

Others

Guinhangdan (Philippines)—insufficient data

Tarong (Philippines)—recently began to grow tobacco but still classified low on the scale since the ramifications of the change are not yet apparent.

outside and against increased involvement in commodity markets. On the other hand was the strong pressure to find alternative sources of income. Industrialization often itensified this opposition of forces. Prior to the Industrial Revolution in the West, the vast majority of the value produced in practically all societies had been in the rural areas—agricultural production plus animal husbandry and handicrafts. Although there had been some value produced in the city, the overall percentage had been low and the disproportionate power of the city made peasants view urban areas as almost totally exploitative, taking much and giving little in return.

The imperialists who set in motion the forces that caused economic crises also created other changes which offered additional economic alternatives to certain people. (The new stratification is the topic of Chapter VIII.) These imperialists often created a situation in which classes other than that of peasants were producing a considerable amount of wealth.

121

Urban wealth no longer stemmed from a small, fixed resource base. With the beginning of some indigenous industrialization and with the linkages to the industrialization process of the West, there developed an expanding resource base in the cities. Moreover, imperialism often imposed a kind of order on an area. Although often very arbitrary in the methods they used and the boundaries they established, the imperialists through their force did often make outside institutions somewhat more stable and predictable for peasant participation. In different areas, market performance was improved, inter-village warfare was stopped, and banditry was almost totally eliminated.

This growth of the urban economy and the increasing outside security presented two opportunities for peasants. First, some industrial and service jobs opened for villagers. Second, there was a great influx of people into the cities which raised urban demand for rural products. The link to the West through imperialism further increased demand for rural products as exports and as raw materials for the industrial process. Also, the stability needed to ship those products increased. Thus, those who set in motion the forces that caused the peasants' economic crises also opened new national markets and work opportunities which made it possible for villagers, or at least some of them, to *gain additional value* outside the village. They were also constantly developing new technological tools to increase productivity both in the industrial and agricultural spheres to meet the new opportunities and demands.

In order to alleviate their crises through this new relationship with the larger economy, peasants had to change their patterns of earning income. In the agricultural sphere, the first step in this direction, it seems, came through changes in patterns of "distribution." This meant simply producing what they had always produced. But instead of reserving the vast majority (after taxes or rent was paid) for use within the village, certain peasants began to put most of it on the market.

Often this was followed by a second kind of decision which enabled certain peasants to gain even more outside value by changing patterns of "production." In this case, they could engage in outside daily work opportunities, adopt new techniques to increase agricultural production, or change to crops more in demand on the outside (or some combination of these). Both changes in distribution and production patterns entailed an exchange of either wealth or labor with the outside on a much more regular basis. The exchange mechanism was the market, through its myriad of institutional components.

The opposition of forces is now perfectly clear. An inward-orientation, by definition, meant a severe limitation on market participation—keeping the market at arm's length. The increasingly severe economic crises, as we shall see in the next chapter, undermined the ability of the village social and political organization to restrict certain peasants from *penetrating the market much more fully in order to gain new value.* Penetration of the market entailed becoming increasingly involved in complex relationships beyond the village, relationships with people the peasant never even saw. Peasants began to participate in new markets and in older markets which may have existed for centuries but where the major participants had been primarily rich landlords. To accommodate this new activity, the market had to grow in scope, it had to become more diverse, and it had to become more complex if it was to serve as the link for peasants to gain added value.[13]

Throughout history, peasants expanded and contracted their degree of market participation according to the stability of market conditions. Such changes were primarily ones of distribution patterns of their goods. In recent decades, however, peasants have increasingly dealt with the incredible se-

[13] See comment by David A. Preston on the development of a market in Bolivia following patron withdrawal, quoted in Andrew Pearse, "Peasants and Revolution: The Case of Bolivia: Part II," *Economy and Society* 1 (August 1972), 412-413. Also see G. William Skinner, "Marketing and Social Structure in Rural China, Part II," *The Journal of Asian Studies* 24 (February 1965), 216.

verity of population growth by changing patterns of production as well as of distribution. They have gone considerably beyond using the market as a mere distribution mechanism. For some this new type of market participation has come through a capital intensification of their agriculture, which has changed their whole method of production. In varying degrees, they have traded the security of growing staples for the greater returns of cash crops.

Given their stake in the market through capital investments and the little subsistence value of such crops as coffee, rubber, and sugarcane, many peasants can no longer contract their degree of market participation as they had done before. It becomes increasingly difficult (though not entirely impossible) for such peasants to maintain the security of a possible reversion to subsistence during short periods of crisis. For others, increased market participation has come about mainly through daily wage labor in the production of industrial wealth or in service occupations. No longer is outside work a secondary activity since now a portion of the village gains its primary source of income from daily participation in the larger economic hierarchy.[14] The increase in external relations no longer involves merely using the outside economy to maintain the village social and political organization and its status system—all predicated on individual farming or service households. With some members gaining their primary livelihood within the national status hierarchy—with perhaps some additional income coming from part-time farming or vegetable gardening—the two status systems come into much more direct conflict.

Movement from an inward- to an outward-orientation through greater involvement in cash and factor markets takes place along a continuum in which cautious peasants are constantly weighing the stability of participation within the various market components against their own perceived needs

[14] See, for example, Ramon H. Myers, *The Chinese Peasant Economy: Agricultural Development in Hopei and Shantung, 1890-1949* (Cambridge, Mass.: Harvard University Press, 1970), p. 164.

and desires. Much of this involves a cost-benefit and risk analysis on the part of each household.

Although peasants have always responded over time to the stability or instability of the market by increased outside participation or a withdrawal inward, in the nineteenth and twentieth centuries an additional element was added. Because population began to grow independently of any changes in peasants' productive capacities and because colonial and national governments were often demanding taxes in cash, peasants were forced rapidly and almost universally into outside participation in cases where there still remained significant insecurity in such involvement. In fact, one of the world's most pressing crises is that the *need* for gaining new value has been expanding more rapidly than the *means* for gaining new value. In these cases, they attempted to maintain some foothold on self-sufficiency even though involved in fairly extensive market relations.[15] They abandoned that foothold only when the risks of outside participation decreased, in other words, when convinced of relatively consistent and fair treatment for them in the market.

SELECTING MEANS TO RELIEVE THE STRESS

No neat analyses can predict whether particular peasants will become wage laborers or capital-investing farmers as their communities change and they seek to gain added value in the growing economy outside. One of the most important factors in determining the avenue of economic change is the amenability of the village's land to new agricultural practices. The types of stratification patterns that emerge in differing cases of land-use will be discussed in Chapter VIII.

Though there still are no definitive answers to this question

[15] See the account on Pelpola, Ceylon. Bryce Ryan, *Sinhalese Village* (Coral Gables, Fla.: University of Miami Press, 1958). Also see Henry Orenstein, *Gaon: Conflict and Cohesion in an Indian Village* (Princeton, N.J.: Princeton University Press, 1965), pp. 237-244.

125

of the route for new economic activity, there seem to be several other elements besides land-use which influence the solutions peasants take to relieve their crises. One crucial factor appears to be the rate and extent of change which brought about the crisis. Although we have spoken of the universal rapidity of change during the last two centuries, some factors produce crises more rapidly and extensively than others. Wars, sudden demands of lords for more rent, and changes to money taxes have been sudden jolts to household accounts, affecting large numbers of peasants simultaneously. Wars and new demands by lords were faced by peasants many times before—often by accepting lower standards of living—but the demands for money taxes have made peasants suddenly seek a rare commodity, cash. Other factors, such as population growth and decreased income from handicrafts, have been slower in creating a sense of desperation among peasants. Also, their effect is felt at different times by different households.

In the more rapidly produced crisis of demand for money taxes, two separate responses by peasants can be predicted. First, short-term out-migration and then daily wage labor are sought. Second, changes in distribution patterns of agriculture (but not necessarily of production patterns immediately) occur in order to convert crops into the needed cash. In these cases, the delay until money is sent back that follows long-term emigration is simply too long for many to wait. Also, there is a lag until changes in production patterns are introduced because of a delay until returns come in and also because the crisis at first does not necessarily demand more total income but more of a certain type of income, cash.

Factors slowly creating crises (e.g., population pressure), on the other hand, are more likely to induce peasants toward long-term out-migration and changes in both distribution *and* production in agriculture. In this case, overpopulation means that long-term migration does not leave the remainder of the household shorthanded in farming. Also, because some have left the village, there are fewer people to support at the mo-

126

ment. Changes in distribution patterns in agriculture are not sufficient. Peasants, in such cases, usually need long-term gains in income through increased output.

Another crucial factor in determining the way peasants face their crises is the proximity of outside economic opportunities. This influences whether they relieve the stress through participation in outside labor or through agriculture. For example, in Pelpola in Ceylon, the peasants have taken advantage of the opportunities in the nearby town and commute as workers, traders, and businessmen. Interestingly, the existence of such nearby outlets has meant that the peasants have not felt compelled to adopt a more capital intensive type of agriculture: "Agricultural practices are constant, and when this constant is inadequate, supplementation is sought outside agriculture."[16] Conversely, where outside labor opportunities are very limited, the pressure remains strong enough to force adoption of new agricultural techniques and a capital intensification of farming, if possible. In Thyagasamathiram (Madras State, India), for example, only the more educated Brahmins have gained government jobs, such as clerks or policemen. The rest have been double-cropping rice and using higher grade fertilizers.[17]

Finally, combinations of responses are typical. External wage labor may be taken up extensively after changes in agriculture distribution and production have proven insufficient to solve crises. The peasants of Hang Mei in Hong Kong, for example, have been switching their farming practices from the traditional staple of rice to truck farming of vegetables. They have used their rich lands wisely, increasing yields through more intensively grown crops. Yet, these yields have still been insufficient so people have looked outside the village for sources of income. As a result, now more than half the

[16] Ryan, *Sinhalese Village*, p. 177.

[17] Dagfinn Sivertsen, *When Caste Barriers Fall: A Study of Social and Economic Change in a South Indian Village* (Norway: George Allen and Unwin, 1963).

127

villagers have salaried jobs (mostly commercial and service) in the nearby cities or towns, while only one-sixth of the manpower is involved in agriculture.[18]

Many villages combine not only increased external wage labor and cash cropping to relieve the stress, but also use the means of long-term out-migration to secure jobs wherever possible. The peasants of Sha-ching (North China) were forced in the first half of this century to look outside the village for employment as population doubled and holdings became increasingly fragmented: "They used their land for crops which commanded the highest price and carefully allocated labor between farming and working outside the village to earn whichever income was greatest."[19] Most labored outside for short-terms (*tuan-kung*) but the poorest were, at times, forced to accept long-term employment outside the village (*ch'ang-kung*).[20]

SUMMARY

All too often analysts have confused culture contact (exposure to a technical innovation or improvements such as the building of a new highway) with the social, economic, and demographic forces impelling peasants to make use of that innovation.[21] Such cases as Hualcan, Ban Ping, and Buarij demonstrate that even participation in aspects of the modern, national sector could be used as a means to sustain the al-

[18] Jack M. Potter, *Capitalism and the Chinese Peasant: Social and Economic Change in a Hong Kong Village* (Berkeley: University of California Press, 1968).

[19] Myers, *The Chinese Peasant Economy*, p. 53.

[20] *Ibid.*, p. 50.

[21] See, for example, Guy Hunter, *Modernizing Peasant Societies: A Comparative Study in Asia and Africa* (New York: Oxford University Press, 1969), p. 140; and Shepard Forman and Joyce F. Riegelhaupt, "Market Place and Marketing System: Toward a Theory of Peasant Economic Integration," *Comparative Studies in Society and History* 12 (April 1970), 198.

ready established patterns of village life.[22] Without the dynamic forces of population growth or loss of income, peasants did not face sustained economic crises. Even when these crises struck, the outlets of frontiers, short-term seasonal wage labor, and long-term out-migration could provide outlets to relieve the stress. In the nineteenth and twentieth centuries, however, these outlets have dried up. The severity of household economic crises has caused a collision of the inward- and outward-oriented forces. Once this collision is at hand the means to gain additional value such as new roads, improved communications, and guaranteed price,[23] begin in themselves to play a prominent role in peasants' lives.

The nature of the interaction between the inward- and outward-oriented forces is the subject of the next two chapters. However, the overall result is clear. Peasants have increasingly moved toward an outward-orientation in which some have become daily wage laborers and others have become increasingly involved in a complex agricultural market. The inward-oriented peasant village has quickly become an artifact of history. The center of peasant life has shifted from the village square to the national capital.

[22] For another example, see Zekiye Eglar, *A Punjabi Village in Pakistan* (New York: Columbia University Press, 1960). Mohla was a 20-minute walk from the railway station for many years but continued to be inward-oriented.

[23] See Paul Stirling, *Turkish Village* (London: Weidenfeld and Nicolson, 1965), pp. 77-78, for the effect of government guaranteed price on peasant propensity to grow for the market rather than for subsistence.

PART THREE

The Triumph of Outward-Oriented Forces

CHAPTER VII

Who Risks Change?

INTRODUCTION

The analysis in this book has viewed certain inward-oriented peasant villages as effective political and social units. As such, the local community delimited the actions of the individual. The peasant was a person within a polity which had a system of justice and a distribution of values, not at all identical with those of society as a whole. The community had norms and sanctions which made the peasant, whatever his resources, less than an unimpeded actor. The community, then, is a key intervening variable when one attempts to assess who innovates, when, and how.

Each village's particular social and political organization related to a wide variety of factors that the community faced —from the insecurity of relations with other classes to the tensions generated within the village itself. As economic crises plagued the community, the political and social organization did not simply disintegrate in their wake. Peasants did not suddenly find themselves unhindered to seek means of increasing income through outside market involvement. Rather, each social and political organization presented paths and obstacles for the peasants as they faced these crisis-producing forces. The actual results of the interaction process between such village social and political organization and externally generated forces may be quite diverse. They ranged from the totally tragic to cases where peasants seemed little harmed by the interaction.

133

The Interaction of Village Organization and External Forces

Some of the most tragic cases have come with outside changes in the land tenure system. In nineteenth century Mexico, for example, the Indians faced disastrous consequences when laws were passed that made the political and social organization of villages impotent in insulating and defending the peasants against rapacious outsiders for the *Ley de desamortización* (Law of Expropriations) in 1857 resulted in all communal property being granted to the individual Indians holding the different plots. With the most basic function of the communal social and political organization, that of land control, no longer possible, there was an undermining of the system of distribution of justice within the villages. The result was that the Indians, dealing in a system of private ownership with which they were unfamiliar, were easily exploited by ready speculators and hacendados. "By 1910 less than 1 percent of the families of Mexico controlled 85 percent of the land, and 90 percent of the villages and towns on the central plateau had almost no communal land."[1] Village independence was replaced by near serfdom on haciendas located on former village communal lands.

Such changes in the system of land tenure have had similarly pernicious effects in other places as well.[2] In Saucío, Colombia, the "liberal" laws of the Spaniards which opened the village to private ownership resulted in increased frag-

[1] Robert A. White, S.J., "Mexico: The Zapata Movement and the Revolution," in *Latin American Peasant Movements*, ed. Henry A. Landsberger (Ithaca, N.Y.: Cornell University Press, 1969), p. 115.

[2] Eric R. Wolf, *Peasant Wars of the Twentieth Century* (New York: Harper and Row, 1969), pp. 277-278, cites changes in the land tenure system as one of the most dislocating experiences to the peasant and to peasant social organization. Also see Samuel P. Huntington, *Political Order in Changing Societies* (New Haven: Yale University Press, 1968), pp. 296-297.

134

mentation of the land and the selling of plots by hard-pressed peasants.[3] Richard N. Adams writes of some cases in Guatemala that

> political action, initiated outside the community, brought about a destruction of or violent alterations in the socio-political structure (whether purely Indian or Ladino-Indian) and with this change, the Indian's resistance to culture change began to disintegrate. His insulation was gone.[4]

In the Middle East, the Law of Tapu in 1858 and in Bolivia, the Laws of Ex-Vinculation had a similar effect of giving large landowners an opportunity to create new kinds of inequalities.[5]

In all these cases, those groups outside the village, ready and willing to exploit the new laws, were powerful and quite near at hand. They simply overwhelmed the village social and political organization. Because these new forces were externally applied and did not result from any building pressures from within the peasant community itself due to long-growing economic crises, there was little chance for any individual peasants to use the new laws for their own advantage. Also, there was little chance for the village institutions to adapt to the new forces. Powerful sheikhs, zamindars, and hacendados were the beneficiaries of this penetration of the village's insulation against the outside.

Freeholding inward-oriented villages had maintained their autonomy in large part because of the lack of powerful out-

[3] Orlando Fals-Borda, *Peasant Society in the Colombian Andes: A Sociological Study of Saucío* (Gainesville: University of Florida Press, 1955), p. 65.

[4] Richard N. Adams, "Changing Political Relationships in Guatemala" in *Political Changes in Guatemalan Indian Communities, A Symposium*, ed. Adams (New Orleans: Middle American Research Institute, Tulane University, 1957), publication no. 24, p. 48.

[5] See Z. Abromovitz and Y. Gelfat, *Hameshek Ha'aravi Be'eretz Yisrael U'vartzot Hamizrach Hatichon* [The Arab Holding in the Land of Israel and in the Countries of the Middle East] (Palestine:

side forces seeking to administer them from within. When powerful outsiders wanted to administer the village directly, however, there was usually little the social and political organization of the community could do to act as a buffer. New "liberal" laws changing land tenure patterns had this penetrative effect. The reason for peasants' maintaining severely restricted external relations—the insecurity of involvement with outsiders—remained. However, the capacity to withstand the onslaught of the new outside forces became insufficient.

In stark contrast to these tragic instances, there have been other patterns of interaction between the village political and social organization and outsiders which have resulted in much less devastating effects upon the viability of communities. The village of Sirkanda (India), for example, has been able to maintain a relatively low rate of outside participation. The peasants there have remained self-sufficient in agriculture, while growing a surplus for market. As a result, the Sirkanda community has been able to use outside resources to maintain its internal prestige system. Though it has inched up on the scale of external relations over the course of the twentieth century, it has been able to continue holding the market at arm's length, avoiding, to a great degree, extensive participation in outside institutions.[6]

Between these two extremes are various patterns of interaction (between community organization and externally generated forces) which have resulted in considerable change for the village social and political organization. T. Scarlett Epstein has compared two neighboring villages in another part of India which differ in the nature and quantity of recurrent outside contacts.[7] Although Dalena has not shared in the ex-

---

Hakibutz Hameuchad, 1944), p. 16 (Hebrew); and Andrew Pearse, "Peasants and Revolution: The Case of Bolivia: Part I," *Economy and Society* 1 (August 1972), p. 258.

[6] Gerald D. Berreman, *Hindus of the Himalayas* (Berkeley: University of California Press, 1963), pp. 55-56.

[7] T. S. Epstein, *Economic Development and Social Change in South India* (Manchester: Manchester University Press, 1962), p. 85.

panded water supply system from the region's new irrigation system, its higher caste members have been able to secure many outside jobs in building and maintaining the system. The village economy diversified, and there were increasing lines of daily cash interaction with the outside. The structural changes in Wangala, on the other hand, have been far less significant than in Dalena. Wangala used the new water supply to intensify its agriculture, and practically its only line of cash economy penetration has come from the sugarcane which the villagers have now been able to grow and sell seasonally to the nearby factory. The Wangalans have continued to grow subsistence staples. Their more precarious tie to the larger national economy has warranted methods that still guarantee self-sufficiency. Their confidence in the local sugar factory and the world sugar market has not grown enough for them to stake their entire livelihood on the expectation that these outside institutions will continue functioning smoothly.

In general, we can state that the rate and degree of structural changes within villages depends upon the *number, periodicity*, and *intensity* of the lines of outside penetration and involvement. By limiting external relations, a strong social and political organization, in many cases, kept all three of these factors low. In such instances, there were only small degrees and a slow rate of structural change. Even with such a viable organization, however, forces from within or without might have been strong enough to increase any or all of the three factors. Changes in land tenure systems so increased the intensity of outside penetration that even a strong social and political organization was helpless.

Crisis-producing forces, however, are not always applied directly by outsiders. What are the process and results of the situation discussed in the previous two chapters: an economic crisis which can be alleviated only by substantially increasing the number, periodicity, and intensity of lines of penetration by the peasants themselves? The remainder of this chapter will analyze two dimensions of the interaction of village organization and externally generated forces. First is the question of what occurs to the social and political organization itself to allow villagers significantly increased interdependence with outside institutions? A second question, implied in the first, is who is it that is able to react to this change in village policy? The next chapter will continue to pursue the interaction of social organization and external forces by analyzing the new kinds of stratifications and the change in village institutions that occur as villages greatly increase their external relations.

TENSIONS, SANCTIONS, AND PRESSURES FOR CHANGE

"To put the matter baldly, it is not uncommon that villagers who are ambitious, enterprising, or successful are, in the eyes of their fellows, 'sons of bitches.' "[8] Resentment also runs the other way: the more enterprising and successful peasants in villages with limited outside participation had to pay a disproportionately high share for the maintenance of an inward-orientation. Often, these wealthier villagers resented spending parts of their surpluses for ceremonies that were purely for consumption, or for the redistributive mechanisms that kept the less fortunate alive. These underlying tensions and resentments made such villages places of strain. On the one hand were those who had begun to tire of their commitments to their neighbors and saw the village social and political organization as oppressive and stifling.[9] Their sporadic contact with the market made them aware of an alternative status system in the outside world. On the other hand were the somewhat poorer households which perceived any attempts to undermine these mechanisms of redistribution as threatening their very survival.

[8] Michael Moerman, *Agricultural Change and Peasant Choice in a Thai Village* (Berkeley: University of California Press, 1968), p. 144.
[9] Mehmet Beqiraj describes repressed internal dissent. *Peasantry in Revolution*, Center for International Studies, Cornell University, Cornell Research Papers in International Studies, vol. v (1966), ch. 1.

Historically, as long as outside exploitation persisted, such strain could usually be repressed. When there had been instances, however, in which the reasons for limiting outside participation decreased, such as lessened exploitation and growing stability of markets, then dissatisfied villagers at times had risked the condemnation and sanctions of their neighbors to establish outside alliances.[10] There were cases of the wealthier peasants using their resources to escape the peasantry, becoming minor lords and exploiters of other villagers. More recently, two interdependent factors have undermined the ability to repress the strain which resulted in an increase in outside participation—and much more rapidly than in the past: (1) within the community the severe economic crises led to a change in the village's power structure and its ability to apply sanctions against outside involvement; and (2) outside there was increased security of participation in alternative status systems for the wealthier members.

The first factor, the change in the power structure, came as such factors as population growth were making life increasingly difficult for peasant households. When the poorer peasants were faced with the pressures of these economic crises, they had no sources outside the village to which to turn. Their response to crisis in fact was very traditional: they reluctantly approached the envied few who were not sinking from the new pressures. Households in crisis went deep into debt, borrowing from the wealthier village members. With little relief from the continuing pressure, they lost their land piece by piece to these fellow villagers, either through foreclosures or through sales for needed cash. More and more the social structure became polarized and frozen. The former fluidity of upward and downward mobility disappeared.

The more that the resources of the village came into the hands of a few members, the less effective was the social and political organization of the village in restraining certain peas-

[10] See G. William Skinner, "Chinese Peasants and the Closed Community: An Open and Shut Case," *Comparative Studies in Society and History* 13 (July 1971), 271.

ants from establishing outside ties. The effectiveness of the inward-oriented village's sanctions had depended on the relative equality within the social structure—of the limits on upward and downward mobility discussed in Chapter IV. Now, with a few members as landholders and the rest economically dependent on them, the use of sanctions by the community was limited. Power became much more concentrated in the hands of the wealthy. The capability of suppressing their desire for outside participation declined.

The second factor resulting in new external ties comes, as was noted, from changes outside the village. The repression of tensions within inward-oriented villages depended upon the relative lack of alternative sources of support for those who were dissatisfied. Despite the resentments that such villages' social and political organization bred, as long as the condition which brought about an inward-orientation continued to exist (extreme insecurity of participation with classes and institutions outside the village), there was nowhere for the ambitious man to turn. It was foolhardy to risk incurring village sanctions. Ostracism meant that communication ceased with almost the totality of the peasant's world. Ridicule indicated a social rejection with almost no one else to turn to for acceptance.

The same factors which caused economic crises for the poorer peasants also changed the nature of the outside environment for the wealthier. Imperialism's penetration of the rural areas caused not only such things as competition for handicraft products but also new institutional security and economic opportunity *for those with the proper resources.* The new conditions brought stability and promise for those with the needed skills and capital. Because peasants were always somewhat involved in the market, these wealthier members had some sense of when outside conditions were propitious for increased participation or when the means to such involvement no longer presented insuperable obstacles. A new road which allowed wholesalers to come directly to

140

the village, for example, could be one way in which new relationships could be forged.

Thus, in the village a minority was at the top of a new economic structure entering into a new status system through recurrent interactions with outsiders. This new status system, with its different sources of prestige and rank, itself demanded even more new patterns of behavior and further weakened the old village organization.[11] In Namhalli (Mysore, India), for example, population pressure had caused a desperate competition for land and a consequent breakdown of consensus. With increased outside involvement, the adoption of some of the conflicting values associated with the outside resulted in villagers acting upon different criteria and this too furthered the breakdown in consensus.[12]

Who Increases Outside Participation?

Greater involvement with outside classes and institutions usually has come at a high risk to those who take the first steps. Conditions were not totally changed. Despite the redistribution of resources and power within the village, the political and social organization still existed, and there continued to be some application of sanctions. And despite conditions that might have indicated a decrease in the lord's will or ability to limit outside contacts, his mere presence remained a significant deterrent to new forms of behavior. Also, though there may have been seeming changes in the security of outside participation, extensive outside involvement had yet to be tested conclusively. A failure of outside groups to

[11] Charles Tilly, *The Vendée* (New York: John Wiley, 1967), pp. 59-65, for a discussion of the growth of the influence of outside norms.

[12] Alan Beals, "Leadership in a Mysore Village," in *Leadership and Political Institutions in India*, ed. Richard L. Park and Irene Tinker (Princeton, N.J.: Princeton University Press, 1959), pp. 432-433.

fulfill expectations and to provide support to the peasant taking the first steps could lead to his ostracization or even expulsion without anywhere for him to turn; it could lead to the eviction by the landlord or an elimination of vital credit by the moneylender; or it could lead to the subjugation by a lord of a formerly independent peasant. Who within the village has best been able and most likely to risk the dire outcome of any possible failure?

An account of a caste in the Indian state of Orissa helps shed some light on this question. In the village of Bisipara, the Ganjam Distillers have been the shopkeepers of the village and probably its wealthiest caste. Unlike those in other castes, however, they have remained as aloof as possible from strictly village affairs, and they have not associated intimately with other peasants. Because of their contacts with middlemen and peasants from the hill villages who buy in their shops, they have found the Bisipara dispute handling mechanisms useless for their differences with these outside groups. They have used or threatened to use government courts, and their threats have been taken seriously because of their money to hire lawyers. Also, the Ganjam Distillers' ties with the middlemen and hill peasants have enabled them to be somewhat immune from the village council's most effective sanction, social ostracism.[13]

This account of the Ganjam Distillers highlights the three factors characteristic of those who initially break village norms: (1) they have already removed themselves somewhat from the village status system by developing outside reference groups and have thus been better able to withstand the application of sanctions; (2) they have had the necessary outside connections which they could use as bases for the formation of alliances; and, most importantly, (3) they have sufficient resources to enter into such alliances, e.g., with lawyers.

[13] F. G. Bailey, *Caste and the Economic Frontier: A Village in Highland Orissa* (Manchester: Manchester University Press, 1957), ch. x.

The shopkeepers have withdrawn from many aspects of the social life of the village and have established other reference groups by whose standards they could measure their behavior and among whom they could achieve social acceptance. In this particular case, two reference groups have substituted for extensive participation in the village status system. First and most important has been the in-group of the Ganjam Distillers themselves, reinforcing each other's behavior and deviance (by village standards). Second have been the lawyers and court officials of the larger social system. The establishment of a reference group with which those who deviate from village norms could identify and from whom they feel they could achieve normative acceptance (even if not openly or directly expressed) is a prime requisite for risking the wrath of the dominant social system, that of the village itself.

The second factor which has characterized those who risk the establishment of new ties is not independent of the first factor. Having outside reference groups may also mean using these reference groups to serve as contacts for forming outside alliances. Certainly the connections of the Ganjam Distillers with town lawyers must have made them more secure in their unusual behavior. The alliances with outsiders greatly reinforced their immunity to the application of village sanctions by giving it an institutional basis.

And this is precisely why the existence of significant "others," an outside reference group, generally has been feared by the village community.[14] In effect, such alliances changed the whole relationship of the village to the outside world. When the village had restricted external relations, the political and social organization served as buffers to outside forces. Village leadership attempted to deal with impinging forces by funneling them into a single channel. Government

[14] One only need think of the grocer in Lerner's parable. Daniel Lerner, *The Passing of Traditional Society: Modernizing the Middle East* (New York: The Free Press, 1958), p. 25.

officials thus dealt not with various strata of the village population but with brokers of the entire village population.

The new alliances, however, have created differentiations among the village populace. Those with resources or attributes more appealing to the outside forces have been brought into relationships from which other villagers have been excluded. Old differences which meant little in the village's relations to other classes gained in importance and served as the basis for stratification of village population in relation to the outside. Even more unsettling, the value ascribed to these old differences has been turned upside down. In these new specific relationships, youth has become valued over old age; secularism over religiosity; individualism over communalism; tightfisted savings over conspicuous consumption. The village political and social organization no longer serves the function of spreading the risks among all. Differences which meant little in the past have grown enormously in importance.

The result is that there are increasing conflicts within the village "between individuals, families, or entire neighborhoods. Such a community," Wolf writes, "will inevitably differentiate into a number of unstable groups with different orientations and interests."[15] The Wisers have spoken of the changes occurring in one Indian village as a result of alliances formed by diverse government agencies with certain villagers through programs they have initiated.[16] These alliances have had an effect upon the village political organization with the government's efforts resulting in new village leadership. This Indian village population has been sorted out by outside agencies attempting to institutionalize it. The result is that there has been a passing of power from the hands of the village elders.[17]

[15] Eric R. Wolf, "Aspects of Group Relations in a Complex Society: Mexico," *American Anthropologist* 58 (December 1956), 1073.

[16] William H. and Charlotte Viall Wiser, *Behind Mud Walls 1930-1960* (Berkeley: University of California Press, 1964), p. 197.

[17] *Ibid.*, pp. 205-206. Ryan also speaks of government's initiative in penetrating the village. Bryce Ryan, *Sinhalese Village* (Coral Gables, Fla.: University of Miami Press, 1958), p. 138.

Who within inward-oriented villages had the connections with which to institutionalize increased external involvement by forming such outside alliances? Wolf has identified such people as the "nation-oriented" members of the village. Those who had been the brokers of the village to the outside world were most likely to know the channels of communications and patterns of outside behavior well enough to operate in the new milieu.[18] It was the broker who knew where to make the brides,[19] which officials to see, where to get the best prices, how to speak the outside culture's language. Moerman speaks of the development of a stratification of knowledge—"news of special prices, insecticides, fertilizers, changes in the law. . . ."[20] "Knowledge of tractor agriculture depends not on position within the household and village but on contact with outsiders."[21] Such brokers may have been merchants, traders, craftsmen, factional leaders, or any number of others who had more regular contact with outsiders. In many cases these brokers were distrusted by the villagers. Yet, despite this distrust, for handling relations with outside economic and political institutions, peasants went to these men, rather than to their old leaders, because these brokers had the right contacts.[22]

Besides the use of particular types of knowledge in making contact, certain ascriptive factors also became important. In Epstein's village of Wangala (India), for example, the new irrigated lands did not help the Untouchables very much, either in getting cultivable land or outside jobs. They were

[18] Wolf, "Aspects of Group Relations," 1065.

[19] F. G. Bailey, "The Peasant View of the Bad Life," *The Advancement of Science* 23 (December 1966), 403-404.

[20] Moerman, *Agricultural Change*, p. 77.

[21] *Ibid.*, p. 76.

[22] F. G. Bailey writes that anyone who had such contacts had already forfeited the confidence of the villagers. *Politics and Social Change: Orissa in 1959* (Berkeley: University of California Press, 1963), pp. 58-59. Also, for a discussion of cultural brokers at the time of the French Revolution, see Tilly, *The Vendée*, p. 93 and *passim*.

145

shunned because of their untouchability. They lacked not only the bribe money, but also the caste connections to get the jobs.[23] Similarly, in the highland village of Aritama (Colombia), the low caste Indians have lacked the knowledge and ascriptive associations which would enable them to manipulate the outside for their own purposes. Instead they have had to continue to deal through the village storekeepers to get the new prestige items, while their neighboring Creoles have entered into a wide variety of direct interdependent relationships with lowland Creoles.[24] Even if one had outside connections, they became important only if they were with the "right" outsiders, ones who could help gain value.

These last two cases of Wangala's Untouchables and Aritama's Indians are particularly interesting because both involved cases of patron-client relationships among peasants themselves. In Aritama, the storekeepers had long served as the community's monopolistic links to the goods and ideas of the lowlands. With the development of alternative means to gain the products of the lowlands, however, only a portion of Aritama's peasants had the connections and knowledge to take advantage of them. The remainder still have had to use the services of the peasant-patron. John D. Powell states that it was the small-scale patron who was, at times, changed increasingly into the role of broker in the course of state and market centralization.[25]

Within the community, new resources grew in importance. A number of peasants may have learned Spanish in Latin American countries or accumulated some capital. These differences, which may have been insignificant while the village was not riddled by economic crises, now became the basis for important differentiations of the village population in rela-

[23] Epstein, *Economic Development and Social Change*, p. 182.

[24] Gerardo and Alicia Reichel-Dolmatoff, *The People of Aritama: The Cultural Personality of a Colombian Mestizo Village* (London: Routledge and Kegan Paul, 1961).

[25] John Duncan Powell, "Peasant Society and Clientilist Politics," *The American Political Science Review* 64 (June 1970), 414-415.

tion to the outside. Larson and Bergman write of Peru's peasants that where there was low hacienda hegemony, it was the middle peasant who assimilated the urban traits of bilingualism, literacy, commercial orientation, religious cynicism, and the like.[26]

Also, just as in freeholding villages and villages with weak lords, restrictions on peasants' behavior by strong lords did not disappear overnight. There usually was not a sudden change from high risk to total security in establishing relations with outsiders. Some peasants had more of the kind of contacts useful in the market place and in dealings with outside officials or had key ascriptive associations. Such villagers were better able to judge when the lord had withdrawn vigilance sufficiently to make a move or when the lord's competitors, be they government officials or other lords, were sufficiently strong to serve as alternative sources for that which the lord had previously supplied exclusively.[27]

Besides the factors of having outside reference groups and external connections, the third factor characterizing those who have risked deviating from accepted village social behavior is the possession of sufficient resources to enter into outside alliances. An alliance is a mutual relationship, and there must be some basis of exchange to solidify the association. In markets, which are the most common means of increasing the degree of one's external relations, the peasant usually has needed sufficient capital as a basis for forming

[26] Magali Sarfatti Larson and Arlene Eisen Bergman, *Social Stratification in Peru* (Berkeley: Institute of International Studies, University of California, 1969), p. 67.

[27] Charles J. Erasmus points out that once the blockage of the hacendado is gone in Latin American countries, there tends to be some pressure towards reconsolidation of holdings, which indicates that even within patron-client communities some are better able to respond to new opportunities. "Agrarian vs. Land Reform: Three Latin-American Countries," in *Peasants in the Modern World*, ed. Philip K. Bock (Albuquerque: University of New Mexico Press, 1969). Also see Wolf's discussion of the Russian *mir* in *Peasant Wars of the Twentieth Century*, pp. 51-99, *passim*.

147

alliances. Other times scarce skills have been important. Political parties or bureaucratic agencies may look for other attributes in their attempts to penetrate the village.

Capital accumulation necessary for market participation usually came through the route discussed earlier in this chapter. The crises of most households in the village led to their turning to those who had been fortunate enough to escape crisis. Interest collected from other villagers and income gained from newly acquired land became the basis for increased market involvement. The innovator's initial major outlays of accumulated cash have been used both as a means to forge relationships with outsiders and to gain the products of outside technology which could ensure a continuing surplus for enduring alliances. Thus, outside alliances were used to maintain the new stratification.

Epstein's Indian villages again serve as a good illustration. It was the wealthier peasants with the cash to make the necessary outlays who were the ones taking advantage of a new opportunity to gain new sources of income. "By creating the need for larger investment in agricultural capital before the benefits from irrigation could be fully enjoyed, irrigation re-emphasized the economic predominance of the richest farmers."[28] Previous to the development of the new irrigation system, the peasants of Wangala had grown the staple dry crops of ragi and jowar and a wet crop, paddy. All of these were half-yearly crops. The new water system allowed them to grow sugarcane, a much more lucrative crop. Sugarcane, however, takes more than a year to mature and the more wealthy, at first, were the only ones who could last through the longer maturing period. Also, sugarcane demands a considerably higher investment to grow than the dry crops or paddy. "Only those few farmers who had some ready cash and the necessary enterprise ventured into sugarcane cultivation immediately after their lands were irrigated. These men are to-day the richest in Wangala."[29]

Those in the village who lived in and out of debt and who

[28] Epstein, *Economic Development and Social Change*, p. 53.
[29] *Ibid.*, p. 30.

were suffering most from the economic crises within the village were the ones least likely to have the necessary resources to extract some measure of relief through outside alliance. The fear of failure—leading to starvation or unpayable debts, for example—acted to deter the poorer farmers in a pre-revolutionary Chinese village from placing the resources they did have into crops that could return considerably more income than usual. Despite the possibilities of very lucrative returns, vegetable-growing was avoided by them, partly because of the greater fluctuations in market prices and partly because vegetables demanded investment in heavy fertilizers and additional farming equipment. As a result, the poorer cultivators continued to grow rice, which had a more stable price and in any case could be used for subsistence purposes.[30]

SOCIAL THEORY AND PEASANT INNOVATION

It has been hypothesized here that three factors are associated with those peasants who have initiated far greater outside participation: they have (1) an outside reference group, (2) previous outside connections, and (3) resources valued by the outside social system which could be used as a basis for enduring alliances. Yet it should be emphasized that our knowledge of who within the village first increased outside participation still remains far from definitive, and debates continue on this question. H. G. Barnett has suggested that it usually has not been the elite of the village who have innovated. There are risks involved in engaging in new forms of social behavior, he claims, which a leader, with his obliga-

[30] Hsiao-Tung Fei, *Peasant Life in China: A Field Study of Country Life in the Yangtze Valley* (London: Routledge and Kegan Paul, 1939), pp. 45-46. For an interesting case in a Madras, India, village, see Dagfinn Sivertsen, *When Caste Barriers Fall: A Study of Social and Economic Change in a South Indian Village* (Norway: George Allen and Unwin, 1963), pp. 101-102. Also see McKim Marriott's interesting discussion on innovation. "Technological Change in Over-developed Areas," *Economic Development and Cultural Change* 1 (1952-1953), 261-272.

tion to conform to the expectations of others, could not take.[31] George Foster has countered that in fact it has been the prestige-laden individual who has innovated. He maintains that the innovator characteristically has been a wealthy and respected member of the community.[32]

Everett Hagen has added another dimension to the debate with the novel hypothesis that it has been groups which had been formerly respected and lost that respect which were in the forefront of social change. The key, in Hagen's view, is not the static status position of innovators in respect to others in the community but their fall in relation to their own previous standing. "Indeed," he writes, "withdrawal of status respect is at the root of the world's turbulence today."[33]

The discussion here has put the question of peasants' increases in outside participation into a somewhat different context. By recognizing the viability and relative autonomy of the village's social and political organization, we have been led to speak of two distinct status systems, that of the village and that of the larger society. Though not mutually exclusive, the two status systems often tended to have very different criteria for such concepts as "elite" and "prestige-laden." The reference group that a peasant looked to for social acceptance was local since his external relations were so restricted. Yet there was an underlying tension within that community status system, for the village was never in perfect isolation: the larger social system tantalizingly offered alternative sources of respect often based on wholly different criteria from that of the village. At times, different resources were demanded by the outside system as a basis for the prestige it was prepared to bestow. In other cases, a resource like land which may have brought some measure of prestige within the village

[31] H. G. Barnett, *Innovation, The Basis of Cultural Change* (New York: McGraw-Hill, 1953), pp. 318-319.

[32] George M. Foster, *Traditional Cultures: and the Impact of Technological Change* (New York: Harper, 1962), p. 114.

[33] Everett E. Hagen, *On the Theory of Social Change: How Economic Growth Begins* (Homewood, Ill.: The Dorsey Press, 1962), p. 192.

could be used to gain even greater respect outside and from a much larger reference group.

Tension mounted within the village status systems because those peasants who recognized and sought these alternative sources of prestige faced the sanctions of the local community. Coupled with the insecurity of outside participation, such restraints usually had been sufficient to inhibit such peasants from risking a jump to much more extensive participation in the larger status system. Once the control of the village social and political organization or of the lord lessened and the stability of outside participation increased, however, changes occurred. Those who were best able to withstand the application of any remaining sanctions and already felt deprived of the larger social system's sources of prestige were the ones most likely to initiate new forms of social behavior through outside participation. They had the "prestige" resources of the outside.

Adoption of new technology and procedures from the outside by peasants, then, depends on a dynamic historical process. Aspirations and resources for increased outside participation may have long existed, but the restrictions from within thwarted potential innovators and resulted in use of a rather fixed level of technology. With the dynamic forces creating numerous economic crises, and with any changes in the security of outside participation, the innovators got their chance to establish new ties.

This is the outline of the model for change in external relations developed here so far. Both the sociologists and political scientists, using a diffusion of innovation model in which innovation is determined by who has available knowledge, and the economists, who assess who will innovate by noting who has available inputs, have often failed to take this dynamic historical process into account. The factors they consider are important but only at a particular moment in each village's history. Their failure has stemmed from an approach which focuses on the individual outside of history and community.

Everett Rogers' analysis of peasants, while far superior to

151

many, shows the inherent weaknesses of such an approach. He is interested in analyzing "innovativeness," the degree to which an individual adopts new ideas relatively earlier than others in his social system. To do this, he identifies its antecedents: literacy, mass media exposure, empathy, social status, achievement motivation, educational aspirations, occupational aspirations, change agent contact, cosmopoliteness, opinion leadership.[34] Nowhere in his study, however, do we find an integration into the analysis of the barriers and obstacles to "innovativeness" within the peasants' own social world, the sanctions and restraints applied by lords and fellow peasants. Rogers compiles a list of attributes associated with innovators and assumes these are always the trigger to change. Nowhere in his book do we get the sense that potential innovators may be frustrated and repressed in their attempts at change—even when they have all the necessary attributes.

Even so astute as observer of peasant agriculture as the economist Theodore Schultz has focused on individuals without noting the communal and class restraints they have faced. His analysis instead goes directly to factors such as the low marginal productivity of both labor and capital.[35] Boserup's theory has the same shortcoming. She assumes that once the incentive of overpopulation is present, the only constraints on economic innovation are access to inputs which would make the investment worthwhile. She neglects any restraints placed by communities or lords on the individual household.[36]

Among these sociologists and economists, the stability of outside institutions and the viability of village structures are not considered as integral components of an explanation of when and why men change their social behavior and even the dominant social system within which they act. Shahid

[34] Everett M. Rogers, *Modernization among Peasants: The Impact of Communication* (New York: Holt, Rinehart, 1969), p. 292.

[35] Theodore W. Schultz, *Transforming Traditional Agriculture* (New Haven: Yale University Press, 1964), p. 28 and *passim*. Schultz has been criticized for his position by Thomas Balogh, *The Economics of Poverty* (London: Weidenfeld and Nicolson, 1966), pp. 74-78.

[36] Ester Boserup, *The Conditions of Agricultural Growth: The*

Javed Burki found in West Pakistan that the focus of sociologists and economists on the individuals' resources tended to make them over-aggregate and therefore lose sight of important distinctions by failing to note the old and new social and political positions of groups.[37]

Unless one sees peasants as acting within polities that are greater than the sum of the individuals, polities that have power to circumscribe severely the actions of the individuals within them, unless one sees villages as shaping themselves on the basis of historical forces and pressures, he runs the danger of "over-aggregating." It is futile to attempt a static, ahistorical analysis of peasant behavior by merely surmising its culture from the attitudes and acts of its populace. Rather, the differences, the stratifications, the tensions of the sum of the individuals are tied up with the local political and social organization that, on the one hand, adapts to the history of the social and physical environment and, on the other, limits the actions of any one of its individual members. The attributes of individuals who innovate are valuable to know if placed within the context of the particular interactions of village structures and external forces that the community has experienced and continues to experience.

Summary

There is an irony to the process of ending a village's limited outside involvement, of moving from an inward- to an outward-orientation. The most prominent factors in this worldwide change have been the severe economic crises that struck and threatened significant numbers of households. Yet initially it was not those households most severely affected by rising

---

Economics of Agrarian Change under Population Pressure (Chicago: Aldine, 1965), p. 88. For an interesting critique of the economists' neglect of the historical development of the market and the barriers to participation, see Matthew Edel, "Innovative Supply: A Weak Point in Economic Development Theory," *Social Science Information* 9 (June 1970), 9-40.

[37] Shahid Javed Burki, "Development of West Pakistan's Agriculture: An Interdisciplinary Explanation" (paper read at the Work-

populations and falling incomes which first used outside institutions, such as the market, government agencies, and political parties, as sources for gaining relief from these crises. Rather, the pressure put upon such a village's social and political organization and the competition faced by the formerly monopolistic lords often afforded those *least affected* by the new crises an opportunity to act first. It was this fortunate minority which gained from others' desperate need for cash. With the proper resources and with outside reference groups and connections, they could take advantage of the weakened village organization as well as any increases in outside security. With a decline in social control of the community's institutions, these villagers were willing, in forming alliances, to risk engaging in recurrent exchanges with other outside institutions.

Subsequently, a whole host of changes ensued for the remainder of the community as well. It has not simply been that the barriers have fallen and all have jumped into increased relationships with outsiders in order to relieve their crises. Those who made the initial contacts have gotten control of vital resources and have entrenched themselves at the top of the status hierarchy. What happens to the remainder of the peasants depends on such factors as how much land is gobbled up by the few at the top, what kinds of outside opportunities exist, etc. In Chapter VIII, we shall delineate the major patterns of stratification which have emerged and which have determined the orientation of various sectors of the peasantry to the outside economy.

In the course of the discussion (Chapters II-IV) of how restrictions on outside involvement were maintained, two continua were implicit throughout. One was the scale of external relations (inward- to outward-orientation) and the other was a spectrum ranging from communities with an almost completely equal differential allocation of economic and political powers among households to ones in which one man or house-

shop on Rural Development in Pakistan, Michigan State University, East Lansing, Mich., July 16, 1971), p. 24 and *passim*.

hold completely monopolized such powers (corporate, free-holding villages to haciendas). The attributes that social scientists have devised to explain innovation are most pertinent at the moment in history when there is a particular relationship between these two scales.

On both ends of the allocation of power scale, there are likely to be inward-oriented communities. A vigilant lord with a complete monopoly over a wide scope of high primacy resources could shut the peasants off from significant contacts with the outside. At the other end, a freeholding village, such as a corporate community, could bar involvement by its members with the outside as long as no person was strong enough to flout its sanctions. It is the middle range of this spectrum of allocation of power—that is, where there is a somewhat unequal distribution of powers—that some peasants may have had sufficient resources, given the proper opportunities, to establish links with groups or institutions outside the village. It is in the middle range that some can withstand the weakened sanctions of peers or patrons. Figure 1 demonstrates this relationship between the degree of outside involvement and the way power is distributed.

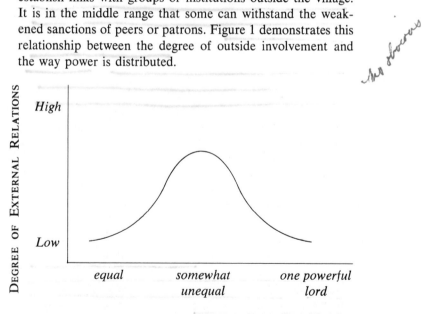

DIFFERENTIAL ALLOCATION OF POWER

FIGURE 1

CHAPTER VIII

Social Structure and Social Institutions

INTRODUCTION

IN THE LAST CHAPTER, we began the consideration of the interactive process between the village's social and political organization and externally generated forces as peasants increase their outside relations. The actions of a significant minority in the village, we saw, bring changes for the entire community and greatly reduced the relatively fluid nature of the old social structure. This chapter continues the analysis of this interaction, showing that the nature of the relationships built with outsiders by the rest of the peasants, the non-innovators, are in large part shaped by the earlier actions of the innovators and by the ecological limitations on the innovators. The outward-oriented village has a social structure and social institutions which relate to its past (who innovated first and under what conditions), as well as to the problems its members currently face.

THE POLARIZATION OF SOCIAL STRUCTURE

There is an infinite variety of social structures that have emerged in rural areas as villages have increased their external relations. However, three basic and necessarily simplified patterns of stratification can be identified for analytic purposes. They differ in their degree of polarization and in the kinds of resources used as a basis for that polarization. They are: (1) the mechanized and extensive agriculture pattern, (2) the intensive agriculture pattern, and (3) the marginal-land agriculture pattern.

1) *The mechanized and extensive agriculture pattern*

The results of the first pattern can be seen, in their most extreme variety, in pre-Industrial Revolution England. There, the enclosures of the newly business-conscious gentry changed radically the nature of the entire rural social system. Some of these landowners consolidated rural landholdings in order to engage in a more commercial agriculture, based on new levels of technology. Many others rented their lands to businessmen who would use these new methods. In effect, the introduction of large, commercialized farms spelled doom and eventual demise for the English peasantry. Law, wealth, and raw power were used to displace peasant agriculture for a type which increasingly relied more heavily on machine power than on manpower. It relied on capital intensity rather than labor intensity. The farms became huge, extensive tracts rather than small labor-intensive holdings.

The resultant rural social structure, then, was one of extreme polarization. On the one hand were the entrepreneurs who operated or rented out the large mechanized farms and on the other were the landless peasants too old, beaten, or set in their ways to migrate to the city. In the course of two centuries, most families made their way to urban areas, and those remaining became part of an impoverished rural proletariat. In England, the peasants not only lost their land but also over time lost their role in the rural areas because of changes in farming methods. Little differentiation among the English peasants emerged, since few remained peasants.

Such a demise of the peasantry need not be associated only with growing mechanization. The key to this pattern is the great economies of scale which make large holdings much more competitive than small, peasant-owned ones or ones parceled out to tenants.[1] In the Caribbean islands, preindus-

[1] See Arthur L. Stinchcombe's discussion of the "ranch" in "Agricultural Enterprise and Rural Class Relations," in *Political Development*

trial consolidation resulted in huge sugar plantations so that there were no (or few) small farms. The displaced white farmer was forced to emigrate from Barbados, for example, after the importation of cheap slave labor. Only those with no other alternatives of gaining income remained in the rural areas (in this case, the slaves and, later, the Negro freedmen). They became part of a work force organized much differently from that in peasant agriculture. The stratification pattern, as in England, was highly polarized. It was made up of rich plantation owners or managers and wretched slaves and freedmen, with no class of small, independent farmers or tenants.[2]

In recent decades, the British pattern has also begun to occur in parts of Asia and Latin America. For example, Hinderink and Kiray's study of four Turkish villages shows a similar, if less severe, pattern compared to that of England and Barbados. Of their four villages, the most "primitive" one has the least amount of social inequality. In contrast, the two most "developed" villages have changed in composition from small independent and medium-sized farmers and sharecroppers in 1940 to communities where now barely a quarter of the population is still in farming. In these two villages, 27 out of 42 farms are smaller than 25 dunams, comprising only 1.7 percent of the cropland. On the other hand, 10 farms make up 92.6 percent—13,348 dunams. These are large-scale, mechanized farms, sizable enough to make many improvements much more worthwhile. Their owners have access to knowledge of innovations. With the increasing importance

---

and Social Change, ed. Jason L. Finkle and Richard W. Gable (2d ed.; New York: John Wiley, 1971), pp. 369-371.

[2] Ramiro Guerra y Sánchez, *Sugar and Society in the Caribbean: An Economic History of Cuban Agriculture* (New Haven: Yale University Press, 1964), p. 19. "Sugar, tobacco, and cotton required the large plantation and hordes of cheap labor and the small farm of the ex-indentured white servant could not possibly survive" (Eric Williams, *Capitalism and Slavery* [London: Andre Deutsch, 1964]), p. 23.

of transportation, credit, new cotton varieties, and tractors, the small sharecropping farmer finds himself less and less able to compete.[3]

Just as home weaving slowly died with the growth of textile factories in the Industrial Revolution, so in this first pattern of stratification does peasant farming diminish with the growth of agro-industries and plantations. Peasant farm land shrinks as the small farms lose their tenancies and sell out their independent holdings. Through this process there is a diminishing number of small peasants owning marginal bits of land. And there is a growing number of out-migrants and poor rural proletarians seeking work on the agro-industries and wherever else possible. Such a social structure is most likely to emerge in areas of fertile land where crops demanding little labor intensity, such as wheat, are grown. These are the conditions that are the most propitious for the use of tractor technology. Economies of scale put the peasant, with his low capital imput, into an extremely unfavorable competitive position vis-à-vis large, capital-intensive farms. The most inexpensive harvesters and combines, for example, available to the wealthy, cost upwards of $10,000 and soon make the hand labor of the poor archaic. These conditions are often accelerated by credit policies which favor the large over the small.

In Europe, the United States and Canada, and increasingly in parts of Latin America and the Middle East, the labor-intensive household cultivation has suffered at the growth of new and relatively costly techniques and tools of farming. A diminishing peasantry remains under these circumstances in villages. Many are forced to relegate farming to a part-time activity on small plots of the village's more marginal land. Others must give up their tie to the soil altogether because of the great pressure by the rich to consolidate as much as they can. This drive to monopolize all the fertile land results because the capital investments necessary for such farming have

[3] Jan Hinderink and Mübeccel B. Kiray, *Social Stratification as an Obstacle to Development: A Study of Four Turkish Villages* (New York: Praeger, 1970), p. 51.

already been made and there are then only marginal additional labor and capital investments that have to be made to get a profit out of an additional unit of adjacent land.

2) *The intensive agriculture pattern*

In those areas of highly labor-intensive agriculture, the imperialists' original changes in land tenure usually did not create a vast displacement of the peasantry from the land. Using the case of India, Robert Birrell explains these background factors which influenced later changes in social structure. With the growth of population in the nineteenth century and the British policy of making land alienable there, Indian peasants were increasingly in debt and forced to give up their lands.[4] Rather than entirely dispossessing peasants, however, the new large landlords in rural India who emerged with British help rented their lands out to tenants of small plots. Those peasants not "fortunate" enough to get a plot at the high rents charged by the landlords became landless laborers. Why was the peasantry not destroyed as in the English case? One reason is that in India

> the economic gains from consolidation are limited, especially in regard to paddy cultivation where few economies of scale have been possible. The paddy field tends to be relatively small due to problems of water control and the necessity of having a level surface. Moreover, paddy is responsive to increased inputs of labor such as careful water control procedures and more intensive, repeated cultivation. Thus by forcing the small tenant to use his labor extravagantly (in the sense that he must compete with other peasants for the use of the land) there seems to be no great gain to be had from letting the land in large farms to fewer tenants.[5]

[4] For a strikingly similar account on Vietnam, see Robert L. Sansom, *The Economics of Insurgency in the Mekong Delta of Vietnam* (Cambridge, Mass.: The M.I.T. Press, 1970), p. 18.

[5] Robert Birrell, "Obstacles to Development in Peasant Societies: An Analysis of India, England, and Japan," in *Peasants in the Mod-*

Some small economies of scale have appeared, especially during the 1960s. There has been a movement toward consolidation but certainly nothing as drastic as occurred in the first pattern. There are several reasons for this increased consolidation. The green revolution's new seeds and fertilizers are most valuable to those who already had irrigation. Also, these new products are most readily available in sufficient quantity to those who can get credit easily and cheaply.

Innovators have been able to take advantage of this situation, to increase their holdings somewhat at the expense of poorer peasants. The result is not an agro-industrial tract by any means. In the Indian Punjab, "the optimum size of holding for the efficient cultivation of the high-yielding varieties assuming a tube-well is about 20 to 25 acres."[6] Peasants with 10 to 15 acres in the Punjab do less well with the new technology partly because of the indivisibility of some of the new technology and partly because they cannot even afford such things as sufficient amount of fertilizer. And the 30 percent with less than 10 acres do worst of all. "It appears likely," write Francine Frankel and Karl Vorys, "that they actually suffered an absolute decline in economic position as a result of the green revolution."[7] This has occurred as larger landowners seeking to consolidate have raised rents by up to one-half. Similarly, in the Sahiwal District of West Pakistan, the 70 percent of the population hovering near subsistence has declined relatively in income (and a good many, absolutely) during the 1960s.[8]

---

ern World, ed. by Philip K. Bock (Albuquerque: University of New Mexico Press, 1969), p. 35.

[6] Francine R. Frankel and Karl von Vorys, "The Political Challenge of the Green Revolution: Shifting Patterns of Peasant Participation in India and Pakistan" (unpublished paper, Department of Political Science, University of Pennsylvania, August 10, 1971), p. 18.

[7] Ibid., p. 19.

[8] Carl H. Gotsch, "The Distributive Impact of Agricultural Growth: Low Income Farmers and the 'System' (A Case Study of Sahiwal District, West Pakistan)" (paper presented to the Seminar on Small Farmer Development Strategies, The Agricultural Devel-

This second pattern of polarization is most often found in the labor-intensive crop areas of South Asia, East Asia, and Indochina. The economic lives of the poorer peasants in the second pattern increasingly become tied to the successes and innovations of the richer peasants. Many of these poorer farmers are forced to give up all or part of their land but still remain part of the peasantry as agricultural workers. Because of the limitations imposed by intensive agriculture, consolidation is more limited and landowning peasants do not necessarily become powerful rich magnates. They become, rather, small capitalist farmers, though there may exist—in addition to poor peasants and small capitalist farmers in the society— separate classes of wealthy aristocrats and large capitalists who also have taken advantage of the new technology.[9]

There are important distinctions from the first pattern. Historically, in the second pattern, the method of peasant household farming remained constant and dominant even though ownership of land increasingly passed to big landlords. These landlords did not mechanize. Rather, they rented land and hired labor to engage in the same type of agriculture as had been used previously. In many countries of Asia, especially, the high labor intensity used by these cultivators in farming such crops as paddy resulted in very high nutritional yields per acre.[10] Population density was higher than it had been in most parts of Europe, and the health advances swelled the numbers of peasants. It became increasingly unlikely that such large numbers could be absorbed in nonagricultural sec-

---

opment Council and The Ohio State University, Columbus, Ohio, September 13-15, 1971). Also see Walter P. Falcon, "The Green Revolution: Generations of Problems" (paper presented at the Summer Meeting of the American Agricultural Economics Association, Columbia, Mo., August 9-12, 1970).

[9] See Stinchcombe's discussion of the "family-size tenancy" in "Agricultural Enterprise," pp. 363-366.

[10] See Doreen Warriner's statement on the role of water control: *Economics of Peasant Farming* (2d ed.; London: Frank Cass, 1964), p. xxxi.

tors (as eventually had occurred in England), even if there were a phenomenal economic growth rate.

The second pattern involved polarization *within* the peasantry itself as well as between poor peasants and those in other classes. Those peasants with sufficient connections and resources to institutionalize outside contacts could consolidate holdings and use new products to solidify their position of ascendance over the other peasants. For example, in the Indian village of Thyagasamathiram, the powerful Brahmins left the village for the towns and cities, even though they continued as absentee landlords. Of the remaining peasants, those who had more cash and other resources took advantage of the new situation to increase their wealth. They commuted the payment of paddy rent into cash at favorable prices and stored the surplus to sell when prices rose. They increased their land and leaseholdings in the village and widened the gap between themse̶l̶v̶e̶s̶ and those who were forced to sell land and who could̶ ̶n̶o̶t̶ ̶s̶t̶ore rice until prices rose.[11]

The polarization̶ ̶o̶f̶ ̶t̶h̶e̶ ̶c̶o̶u̶n̶t̶r̶y̶ ry has been a deepening of the initial divisi̶o̶n̶.̶ ̶A̶t̶ ̶ the moment of the great expansion of outs̶i̶d̶e̶ ̶ se much of such farming remains labor-in̶t̶e̶n̶s̶i̶v̶e̶,̶ ̶ asant has not been placed at so severe a c̶ ̶ ntage that there is no role for him in the ̶ ̶ , many of the inputs associated with th̶ ̶ demand more labor than previously.[12]

The role ̶o̶f̶ ̶ er, may change progressively

[11] Dagfinn ̶ Barriers Fall: A Study of Social and Econon̶ ̶ Indian Village (Norway: George Allen and I̶ ̶ ̶ 102.

[12] D. W̶ ̶ se of the careful methods in vogue and the e̶ ̶ ̶ ed by hand weeding, it is doubtful if the in̶ ̶ achinery would increase production. More lik̶ ̶ less. Certainly the rice paddies would produce ̶l̶e̶s̶s̶ ̶ anting should be abandoned." Derwett Whittlesey, "Major ̶A̶g̶r̶i̶c̶u̶l̶t̶u̶r̶al Regions of the Earth," in Readings in Cultural Geography, ed. ̶P̶hilip L. Wagner and Marvin W. Mikesell (Chicago: The University of Chicago Press, 1962), p. 431.

163

from small holders to landless laborers since market mechanisms and mechanization still give somewhat of an edge to bigger holders. This trend was already visible in India in the early part of the century (see Table 3), and has been even

TABLE 3

COMPOSITION OF AGRICULTURAL POPULATION IN INDIA

| | Numbers in millions | | Percentage increase or decrease |
	1911	1931	
Noncultivating landlords	3.7	4.1	+10.8
Cultivators[a] (owners or tenants)	74.6	65.5	−12.2
Agricultural laborers	21.7	33.3	+53.4

[a] Of the cultivators in 1931, 40 percent were owners.
Source: M. L. Dantwala, "Problems in Countries with Heavy Pressure of Population on Land. The Case of India," in *Land Tenure*, ed. Kenneth H. Parsons, Raymond J. Penn, and Philip M. Raup (Madison: The University of Wisconsin Press; © 1956 by the Regents of the University of Wisconsin), p. 136.

more marked since the green revolution. In West Pakistan, for example, the smaller peasants were less able to compete with the innovative techniques, and thus there was the displacement in the 1960s of a large number of small landholders. Those with less than 10 acres and those with 10 to 25 acres lost 12.2 percent and 6.9 percent of their land respectively from 1959 to 1969, while the holders with 50 to 100 acres gained 19.2 percent.[13]

3) *The marginal-land agriculture pattern*

A last pattern of new polarization has resulted in villages which possess neither the fertile, extensive type of cropland

[13] Shahid Javed Burki, "Development of West Pakistan Agriculture: An Interdisciplinary Explanation" (paper read at the Workshop on Rural Development in Pakistan, Michigan State University, East Lansing, Mich., July 16, 1971), p. 28.

164

amenable to large economies of scale through mechanization nor the kind of land which demands high labor intensity.[14] Rather, these villages of small landholding peasants exist in areas of marginal lands.[15] Here, the peasants are not able to mechanize and consolidate holdings in order to grow extensive crops as is done in the United States. Nor are they able to make best use of new seed varieties and fertilizers through multiple cropping because of their rocky land or its location which makes irrigation impossible. Any intensive labor practices are usually put into raising delicate crops (e.g., olives, grapes, and tree fruits).

In villages with such marginal lands, those who first established contacts with outsiders may have switched their production from subsistence crops to fruits high in demand by an increasingly affluent urban center. In this case, the jump the innovators get on their fellow peasants in participation in the wider social system does not help them too much if they remain farmers. Their crops are more limited in their economies of scale than those in both the first and second patterns. Moreover, they often coexist in a society which has other areas which are more conducive to more economically competitive agriculture.[16]

[14] Of our cases, Sakaltutan is a good example. It is a village of dry lands. Almost half the village land is entirely uncultivable. The other half gives poor yields and half of that must be left fallow each year. Paul Stirling, *Turkish Village* (London: Weidenfeld and Nicolson, 1965).

[15] Such land is not only rocky land or land with poor soil. Theodore W. Schultz, *The Economic Organization of Agriculture* (New York: McGraw-Hill, 1953), p. 147, hypothesizes that within a country, economic development occurs within a specific urban-industrial locational matrix and that agriculture develops best in areas situated favorably relative to that matrix and develops poorly at the periphery of such a matrix.

[16] Yet, there are some pressures for a limited amount of consolidation. See Shepard Forman and Joyce F. Riegelhaupt, "Market Place and Marketing System: Toward a Theory of Peasant Economic Integration," *Comparative Studies in Society and History* 12 (April 1970), 206.

In such cases, if the peasant who made the initial move to outside involvement is to ensure his ascendancy over his fellow villagers, he must use his resources as a basis for gaining entrance into some other work activity besides agriculture. Some use their initial advantage to escape the village altogether, followed by poorer peasants suffering from economic crises. A frequent result for such villages is a high rate of both long- and short-term emigration.[17] Entire villages, for example, have been abandoned in parts of the rocky plateau in Northern Spain.

Stratification within villages which have not suffered such extreme desertion has been based on the quality of non-agricultural work situations the people have access to in nearby towns. Those who first furthered the degree of their external relations may have used their surplus as a stake in a business or occupation while having laborers farm their land. The others in the village remain poor farmers or many become part-time cultivators while taking on low-paying jobs in town. Whoever had access and resources to gain the best opportunities in external work situations is often determined by who made the initial outside alliances. Such was the case in Sakaltutan, Turkey, where 58 of 130 working adult males are employed outside the village.[18]

The Druse village of Yarka, located in northern Israel is a good illustration of a village on such marginal lands. Situated on a hilltop with a breathtaking view of the lush hills and coastal area, Yarka has much of its land covered by big white rocks which make cultivation nearly impossible. Moreover, the farmers have to compete in a society which is dominated by kibbutz and moshav agriculture, using the most sophisticated products and farming techniques known in the world. Like the Arabs in villages on the West Bank of the Jordan

---

[17] See, for example, Ramon H. Myers, *The Chinese Peasant Economy: Agricultural Development in Hopei and Shantung, 1890-1949* (Cambridge, Mass.: Harvard University Press, 1970), pp. 40-66.

[18] Stirling, *Turkish Village.*

River, the Druse of Yarka have remained in the one area of agriculture where such new technology has done relatively little, the raising of fruits (in the case of Yarka, the main product is olives). Yet the return for labor invested remains quite low, and as a result, young men of the village have looked to their stint in the army as an opportunity to explore other, more profitable work experiences. One of the richest and most prestigious men in the village used his secondary school education to become principal of the village schools. Few of those from families which were wealthy in British mandate times have remained solely in agriculture. Instead, they rent out their lands or hire a manager and workers so they can engage in other work experiences in order to gain wealth.[19]

This third pattern of polarization, found predominantly in parts of the Middle East and highland areas of Latin America (and Europe), also tends to accentuate gaps in resources and power within the peasantry that existed when the large increases in outside involvement began (just as the second pattern did). In this case, however, stratification tends to be centered around a variety of work experiences rather than almost totally around agriculture. Those who first made outside alliances and recognized the severe limits on the wealth that can be earned in respect to investments of capital and labor on the land used their resources to gain a foothold in relatively lucrative experiences on the outside. The poorer members have no such resources and many become unskilled workers. Others remain on the land but must compete in their agriculture with those in the society having more fertile lands on which there are greater economies of scale.

In all three patterns (see Figure 2 for a summary of their characteristics), the fluidity of social mobility, which had been characteristic within the peasant class in inward-oriented villages, is greatly reduced. Those who had the resources and

[19] For another interesting account, see Charles Tilly, *The Vendée*, Science Editions (New York: John Wiley and Sons, 1967), pp. 141-142.

FIGURE 2

PATTERNS OF POLARIZATION OF SOCIAL STRUCTURE WITH INCREASING DEGREES OF EXTERNAL RELATIONS

First Pattern

Stratification: two classes—rich entrepreneurial farm owners and poor rural proletariat

Social Mobility: little mobility between these two classes but among proletariat much mobility with great competition for jobs; much emigration of surplus labor

Occupational Structure: a very small group working on the soil and the remainder seeking low level industrial or service employment

Fertile lands, extensive crops, good transportation and communications, readily available technology

Villages with Low Scale External Relations

Second Pattern

Stratification: increasing divisions within peasantry with a widening gap

Social Mobility: less mobility than before but still some mobility between groups in peasantry; no limits on upward or downward mobility

Occupational Structure: large numbers in agriculture but with increasing differentiation between consolidating owners and landless laborers or tenants

fertile lands, intensive crops, good transportation and communication, available irrigation and technology

Stratification: peasants fairly homogeneous living as freeholders or under lords

Social Mobility: fluid with absolute limits on upward and downward mobility

Occupational Structure: small holders or tenants with a few artisans working locally; agriculture primarily for subsistence

Third Pattern

Stratification: differentiations within peasantry but less based on relation to agriculture than on types of external wage labor

Social Mobility: less mobility than before but still some mobility within the larger social system; no limits on upward and downward mobility; much emigration

Occupational Structure: small farmers and variety of outside work experiences

Marginal lands, intensive crops, poor transportation and communication, technology and irrigation not readily available or useable.

connections valued by outside institutions are able to use their initial foothold as a basis for solidifying their position. In fact, they can usually bring about a redistribution of wealth and land in the village so the new structure is not only more rigid but the gaps get continually greater. The differentiations, once villages are outward-oriented, may become quite long-lived.[20] Whether the continuing growth of such gaps in status means absolute deprivation or not for those on the bottom of the social hierarchy depends on certain factors. These include the rate of population growth and the availability of outside work activities.

The innovators who risked the village's or the lord's sanctions and the possibility of failure on the outside now have established the types of relationships where they no longer need to worry about such sanctions.[21] Their reference group, their interests, their sense of effective community all are now in a greater area than the boundaries of the village. And this has an added impact on the village, for it further reduces its capacity to resist outside forces and pressure.[22] The village is no longer inhabited by a highly homogeneous group of inward-looking peasants with rather similar relations to agricultural production. Rather, there are numerous work experiences both in the village and outside, and each of these tends to separate people along the lines of their reference groups

[20] On village differentiation, see Eric R. Wolf, "Aspects of Group Relations in a Complex Society: Mexico," *American Anthropologist* 58 (December 1956), 1070-1071. Wolf is speaking of Mexico but his description has much wider usefulness.

[21] A. Aiyappan writes that in Mayur (Kerala, India), the result has been almost a total disappearance of the old forms of social control (*Social Revolution in a Kerala Village: A Study in Culture Change* [New York: Asia Publishing House, 1965]). Also see William McCormack, "Factionalism in a Mysore Village," in *Leadership and Political Institutions in India*, ed. Richard L. Park and Irene Tinker (Princeton, N.J.: Princeton University Press, 1959), p. 444, for a discussion of how the wealthy have freed themselves from the sanction of a boycott of cooperative labor.

[22] Wolf, "Aspects of Group Relations," 1072.

169

and their interests. Mass media and other communication and transportation networks become increasingly important means for each group within the village to maintain adequate ties and regular channels of social and economic exchange with its outside contacts.[23] The locus of the status hierarchy is no longer within the village.[24]

Now, even when labor is tied to those who control the means to produce wealth, agricultural or otherwise, many of the patron-client overtones disappear. As long as there is free movement in the labor market, laborers do not usually become tied to specific employers, and employers have no prior obligations to specific laborers. "The client has become the workman of anyone who will pay him a daily wage."[25] Such a process frees the poor peasant from specific bonds to patrons but does not, in most cases, at the same time allow him to increase his wealth since he lacks the skills and resources to take advantage of outside opportunities. (See Figure 3 for the change in peasant status.)

In fact, the end of such personalistic and binding ties is often most adamantly resisted by the poorest who found in it a sense of security that a free labor market does not afford. One Washerman in a village in Uttar Pradesh, India, expressed this. He stated that he had a job in the laundry in the city but had to return to fulfill his caste labor and ritual obligations in the village. Despite the fact that the upper castes in the village were really tiring of their obligations to give a

[23] See Bernard Gallin, *Hsin Hsing, Taiwan: A Chinese Village in Change* (Berkeley: University of California Press, 1966), pp. 45-46.

[24] In many Indian villages, even the internal community status system based on caste can be affected. See, for example, Oscar Lewis, *Village Life in Northern India: Studies in a Delhi Village* (Urbana: University of Illinois Press, 1958); and Gouranga Chattopadhyay, *Ranjana, A Village in West Bengal* (Calcutta: Bookland Private, 1964).

[25] F. G. Bailey, *Caste and the Economic Frontier: A Village in Highland Orissa* (Manchester: Manchester University Press, 1957), p. 144.

170

FIGURE 3

CHANGES IN STATUS OF PEASANTS IN VILLAGES MOVING
FROM LOW TO HIGH ON THE SCALE OF
EXTERNAL RELATIONS

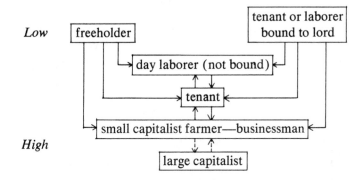

set portion of their harvests to the lower service caste people,
the Washerman insisted that he was needed in the village and
the upper castes would not let him go permanently even if he
wanted to.

The "freeing" of labor puts the poor peasant into a social
system for which he has few resources for success, and he
lacks the means of getting such resources. The sanctions—
ridicule and gossip and holding back cooperative labor—
applied against those who had first attempted to expand outside involvement were applied with good purpose, for the
poor peasant now finds himself devoid of village political and
social organization which can shelter him somewhat from exploiters. He now competes in a wider social system whose
criteria for success seem as difficult as ever to achieve.

COMMUNITY INSTITUTIONS AND THE CHANGE TO
INVOLVEMENT IN THE WIDER SOCIAL SYSTEM

Bryce Ryan has spoken of the effect of the new differentiations and interests upon the Sinhalese village he studied.

171

Over the long run, . . . there is no doubt of a decline in established primary group functions. The very introduction of wage labor on a wide scale has implied the diminution of the nuclear family as a production group. It seems incontrovertible as well that the growing market economy has emphasized impersonal sources for commodities which were once produced within the family. Reliance upon kinsfolk has been evidently reduced through government maternity hospitals, just as dependence upon a medical practitioner has shifted from the village "native doctor" toward the government dispensary. Even the limited credit facilities sponsored by the government mean less necessary reliance upon kinsmen and neighbors. These are the logical, though seldom visibly disorganizing, effects of money economy and socialistic government.[26]

Others have noted similar trends in other villages concerning the decline of groups within the community which emphasized primary, face-to-face relationships. Potter has spoken of a change from a "collectivity orientation" to an "individualistic orientation." This has involved a move away from obligations toward family, lineage, and village to a situation in which the peasant's own economic interests take precedence.[27]

These and other accounts indicate either an end to or a great dimunition in the functioning of kin and non-kin institutions as peasants increase their outside participation. What is striking in viewing the case studies is the persistence and continued importance to the peasant of a number of these institutions long after villages have greatly extended both the range and frequency of their outside relationships. Although there are pressures from the diverse range of new, outside organizations for a more individualistic orientation, it is in many ways

[26] Bryce Ryan, *Sinhalese Village* (Coral Gables, Fla.: University of Miami Press, 1958), p. 145.

[27] Jack M. Potter, *Capitalism and the Chinese Peasant: Social and Economic Change in a Hong Kong Village* (Berkeley: University of California Press, 1968), p. 3.

172

counterbalanced by the low status which most peasants continue to hold in the larger society.

Aside from the relatively few who have risen appreciably on the larger system's status scale, most peasants remain without —or more important, without access to—the skills and resources very highly valued outside. As we shall discuss later, many of the continuing insecurities of outside participation from which they were sheltered by the village social and political organization and by subcommunity institutions must now be confronted directly. New forms of exploitation of these weak peasants lead them to find ways to mitigate the effects of the individualistic orientation. The peasant as an individual on the free market often finds he needs security and buffers against all that "freedom."

Let us first look at some of the institutions in which there is a significant weakening as outside relations increase. Village mutual aid projects and cooperative labor are among the first to suffer in an expanding network of economic and social ties. Table 4 compares the prevalence of mutual aid and cooperative labor for agriculture and housebuilding in inward- and outward-oriented villages.

TABLE 4

MUTUAL AID IN VILLAGES LOW AND HIGH ON THE SCALE OF EXTERNAL RELATIONS

| | Mutual aid and cooperative labor | |
	Prevalent	Rare or never
Inward-oriented	13	2
Outward-oriented	14	22

Only slightly more than one-third of the more open villages engage in such cooperative practices compared to more than 85 percent of the villages low in outside relations.

173

The widening of the stratification gaps and the increasing consolidation of holdings by peasants often results in a readily available, cheap labor force for the wealthier peasant. Previously, the lack of great social differentiations among the peasants may have made hired labor scarcer or even entirely non-existent. In such cases, the only way one could garner a labor force large enough to accomplish something so intricate and time-bound as transplanting of rice was through cooperative labor mechanisms. With the new, cheap labor, such cooperation becomes much less necessary for the wealthy.

There is also another reason for the weakening of mutual aid. One of the most potent barriers in villages restricting outside involvement was the withholding of cooperation by the other members. Anyone who greatly expanded his outside relations had to plan how to do without such aid. The result of the increasing ties was a withdrawal-exclusion of some from these exchanges which had previously helped create a village-wide solidarity. Later, with the differentiation of the peasants into cultivators and wage earners, there was much less to be gained by those who worked outside the village from institutions such as mutual harvesting teams.

Other solidarity-producing institutions within villages with low outside involvement, such as ceremonies and fiestas, also suffer a decline as outside participation increases. With the new value on resources needed for successful participation in outside institutions, there is little support by the more wealthy for ritual and ceremonies resulting in consumption or redistribution of their surplus solely within the village.

With the emergence of new, outside reference groups and clear-cut differentiations in work experience, there is little inclination to gain prestige based on the village's old criteria and mechanisms. This is especially true if these involve sacrificing the means of gaining prestige in the larger social system. Nine of the 15 (60 percent) cases of inward-oriented villages mention the operation of some kind of conspicuous consumption or redistribution through the mechanisms of ceremonies,

174

festivals, or gift-giving, while only 13 of the 36 (36 percent) cases of more open villages do. Potter has noted such a decline in ritual and ceremony in Hang Mei (Hong Kong). "In the wider society of the colony," he writes, "social status is largely determined by education, occupation, and personal wealth, and hence the traditional means of validating status in the village are no longer as meaningful as they once were."[28]

On the subcommunity level, there has been significant change in institutions, as well, as villagers have increased their external associations. But the total disappearance or severe diminution of functions as occurred with mutual aid and fiestas is much less prevalent. In many cases, there has been a reorientation of the old institutions to cope with a new set of problems associated with participation in a social system which demands new criteria for success under much more impersonal circumstances. Some of the most substantial alterations in orientation and composition have occurred in the peasant household. As peasant farming shifts from an enterprise of high labor inputs and low capital inputs to one in which capital inputs are more substantial, a change occurs in the economic function of the household. In areas of extensive farming (e.g., Europe), where joint families were always rarer and where the number of people in a household was generally small compared to labor-intensive crop areas, there is even a further contraction in family composition and size.

Large mechanized farms (first pattern) demand decreasing amounts of labor as tractors and other machines take over a greater share of the work. Farm work becomes less based on the division of labor within the household and more on a division of labor between classes. Household servants and orphan children were brought in formerly as a means to increase the labor input on a given unit of land; now that is no longer done. One description of peasant change in seventeenth and eighteenth century Sweden highlights this point. Only

[28] *Ibid.*, p. 171.

175

with growing prosperity and increasing numbers of outside ties there did farmers relegate farmhands who had been members of the household to quarters in the stable.[29] It is hypothesized, for the same reason, that the mean number of children per household slowly decreases as the degree of external relations increases.

Indirect evidence for this hypothesis comes from Hinderink and Kiray's four Turkish villages. There, the more developed villages had a lower mean number of children per household and a lower mean number of children preferred (see Table 5). Hinderink and Kiray point out that where child labor (for

TABLE 5

THE MEAN NUMBER OF CHILDREN AND CHILDREN PREFERRED IN VILLAGES LOW AND HIGH ON THE SCALE OF EXTERNAL RELATIONS

	Inward-oriented		Outward-oriented	
	Orçclu	Karacäoren	Sakizili	Yunusoğlu
Children/household (mean number)	5.02	5.07	2.81	2.95
Children preferred (mean number)	6.3	5.2	3.8	3.8

Source: Jan Hinderink and M. B. Kiray, *Social Stratification as an Obstacle to Development* (New York: Praeger, 1970), p. 122.

instance, picking cotton for wages or doing small tasks at as early an age as six) is no longer needed or tolerated, there is likely to be a decrease in the number of children per household. Similarly, in those cases of extensive crop areas where joint families did exist, there is likely to be a contraction to a

[29] Börje Hansen, "Group Relations of Peasants and Farmers," in *The Peasant: A Symposium Concerning the Peasant Way and View of Life*, ed. F. G. Friedmann, no. 8 (February 1957), mimeo, p. 15.

greater proportion of nuclear families.[30] Only on the small holdings which resist being gobbled up as parts of mechanized farms, but which become increasingly uncompetitive, does the household retain its role as an integrated, economically productive unit.

Patterns of household change in areas of intensive crop cultivation (e.g., paddy) show somewhat similar, though often less dramatic, trends. Because of the nature of these crops, the organization of the farm work becomes a combination of high capital input along with continued high labor input. The lesser consolidations of farms and growing population in such areas lead to some motivation to decrease the number within the household. Many of the labor-intensive tasks are increasingly performed by day laborers, rather than by members of the landowning household. Moreover, the fractionalization of that land which is not yet consolidated is another motivation for smaller household size. In Bisipara (Orissa, India), for example, there used to be servants as part of the household but the fractionalization has made such extra labor unnecessary.

Despite these pressures for a reduction in household numbers, there are opposing forces as well. Many holdings continue to be run on a household basis. There still is a need for high inputs of labor on all holdings, which leads even laborers to have children who can work in the fields and collect pay. As mentioned in Chapter v, parents also want to guarantee the survival of a son in their old age. Thus families continue to have a large, though slowly falling, number of surviving children.

[30] *Social Stratification*, pp. 172 and 185-186. Here are the figures for family composition of their four villages, showing the scale of external relations:

	low		high	
	Oruçlu	Karäcaoren	Sakizli	Yunusoğlu
Percent Extended	41.2	29.2	18.6	13.3
Percent Nuclear	55.9	64.5	67.5	79.1

177

More visible in these areas than a drop in the number of children per household is the strain under which households consisting of joint families (often quite a high percentage in such areas) come. Epstein has noted this trend for the village of Wangala where there has been a significant number of joint family dissolutions among the Peasant caste. Young men in Wangala want cash and independence from the parental unit in order to buy bicycles, watches, and other products and prestige items of the new technology.[31] They rebel against the kind of rigid control still found in villages of restricted outside contacts, such as Tarong (Philippines) where money is spent only after the joint family decides upon its best use.[32]

In these areas of intensive cultivation, it is not so much a shift away from household farming which is responsible for the strain in the joint family (though certainly this has an impact). Rather, though the household may remain the most common organization of farming, population growth and land fractionalization have meant that there is more labor than can effectively be used on the holding. Where other work opportunities are available either locally or nationally, they result in a household's having several sources of income: that produced on the farm by a cooperative effort of several of its members and wages earned on other individual jobs. It is this widening of the scope of sources of income which puts a tremendous strain on the joint family (and to a lesser extent the nuclear family, as well). Such strain can be understood if the family or household is seen as an institution with particular distributions of power. It is the diversification of sources of income which acts to alter radically that distribution of power within the households.

[31] T. S. Epstein, *Economic Development and Social Change in South India* (Manchester: Manchester University Press, 1962).

[32] William F. and Corinne Nydegger, *Tarong: An Ilocos Barrio in the Philippines* (New York: John Wiley and Sons, 1966). In Sakaltutan and Elbaşi, Turkey, the pattern is even more rigid. There, the father runs the household budget even giving his adult sons money for specific expenses. Even sons with independent incomes give their wages to their father. Stirling, *Turkish Village*.

Previously, in most inward-oriented villages, women and even married sons had little visible power within the household.[33] Often cut off from direct participation in most aspects of agricultural production, women came under the domination of their husbands, the principal producers. As in patron-client relationships, there was a system of exchange based on an inequality in control of the critical resources which resulted in a very skewed distribution of power within the household.

Tenure of land came to be associated with males, as a result, and grown sons often had to wait until their father's death or voluntary bequeathal of his land until they had control of the resources which allowed them to assert themselves within the household. Wives often never got this chance and were particularly vulnerable in the patrilocal societies, far from the family members and friends among whom they had grown up. One young Indian wife, whose father-in-law is a wealthy landowning member of an untouchable caste, expressed this sense of vulnerability when she said, "In my father's village I was free. Here I am a prisoner."[34]

With an increase in the sources of income for households in peasant villages, the head for the first time is challenged in his monopoly of control over the household's wealth-producing resources. This can be seen, for example, in a prerevolutionary East Chinese village, Kaihsienkung. The women there had previously worked on the production of silk at home as part of the household's economic functions. Each husband, extremely dominant in his household, would carry the mulberry leaves to the woman in the house. Radical changes in the role of women were brought about, however, as the loca-

[33] In 11 of the 15 cases of inward-oriented villages, there is no mention of married women either owning or administering the land nor of their having a dominant role in household decision-making. In four cases, there was separate ownership, but, in two of these, the man administered the land of both.

[34] For a moving quotation on the plight of a young peasant wife in prerevolutionary China, see William Hinton, *Fanshen: A Documentary of Revolution in a Chinese Village* (New York: Monthly Review Press, 1966), pp. 40-42.

179

tion of their silk work switched from the home to the new factory. Fei wrote then, "Wage earning is now regarded as a privilege, because it makes an immediate contribution to the domestic budget. Those who have no adult daughters begin to regret it. The woman's position in society has undergone a gradual change. For instance, a girl who was working in the village factory actually cursed her husband because he forgot to send her an umbrella when it rained."[35] Women factory workers, then, became more assertive as decision-makers within the household because of the crucial wages they brought home.[36]

The effect of an independent source of income for women on the distribution of power within the household can be seen readily in a comparison of the roles of the women in two different castes in the village of Bagerawan (Uttar Pradesh, India). Playing a completely domestic role, the women of the generally wealthier caste of the Rajputs are extremely deferential to the males of the household and exercise only minimal influence in decisions concerning cash expenditures. The wives are barred from forming alliances outside the household since they have no independent resources and rarely even leave the joint family's compound. The older women have asserted power only within the household in "women's" activities. Their women neighbors in an untouchable caste, however, play much more equal roles with the men and even interrupt the men in conversation if displeased with what they are saying. Their exercise of power within the household stems from the caste's position of supplying daily wage labor for farming. Women earn the same Rs 1 or Rs 2 (10 or 20 cents) as the men do each day. Some of the strain that this new demand for power has caused is seen in the joint family compound that was recently divided into seven smaller, separate compounds.

[35] Hsiao-Tung Fei, *Peasant Life in China: A Field Study of Country Life in the Yangtze Valley* (London: Routledge and Kegan Paul, 1939), p. 233.

[36] *Ibid.*, p. 171.

In most villages, even those members who still lack any direct source of income and continue to perform agricultural or domestic tasks now have others in the household with whom they can ally against the absolute control of the head. Daughters-in-law are often accused of fostering quarrels between brothers and between fathers and sons, causing the breakup of the joint family. The daughters-in-law's complaints to their husbands and their bickerings are attempts to enlarge their own sphere of decision-making by allying with their husbands and having much more power devolve from the head to the component nuclear parts of the joint family.

Yet, given all these cases of the strain or dissolution of joint families and of the changes in the distribution of power within households, a striking factor in peasant villages is the persistence of households (and, at times, even ones composed of joint families) in performing a wide variety of functions. In other words, the household has not declined as rapidly and universally as some predicted. It often remains the most central economic and social unit in villages that have substantially increased outside relations. In the Jaunpur district of Uttar Pradesh, India, for example, the joint family still remains quite viable. Even with a perceptible shift in the distribution of power within the household there, as one or more sons go outside the village to find employment (leaving their wives and children with the rest of the joint family), the institution still lives on.[37]

Other, even wider kinship and fictive kinship groups have remained viable as well. Lewis found in Rampur, India, "Caste and kinship still form the core of village social organization. . . ."[38] In Hsin Hsing, Taiwan, the *tsu* (lineage) has

[37] Even in Europe, there are reports of the continuing viability of the peasant family in performing numerous social and economic functions not usually done by households outside rural areas. E. A. Hammel, "The 'Balkan' Peasant: A View from Serbia," in *Peasants in the Modern World,* ed. Bock, p. 97.

[38] Lewis, *Village Life in Northern India,* pp. 148-149.

been affected by the rapid expansion of outside relations, yet it has remained a viable unit in the peasants' lives.[39] In Moche (Peru), there has been a survival of *compadrazgo* (ritual co-parenthood) despite an increasing degree of external relations.[40]

The question that arises is, given the hypothesis that as peasants increase their outside relationships their social structure will tend to become identical with that of the larger society,[41] why has there been a persistence of such kin and fictive kin ties?[42] These ties live on though they seemingly are less and less associated with household economic production.

More generally, the question can be put as to why there has been a persistence altogether of a peasantry with cultural traits and institutions somewhat different from those of the larger society? Why has there not been a total integration of peasants into varying institutions, classes, and sectors as they have increased their degree of external relations? Why, despite their increase in outside involvement, does a significant percentage of their crops, in many areas, continue to go for subsistence needs? Would one not expect land to be devoted solely to those crops that give the highest returns on the market? Would one not expect a total demise of smaller, less competitive holdings, with the peasants becoming either small

[39] Gallin, *Hsin Hsing*, p. 272.

[40] Gillin is cited in Sidney W. Mintz and Eric R. Wolf, "An Analysis of Ritual Co-Parenthood (Compadrazgo)," in *Peasant Society: A Reader*, ed. Jack M. Potter, May N. Diaz, and George M. Foster (Boston: Little, Brown, 1967), p. 194.

[41] See, for example, John H. Kunkel, "Economic Autonomy and Social Change in Mexican Villages," *Economic Development and Cultural Change* 10 (October 1961), 58.

[42] In India, some of the differences from the larger society come out in Driver's statistics. In Nagpur district of Bombay, 40.1% of the total couples in agriculture interviewed were within joint families. The next highest occupational category was 32.8% for traders and down to 16.2% for clerical workers. Those in agriculture also had the lowest median age of wives at marriage of all the occupational groups. Edwin D. Driver, *Differential Fertility in Central India* (Princeton, N.J.: Princeton University Press, 1963), pp. 47, 65.

capitalist owners or part of a rural proletariat working for others or for the state?

The answers to such questions are very complex and beyond the scope of any single study. Peasants' lack of total integration into the larger society stems from many environmental conditions they face. In order to understand some of the key conditions, it is important to recall here that peasants had always withdrawn inward because of insecurity of outside participation. Their recent expansion of outside relations comes primarily because of household economic crises. The innovators have responded as well to the much more tentative and scattered changes in the security of outside participation. Yet, some insecurity of participation in outside institutions continues to plague peasants in both subtle and blatant ways and has a great effect on the nature of peasant institutions. The poor peasant is particularly vulnerable. Those who first increased their outside relations may have had sufficient resources to negotiate their way in the outside world, but the poor peasant finds it as hostile as ever. William Mangin recounts a story of the introduction of a type of Merino sheep into an Ecuadorian Indian community. When the peasants overcame their initial suspicion and took the sheep, their wool production increased tremendously. In fact, it increased so much that local mestizos came to the village and stole the sheep.[43]

Peasants have found that institutionalization into the procedures and organizations of the larger society often leaves them, with their lack of highly valued resources and skills, little ability to guarantee the fair operation of those procedures or organizations. Peasants find themselves participating in institutions acting against their interests, in many cases, and thus with as little protection against exploitation as previously. The events in the village of Shivapur (Mysore, India) provide

[43] This story is told by Marvin Harris and recounted by William Mangin (ed.), *Peasants in Cities, Readings in the Anthropology of Urbanization* (Boston: Houghton Mifflin, 1970), Introduction, p. xxv.

an illustration of peasants' vulnerability. The cooperative society bought a tractor with a loan from a local bank, which was granted because the bank director owned shares in the tractor company. Nothing but distaste for tractors emerged from the following series of events. The secretary of the cooperative embezzled some funds, and the chairman's son became the tractor driver. Rather than serving the villagers' purposes, the tractor was used to plough fields for cash, often fields of peasants outside Shivapur. By the end of a year, the tractor had broken down, and each member had to pay Rs 600-700 on the loan.[44]

Numerous writers have noted the widespread prevalence in third world countries of corruption, referring to the use of such dishonest practices as bribery. In several instances, these writers have pointed to the benefits of such practices for economic and political development as well as to the costs.[45] Poor peasants, however, are most likely to suffer the costs of corruption, as well as those of monopolistic practices simply because they are such vulnerable targets. In India, for example, peasants may receive adulterated fertilizer or be presented with bills for fertilizer they never had (the village-level worker having sold it to someone else at a price lower than the set rate and then having pocketed the money). Even what may seem like a small bribe, to a peasant may be a significant portion of his income, and the amount of the bribe may make the cost of raising cash crops prohibitively expensive. By maintaining as much distance from these outside institutions as possible and by guaranteeing themselves at least subsistence needs, peasants are able to survive in such an exploitative milieu.

Besides the prevalence of corruption and monopolistic

[44] K. Ishwaran, *Shivapur, A South Indian Village* (London: Routledge and Kegan Paul, 1968), p. 13.

[45] See, for example, Joseph S. Nye, "Corruption and Political Development: A Cost-Benefit Analysis," *American Political Science Review* 61 (June 1967), 417-427.

practices, peasants also often face a structurally incomplete[46] set of economic and political institutions in such areas. Lack of a passable road in monsoon season severely hurts the chances of Senapur's (Uttar Pradesh, India) peasants from marketing their produce so as to gain the best advantage in price. Transportation costs become so high as to make the costs of cash crop growing border on the prohibitive. Villages also may lack adequate communications about the new, complex market with which they are dealing. The absence of silos may force the farmer to put his wheat on the market just when prices are lowest. Credit facilities may be far short of needs to switch production to cash crops entirely or they may be available only for the wealthy. The costs of certain goods, from bags for packing grains[47] to tractors, may be prohibitively high since the government levies high tariffs in order to protect inefficient domestic industries. Such structural incompleteness tends to keep peasants from giving up some subsistence agriculture.[48] What may, at first, seem a senseless method of action may at a closer look simply be peasants' way of trying to cope with a situation of inadequate resources and opportunities.

With the peasant facing strong buyers who can force down prices, strong suppliers who force up costs, corrupt officials, and inadequate means to get their produce to distribution points at reasonable costs and at the right time, he is unwilling

[46] The concept of the structurally incomplete has been expressed in economic terms. "Suppliers are unable to produce sources of income streams cheaply enough to induce the demanders to purchase any new (additional) sources. The price is high, and in conventional terms the rate of return to investment is accordingly low." Theodore W. Schultz, *Transforming Traditional Agriculture* (New Haven: Yale University Press, 1964), p. 81.

[47] See, for example, James R. Scobie, *Revolution on the Pampas: A Social History of Argentine Wheat, 1860-1910* (Austin: University of Texas Press, 1964), p. 90.

[48] Philip K. Bock (ed.), *Peasants in the Modern World*, Introduction, p. 5.

185

to break many of the ties of the past in order to become a free economic individual.[49] Peasant cooperatives for buying and selling, and peasant credit unions have been very adaptive responses to such problems by well-meaning governments or by peasants themselves. But in some cases, as was seen in Shivapur, these too fail totally, and in other cases, they only mitigate the vast problems peasants face in dealing with the outside. The peasant's attachment to land often remains strong even though a strict cost-benefit analysis would dictate his selling it to a larger owner. Fei wrote, "The incentive to hold land is directly related to the sense of security. The farmer says, 'The best thing to give one's son is land. It is living property. Money will be used up but land never.' "[50]

As in China, so too in the Arab Middle East[51] and Turkey[52] and numerous other places. Even where the use of new technology proceeds rapidly, the desire to maintain the security of knowing there is always a way to earn one's bread despite outside instability leads peasants to hold on to their land. They are then less dependent on the factories and cities of the larger social system or on the working of numerous components making up the national and international market system.

Let us return to the original question of why peasants continue to participate to a greater degree than others in kin and related groups. One of the key factors is this continuing lack of security because of corruption, monopoly, and structural incompleteness outside. The distrust of outside organizations is based on a knowledge of their workings and on a knowledge of the vulnerability of the poor and weak to unfair treatment

[49] On the incompleteness of markets, see Matthew Edel, "Innovative Supply: A Weak Point in Economic Development Theory," *Social Science Information* 9 (June 1970), 23-27.

[50] Fei, *Peasant Life in China*, p. 182.

[51] See, for example, Abdulla M. Lutfiyya, *Baytīn A Jordanian Village, A Study of Social Institutions and Social Change in a Folk Community* (London: Mouton, 1966), p. 102.

[52] Hinderink and Kiray, *Social Stratification*, p. 162.

in them. This leads many peasants to maintain strong kin and
fictive kin ties apart from their relations with outside institutions. Pearse has summarized the peasant's persistence in
clinging to "outmoded" forms of production and social organization.

> The schematic answer to queries about why the subsistence
> orientation of family productive units should survive is
> simple enough: the peasant does not perceive the existence
> of a secure system of distribution of goods and facilities
> necessary for family livelihood based on money-exchange,
> and his perception generally corresponds to the real situa-
> tion. The crisis is not in the long life of the subsistence sys-
> tems, but in the dysfunctional straddle between these and a
> reliable money-market system.[53]

In order to minimize risk in outside participation, the family pools its resources in order to have enough to give one son
the necessary skills to gain some measure of power within the
larger social system. His social mobility is mobility for them
all, and he has clear obligations, both financial and social, to
the rest of the members once he has gained a job. In Jaunpur
district of Uttar Pradesh, India, there are numerous cases of
joint families sending one son to a local university or even
one to America to study while his brothers, wife, and parents
continue to live in the village and work the land. Upon their
graduation, these sons send money back to the village regularly and use their connections to gain special privileges for
their kin (or at least the rights they are supposed to have coming to them).[54] Education is understood to be a key resource

[53] Andrew Pearse, "Metropolis and Peasant: The Expansion of the
Urban-Industrial Complex and the Changing Rural Structure," in
Peasants and Peasant Societies: Selected Readings, ed. Teodor Shanin
(Baltimore: Penguin Books, 1971), p. 73n.

[54] Joseph R. Gusfield talks of the utility the joint family can have
in economic growth in developing states. "Tradition and Modernity:
Misplaced Polarities in the Study of Social Change," *American Journal of Sociology* 72 (November 1966), 356-357.

for power in the larger social system.[55] Dube writes of Shamirpet in Hyderabad, India, "Education is now regarded as important, because it provides 'the key to' the understanding of the 'wide world' and equips one better to assert one's rights and claim one's due from officials and the cunning townspeople."[56]

SUMMARY

The change from an inward- to an outward-orientation among peasant villages greatly affected power relations and stratification in rural areas. Those with the resources and connections to take advantage of opportunities in the changing outside economy were able to widen the social gap considerably. In areas amenable to large capital inputs (pattern 1) the extensive agriculture becomes less and less based on peasant farming. Out-migration is high and the remaining classes are capitalist farmers and a poor rural proletariat. In patterns two and three, the gap occurs within the peasantry as well as between peasants and those in higher classes. With these changes among villagers and with the new lines of contact to the outside economy comes a change in village institutions as well. Some are weakened considerably or disappear altogether. For the poor peasant, however, certain institutions continue to survive, adapting to the insecure conditions of the outside.

Thus, families and fictive kin institutions, such as compadrazgo, serve as "the orienting thread and conduit of mobility."[57] No longer are they coherent productive units or bases primarily for maintaining solidarity and equanimity

[55] Similarly, Robert R. Kerton has written, "One strength of the family that has been noticed is its ability to pool income to purchase training for an able family member. Later, the return is shared among the wider group." "An Economic Analysis of the Extended Family in the West Indies," *The Journal of Development Studies* 7 (July 1971), 431.

[56] S. C. Dube, *Indian Village*, Harper Colophon Books (New York: Harper & Row, 1967), p. 165.

[57] Hammel, "The 'Balkan' Peasant," p. 97.

within the village so outside institutions need not intervene. Rather, as peasants "increasingly face the insecurity of growing incorporation into the national structure and increasing local wage-based, cash crop competition,"[58] they often continue to seek a "collectivity orientation" to the problems posed by individualistic societies.

Whether these adaptations by old institutions to new problems will mean their indefinite survival as they are now constituted is quite doubtful. Certainly an essential point about peasants is the degree to which they operate in the wider social system—one that is fraught with injustice for them—and simultaneously are part of institutions that are described as atavistic, nativistic, and parochial but which, in fact, give them much protection against the injustices they encounter.

[58] Mintz and Wolf, "An Analysis of Ritual Co-Parenthood," p. 194.

PART FOUR

Politics and Revolution

CHAPTER IX

The New Political Community

INTRODUCTION

VILLAGES which had restricted their peasants' market relations outside the immediate community or the local marketing area did so as an adaptation to the threats posed by the classes above. Political relationships with outsiders also were severely circumscribed. Payment of taxes, service in the lord's private army, acceptance of protection from the state against the encroachment of others were a few of the limited political interchanges between peasants and those in other classes. And even in many of these circumstances, the peasants usually dealt with outside institutions through the intermediary of the village leadership.

The primary locus of politics for the peasants, the area within which they looked for commands and participated in decisions affecting their behavior, lay within the peasant community itself. It was there that disputes were settled, actions on behalf of the state were taken, and constraints and demands on everyday behavior were imposed. Both the local lords and the peasant political organization exercised these functions. Although many of the contours of peasant behavior were determined by the power of outside lords, politicians, and administrators, peasants very often felt the weight of such power through the village leadershhip.

The change from an inward- to an outward-orientation brought not only substantial social changes but also a crucial change in the dimensions and locus of the peasants' political

193

world. A number of studies in recent years have examined some of the new political forms in rural areas that have resulted from a changing political orientation by peasants. There has been a particular interest in peasant movements in the form of unions, syndicates, parties, etc.[1] Political anthropologists have increased their research of some of the changes over time of the village government and its relation to district, state, and national political institutions.[2]

Some of this valuable material will be drawn upon, but the goal here is not to focus specifically on these new structures and relations. Instead the purpose of this chapter is to analyze the relationship between peasants' political participation and their degree of external relations. Specifically, it will analyze the effect of the problems stemming from increased outside relations on the dimensions of the peasants' political world and the nature of their political activity. A theory of the *process* of political change among peasants cannot be built

[1] For some of the better examples of this work, see the essays in Henry A. Landsberger (ed.), *Latin American Peasant Movements* (Ithaca, N.Y.: Cornell University Press, 1969). Also, Peter P. Lord, *The Peasantry as an Emerging Political Factor in Mexico, Bolivia, and Venezuela* (Madison: The Land Tenure Center, University of Wisconsin, LTC no. 35, May 1965); John Duncan Powell, *Political Mobilization of the Venezuelan Peasant* (Cambridge, Mass.: Harvard University Press, 1971); and Susan C. Bourque, "Cholification and the Campesino: A Study of Three Peruvian Peasant Organizations in the Process of Societal Change," Latin American Studies Program, Dissertation Series, Cornell University (January 1971). An early attempt to build a framework to analyze peasant movements is found in Henry A. Landsberger, "A Framework for the Study of Peasant Movements" (Ithaca, N.Y.: New York State School of Industrial and Labor Relations, Cornell University, 1966).

[2] Several interesting contributions for Guatemala are found in Richard N. Adams (ed.), *Political Changes in Guatemalan Indian Communities: A Symposium* (New Orleans: Middle American Research Institute, Tulane University, 1957), Publication no. 24; and for India in Richard L. Park and Irene Tinker (eds.), *Leadership and Political Institutions in India* (Princeton, N.J.: Princeton University Press, 1959).

194

simply on descriptions of the old and new political institutions and modes of participation.[3] Instead, it must first be rooted in the dynamic social and economic changes associated with increased outside involvement. A theory must explain *why* institutions change and *why* the frequency, scope, and intensity of participation differ from those of previous times.

This chapter, then, focuses on two crucial questions about the *process* of peasant political change. First, what happened to the peasants' sense of political community (the dimensions of their political world) and to the nature of their political activity as outside relations expanded rapidly? The second question is one that has been largely ignored in the literature. What are the specific incentives and motivations for peasants to engage in new and different political relationships?

THE CHANGE OF POLITICAL COMMUNITY: THE VILLAGE'S POLITICAL DECLINE

One of the important results of vastly increased outside participation has been a growing interdependence with fellow factory workers, with foremen, with fellow farmers selling an agricultural product one needs, with wholesalers, or with various suppliers. Politically, the result of such enduring relationships among segments of the peasantry and with outsiders has been a decline in the importance of the village as a source of peasant identification: "The villagers have become increasingly involved in groups outside the village, with the result that village society as a reference group for confirming social status has declined in importance."[4]

Increases in outside relations by the peasants of Hsin Hsing,

[3] Huntington has lamented scholars' preoccupation with "comparative status" rather than theories of change. See Samuel P. Huntington, "The Change to Change: Modernization, Development, and Politics," *Comparative Politics* 3 (April 1971), 296.

[4] Jack M. Potter, *Capitalism and the Chinese Peasant: Social and Economic Change in a Hong Kong Village* (Berkeley: University of California Press, 1968), p. 171.

195

Taiwan, have also affected their orientation toward their village. One of the most important of the peasants' current contacts is with the Farm Association, a government monopoly, which procures fertilizers for them. Government-operated irrigation systems have also been important because their networks cross village and area boundaries: "Although villagers in premodern Taiwan also had relationships with other villages and areas, it is evident that the recent expansion of agriculture has made the increase in their outside relations both possible and necessary."[5] Internally, the result has been a deterioration of the influence of the village on the lives of the peasants as they have attempted to strengthen their outside relations.

Prestige is based on the criteria of these new, outside groups within which one interacts, and the standards differ from those that existed previously in the relatively closed world of the village. Patterns of peasant social behavior, then, change to conform to these new criteria. This opening of choices of modes of behavior affects the decision-making capacity of the village as a unit. Lewis noted that in Rampur (Delhi State, India) the system of caste occupational specialization (*jajmani*) which entailed an exchange of services and an exchange of grain for services within the village has been declining with the emergence of new and different kinds of work experiences. As a result, there is almost a total lack of village cohesion. Only infrequently now does the village act as a social or political unit.[6]

Such increases in outside relations do not result in a sudden disappearance of village-oriented behavior. There is a differential rate of entry into the larger social system for community members and also different degrees of outside involvement. It is not so much a substitution of one value system for another as a continuing confrontation and tension between two

[5] Bernard Gallin, *Hsin Hsing, Taiwan: A Chinese Village in Change* (Berkeley: University of California Press, 1966), pp. 86-87.

[6] Oscar Lewis, *Village Life in Northern India: Studies in a Delhi Village* (Urbana: University of Illinois Press, 1958), pp. 148-149.

conflicting value systems.[7] In Namhalli (Mysore, India) for example, people choose different criteria upon which to act and upon which to settle disputes, and this has led to a lack of consensus within the village.[8] Alan Beals states, "The implication of this for village-wide leadership is, briefly, that there can be no village-wide leadership." [9]

Thus, one of the most noticeable political results of movement from an inward- to an outward-orientation is a rapid deterioration of the village dispute settling mechanisms. Hsin Hsing in Taiwan, for example, had always attempted to localize its disputes and mediate them in order to minimize outside governmental interference and in order to restore surface harmony as quickly as possible. The decreasing importance of the separate village status system has meant that the old leaders are no longer widely accepted as respected forces in settling disputes.[10] Previously, a dispute in Hsin Hsing over the distribution of values, whether it was water irrigation, land ownership, or expenditure of village funds, was often quite serious, but there was a basic acceptance of the village's system of distribution of justice by all parties to the dispute. Now, the disputes have escalated so that no settlement is possible, since there is no basic acceptance of the village's system of justice and its institutions.[11]

In many areas, outside courts and police have become exceedingly important in peasants' lives with the decay of the dispute settling mechanisms within the villages. Of the fifty-

[7] For the declining unity of a Tanjore (India) village, see E. Kathleen Gough, "The Social Structure of a Tanjore Village," in *Village India: Studies in the Little Community*, ed. McKim Marriott (Chicago: University of Chicago Press, 1955), pp. 43-48.

[8] Alan Beals, "Leadership in a Mysore Village," in *Leadership and Political Institutions in India*, ed. Park and Tinker, pp. 432-433.

[9] *Ibid.*, p. 437.

[10] Gallin, *Hsin Hsing*, pp. 278-280.

[11] Bernard Gallin, "Conflict Resolution in Changing Chinese Society: A Taiwanese Study," in *Political Anthropology*, ed. Marc J. Swartz, Victor W. Turner, and Arthur Tuden (Chicago: Aldine, 1966), p. 267.

one cases in this study, only six have sole arbitration of disputes within the village, and four of these are inward-oriented villages. The expansion of outside participation, differing widely for various village segments, does not therefore result in a sudden replacement of one type of arbitration for another. A choice of methods introduces, rather, new tensions and undermines the village mechanisms as courts of last resort.[12]

These examples in the decline of village influence on the individual peasant and, particularly, the deterioration of dispute settling mechanisms should not be taken to signify that the village becomes a wholly negligible factor in peasants' lives after an increase in their outside relations. The effect of the social and political organization remains quite substantial in many cases, although diminished relative to its importance when the village was more inward-oriented. The village still exists as one of the primary sources of identity in the minds of the peasants, and it often continues to be thought of as a separate entity by others, including the province and the state.

As was the case before peasants vastly increased their outside relations, the strength of a village political organization still depends in great part on the actions of outsiders even after peasants become outward-oriented. The political organization of the village continues to exert control in proportion to the nature and extent of the authority and responsibilities delegated to it by the state. In some areas, the state aggregates demands, exerts its authority, and administers its programs all through village-wide institutions. In such instances, the village leadership and institutions remain strong, and the community continues to be a major source of identity. In Bisipara (Orissa, India), for example, state administrative actions are "routed through the communal institutions of the

[12] In one Lebanese Druse village, disputes have increasingly gone to the courts, once this element of choice was opened. Victor F. Ayoub, "Conflict Resolution and Social Reorganization in a Lebanese Village," *Human Organization* 24 (Spring 1965), 11-17.

village, and not through individuals. A single exception was the agricultural loan. In all other cases, if the village wants something, then it petitions as a village. From the other direction Government orders come down to the headman, who passes them through the village council."[13]

In Baytīn (Jordan), there is a subdistrict police force which is assisted by the village leaders. Moreover, the village council is delegated the authority to mediate in disputes using tribal law and common sense. Only when it fails to resolve the issue will it pass it on to the subdistrict administrator. In some other cases, disputes go on to civil or religious courts.[14] The headmen of Bangkhuad, Thailand, are given guns to maintain order and are still asked to settle interhousehold disputes.[15]

There are numerous other cases, however, where the state bypasses the village hierarchy. In such instances, the state usually is attempting to accelerate the weakening of old ties and bonds. By incorporating individuals directly into new administrative and political procedures and organizations, the state hopes to undermine old avenues of loyalty and promote direct participatory support for itself.[16] Ignoring the community as a building block in administrative actions may have its costs for the state in policy implementation,[17] but it does serve

[13] F. G. Bailey, *Caste and the Economic Frontier: A Village in Highland Orissa* (Manchester: Manchester University Press, 1957), pp. 254-255.

[14] Abdulla M. Lutfiyya, *Baytīn A Jordanian Village: A Study of Social Institutions and Social Change in a Folk Community* (London: Mouton, 1966).

[15] Howard Keva Kaufman, *Bangkhuad: A Community Study in Thailand* (Locust Valley, N.Y.: J. J. Augustin, 1960).

[16] For the conflict of old ties of loyalty and new bonds, see Clifford Geertz, "The Integrative Revolution: Primordial Sentiments and Civil Politics in the New States," in *Old Societies and New States: The Quest for Modernity in Asia and Africa*, ed. Geertz (Glencoe: The Free Press of Glencoe, 1963).

[17] John D. Montgomery has shown the utility of giving land reform implementation to decentralized, local units rather than bureaucratically centralizing the procedure. "Allocation of Authority in

the purpose of weakening rapidly the old political institutions and leadership of villages. The community then falls significantly as a source for peasant identification.

In writing of Guatemalan Indian peasants, Nash observes that previously two conditions for the strength of the political hierarchy existed: the leadership acted in the name of the community while remaining passive agents of the state and the state did not bypass the leadership by direct appeal to individuals. In 1944 to 1954, however, the new progressive Guatemalan government attempted to have the Indians "act as individuals, to be recruited to government organizations, to appear in rallies, vote in elections, join unions, and to sanction leadership oriented away from the local society."[18] This resulted in a crippling of the villages' civil-religious hierarchy and after the introduction of elections, factionalism increased greatly within the communities.

Thus there is a diminution to the peasants in the importance of the village and its political organization. This diminution is proportionate to the extent of the village's external relations and to the extent to which the state uses it as an administrative link. Villagers now operate in a much more complex social world. The result has been a decline in the reinforcement of the political organization by the village social organization. The acceptance of the power of the political organization no longer stems from its identification with the major boundaries of the peasants' social world but from its association with the state, the boundaries of their new social world. For the village to remain a viable political unit, the state must designate it as such.

This diminution stems also from a change in the proportion of political and administrative tasks the village political institutions perform. With the appearance of district courts, state

Land Reform Programs: A Comparative Study of Administrative Processes and Outputs," *Administrative Science Quarterly* 17 (March 1972), 73 and *passim*.

[18] Manning Nash, "Political Relations in Guatemala," *Social and Economic Studies* 7 (March 1958), 72.

agricultural agents, police, health officers, population control agents, marketing cooperative agents, military draft personnel, census takers, and others, numerous and diverse ties are made by the state administration directly to various individuals and groups. Even when the village leadership *is* used for administrative purposes by the state, there are increasing numbers of cases where contacts between state and individual are made without channeling through the village political leadership. Even in cases such as that in Ranjana (West Bengal, India) where the village remains a definite administrative block,[19] the proportion of political and administrative tasks performed for its constituency falls. Though the absolute number of tasks rises for the village leaders and they go from being spare-time to full-time, the proportion falls since there are a growing number of other tasks performed by larger governmental units.

More important than the decline in the proportion of political and administrative actions is the fact that the indigenous leadership is used by the state as the final link in its administrative chain. The village political organization changes from being primarily a political and judicial structure, making decisions about village welfare and settling disputes, to an administrative structure, carrying out the mandate from above.[20] Leaders are increasingly defined as administrators rather than decision-makers, and the community's most respected members may now decline altogether to serve in official positions.

This change is reflected in the incentives for one to serve the community. In Guatemala, previously, men serving on the civil-religious hierarchy gave from one-half to all their work time plus cash outlays for liquor, corn, masses, candles, marimbas, and so forth. The reward was prestige.[21] Now, in out-

[19] Gouranga Chattopadhyay, *Ranjana, A Village in West Bengal* (Calcutta: Bookland Private, 1964), p. 253.

[20] Harumi Befu, "Political Complexity and Village Community: Test of an Hypothesis," *Anthropological Quarterly* 39 (April 1966), 618, writes that in the modern state the village loses its decision-making capabilities and gets more administrative chores.

[21] Nash, "Political Relations in Guatemala," 67.

ward-oriented villages, those serving most often must be paid in order to accept the task. In our cases, only 26.7 percent of the inward-oriented villages cited payment for officials, while 58.3 percent of outward-oriented communities made mention of such payment.

Ishwaran describes the situation in Shivapur (Mysore, India) where one can see the changes that occur as the elders no longer have the final say.

> The fact that there is now a formal bureaucracy, in theory independent of and superior to the informal but traditional power structure, has tended to weaken the informal power structure somewhat. It has become much more dependent on the personal wisdom and integrity of the elders for its successful functioning. Thus, while it has perhaps become more efficient, it has also lost somewhat in effectiveness. If the elders give an unacceptable or unwise decision, it is theoretically possible to appeal to the impersonal bureaucracy.[22]

Villages which have been bypassed as links in the administrative and political chains are even more subject to these changes. In those cases, the leadership loses both its political and administrative tasks and then quickly becomes irrelevant to the peasants' needs and social experiences. In short, the changing internal environment due to increased differentiation and the changing external environment which is making more individualized demands and is creating more interdependencies, combine to make the old political arrangements intolerable for some.[23] This does not mean an end to village government, but the continuing viability of village government stems more than ever from its relationship to a larger political whole, to the broader political community.

[22] K. Ishwaran, *Shivapur, A South Indian Village* (London: Routledge and Kegan Paul, 1968), p. 185.

[23] See Ralph W. Nicholas, "Rules, Resources, and Political Activity," in *Local-Level Politics: Social and Cultural Perspectives*, ed. Marc J. Swartz (Chicago: Aldine, 1968), p. 309.

THE CHANGE OF POLITICAL COMMUNITY: ACCOMMODATION AND ORGANIZATION

Increased outside involvement in market structures inevitably results in new dealings with outside political institutions, as well. The greater scope and frequency of peasants' new social and economic interactions raises problems never before confronted. For example, the peasants of Saucío in Colombia were faced with a government directive stating that all cattle had to be vaccinated because of a scare of hoof-and-mouth epidemic. The peasants resisted because they felt such matters are in the hands of God. In the end, however, they capitulated to the wider political authority for the simple reason that without a vaccination certificate the cattle could not be sold on the national market.[24] Perception by peasants of their political world is shaped, then, by the degree of their external relations and the constraints, demands, and problems that arise in the context of their interactions. Structures and beliefs that are incompatible with the scope of this new participation (such as the belief that epidemics are in God's hands) must be adapted to the new political reality if they are to survive at all.

The contrasts, both in internal and external politics, between the two neighboring South Indian villages of Dalena and Wangala is instructive in showing how the village's position on the scale of external relations affects the peasants' arena of political action and some of their old political structures.[25] Wangala's peasants have much more limited involvement in outside economic institutions than Dalena's who have taken advantage of numerous and diverse work opportunities in the area. Such a difference in the degree of outside involvement resulted because Wangala benefited from the irrigation

[24] Orlando Fals-Borda, *Peasant Society in the Colombian Andes: A Sociological Study of Saucío* (Gainesville: University of Florida Press, 1955), p. 225.

[25] The following accounts are taken from T. S. Epstein, *Economic Development and Social Change in South India* (Manchester: Manchester University Press, 1962).

project and remained an agricultural village while Dalena stayed dry, and its peasants took advantage of the new, outside jobs.

Internally, Dalena has undergone important political changes. Its peasants' various outside ties have led to a new distribution of wealth in the village, which in turn resulted in conflict over the principle of hereditary political leadership. The wealthier members who have prospered with the expansion of outside involvement wielded their increased material resources against the poorer hereditary lineage elders. They succeeded in using the new democratic legislation from above as a lever to gain positions on the village *panchayat* (council). Wangala, on the other hand, has been able to steer free of such direct clashes of values and bases of power, since outside relationships are much more circumscribed and have not resulted in new distributions of wealth. Upon the establishment of its panchayat, consequently, the election turned out to be nothing more than a farcical confirmation of the previous village leadership.

The difference between the two villages on the scale of external relations is reflected in outside political involvement, as well. For the peasants of Wangala, the village with less extensive outside economic involvement, external politics has been uninteresting, on the whole. Their curiosity has been little roused by the district and state political machinations. The Dalena peasants, on the other hand, have become quite involved. When proposed changes raised the possibility that their fellow caste members who originally got them the jobs in the outside would lose dominance, they took part in a planned demonstration against the proposed changes. Membership in local trade union chapters by the Dalena factory workers gave them the organizational wherewithal to create substantial pressure on the state's politicians.

Changes in village political structures and the peasant's effective political world, his area of concern and action, are related to new kinds of political associations within the village and between villagers and outsiders. Dalena's trade union participation is one example. Such associations, which can have an impact on both internal and external politics, stem in great part from the increased economic interdependency and differentiation that occur with expanded outside participation. Shifting, unstable factions still appear—and may even increase in number and intensity as people no longer feel as strong about the possible dangers to village viability by airing differences. More enduring kinds of divisions and associations based on occupational differences and interdependencies also begin to characterize the community.

Enduring organizations are characterized by a significant degree of complexity, a hierarchy of roles performing a variety of interrelated tasks. It is only with the results of significant increases in outside involvement that peasant experience begins more and more to consist of single-interest relationships, rather than multiplex ones. These new, single-interest relationships give the peasants for the first time the social basis to engage in interaction with large numbers of others, each with a specialized task. In other words, many peasants now have the social experience to participate in complex organizations.

The development of such organizations has recently marked life in Thyagasamuthiram in Madras State, India. The social and economic changes of the last decades have been followed by an incorporation of the community into the larger polity. This political integration with the outside has been achieved through two separate organizations, a workers' association and a landowners' association. Under the guidance of several dedicated outside leaders, a number of peasant laborers and tenants quietly began working for a union chapter of the Poor Cultivators' Association in order to resist exploitation of the poor peasants by the landowners. Two of the organizers were landowners themselves, and their presence had a considerable impact. Besides their prestige, they could offer the material incentive of compensatory leases to those potential joiners who were threatened by other landowners with loss of leaseholds.

Infantrymen caste members (Sudras) were first recruited by the organizers, but it was quickly realized that the lowly Pariahs (untouchables) would also have to be brought into the organization if a strike was to be held, since they were numerous and they could withhold ritually important services to the landowners. The Pariahs, in turn, had little chance for gaining the rights promised by the government—use of wells, streets, public places, and temples—without some assistance from other castes. The breakthrough of equal association across caste barriers was therefore made: "The Sudras, in treating the Pariahs as equals *for the purpose of this association*, do so partly as a symbolic concession and partly out of necessity. The main basis of identification is in their work in agriculture, where they do the same jobs for the same pay, thus providing a simple and convincing argument for their joining together—in furthering their interests the one group has to depend on the other, 'Pariah and Sudra are one.' "[26]

Such an association does not translate into a complete abolition of castes. Ritually, they remain distinct, and there is neither interdining nor intermarrying between Infantrymen and Pariahs. In fact, caste membership is still a strong enough source of identity and of effective sanctions that it can be used to reinforce the new social patterns. Some of the traditional leaders of the Infantrymen caste, for example, were pressed into joining the Union because they were told it would be humiliating not to have caste unity. Social ostracism against them by the others in the caste was threatened.

The community of Thyagasamuthiram is thus divided. On the one hand are the Union members and, on the other, are the landlords who joined together as threats of concerted action against them grew. The smaller landowners, caught in the middle, have attempted to remain as unobtrusive as possible, while nominally joining the rather weak landowners' association. Yet, surprisingly, despite the new divisions in the village,

[26] Dagfinn Sivertsen, *When Caste Barriers Fall: A Study of Social and Economic Change in a South Indian Village* (Norway: George Allen and Unwin, 1963), pp. 123-124 (my emphasis).

the old, highly political institutions, the temple assemblies, continue to function. The old leaders of the landowner castes are still being invited as guests of honor to weddings and other social functions of their workers, yet there is a key difference: now their authority within the community has been undermined. People continue to attend temple assemblies (less frequently), but the assemblies are no longer vehicles for the exercise of authority by the old leaders. At harvest time, the division in the village came to a head with a strike by the Union, which was demanding higher wages. During the negotiations, the landowners attempted to divide the strikers by agreeing to the demands except in the case of the Pariahs. The other strikers refused to be split in this way, and the strike action was successful within a few days.[27]

These accounts of the organization of segments of the peasantry in Dalena and Thyagasamuthiram, for both internal and external political goals, should not lead one to believe that organized participation in institutions tied to the larger political system automatically follows participation in the national economic system. Political organizations are not a necessary outgrowth of experience based increasingly on single-interest relationships. Peasants' action in politics may remain merely that of individual accommodation or passive resistance. The Saucío, Colombia, peasants, we have seen, merely yielded to the vaccination decree. Passive resistance is an option when there is low enforcement of laws and rules.

Peasants have two huge hurdles to overcome, however, before they can be an effective voice in national politics. First, they must build a basis of association among a significant portion of their numbers. In the case of peasants who are emerging from the dominance of strong lords, this entails forging ties among themselves where previously the great proportion of interaction came through dyadic ties to the lord and within the household. And in the case of peasants who had a viable social organization, their associations must be reconstituted

[27] This account is taken from *ibid.*, ch. IX.

on the basis of specific interdependencies instead of multiplex ties. For organizations to be enduring, there must now be a complexity in the division of tasks. Second, they must forge (or have forged for them) a basis for political alliances with other classes or groups in the society.

For peasants, the difficulty in overcoming these two obstacles is enormous. Many of the new results of the social experiences of wider participation—greater specificity of relationships, enduring economic interdependency with others, larger ranges of common economic interests, increased importance as essential cogs in the national marketing system— are the bases for an ability to be parts of hierarchical, long-term organizations. Yet, compared to other classes in the increasingly organizational society, such bases are weak. They are involved in household farming, and even when growing crops for the market, their daily experience is one which demands little dependence on others outside the household. In addition, their degree of involvement in the market differs widely, and their participation in economic organizations demanding minute-by-minute interdependency, as does a factory job, remains low.

Although less so than previously, it is still somewhat true that one peasant's fortunes are not extensively tied to the actions of other peasants. This leaves them vulnerable to exploitation, which explains the necessity of outside alliances. Their ability to operate within organizations is greater than when their villages were inward-oriented, but it still is less than for other groups in the society.[28]

All this means that, although peasants now have greater capabilities than before of sustained political participation through organizations, they are generally incapable of institutionalizing such associations themselves. As a result, their degree of sustained political involvement depends, in great part,

[28] For the reasons organizations often fail in peasant villages, see the description of a village in Ceylon. Bryce Ryan, *Sinhalese Village* (Coral Gables, Fla.: University of Miami Press, 1958), pp. 151-152.

on the initiatives of nonpeasants. These may be government administrators, party officials, union leaders, or others. Where the efforts of such outsiders are weak or nonexistent, politics is nothing more than accommodating to (and occasionally resisting passively) a different set of political institutions.

In practically all cases of effective organization of peasants, the initiative is from above, from those outside the peasant class. In Venezuela, there seemed to be indications to the contrary, since 48 percent of local unions surveyed were founded by local peasants. A closer examination, however, showed that in each instance the peasant organizers were party members who had been ordered from above to found the chapters.[29] Often, such peasants became party members when living in the cities for long periods of work. Similarly, national sponsors, APRA and Acción Popular, led the blooming of peasant organizations in Peru's sierra.[30]

For those who organize segments of the peasantry politically, the potential benefits are many. The capacity to bring large numbers of new actors, capable of sustained pressure, through highly institutionalized political groups, into the national arena may tip the struggle in one's favor. Peter Lord has written about the Bolivian, Venezuelan, and Mexican cases:

> In all three countries under study, a political role for the peasantry has developed because political leaders needed its vote, its militia, or its general support in order to promote political stability and to keep political control away from potential opposition groups. Thus, political leaders have organized the peasantry and brought it into the political system to serve their own purposes. . . .[31]

[29] John R. Mathiason and John D. Powell, "Participation and Efficacy: Aspects of Peasant Involvement in Political Mobilization" (revised version of paper presented at the Annual Meeting of the American Political Science Association, September 4, 1969), p. 15.

[30] Borque, "Cholification and the Campesino," pp. 34-37.

[31] Lord, *The Peasantry as an Emerging Political Factor*, p. 94.

Just as the government can organize the peasantry to serve its purposes, whether to keep the status quo or to institute reforms, so too can dissident groups enhance their role in respect to the government by effective organization of the rural population.

POLITICAL ORGANIZATIONS: WHY PEASANTS PARTICIPATE

Less obvious than the gains for outside political groups in organizing peasants is the incentive for peasants to be organized. Too many of the recent works on peasant organization —particularly on Latin American cases—have avoided a close analysis of the process by which peasant organizations are built, focusing instead on structures and the relations among different structures. It has all too often been assumed that the government or its opposition comes to the peasants with a program, which promises more favorable policy in issues affecting them, and it is the specific content of this program which motivates peasants to join the particular political organization. Ignored are the negative experiences that peasants have had with powerful outsiders in the past which would make them quite suspicious of new promises. Also ignored are the costs of political participation, especially to an extremely poor peasant who has time for little more than to scratch a living from the ground or to work at some low-level wage job.

The understanding of peasant political participation in this book is different. As economic crises result in a greater degree of external relations, peasants interact increasingly with an entire network of economic institutions outside the village. What is particularly relevant for the peasants—and especially the less powerful ones—is that this network, as discussed in Chapter VIII, is fraught with shortcomings: it is marked by corruption and monopolistic practices and is structurally incomplete. There may be a system to market produce, but a mile of road is needed for the transportation costs not to be too prohibitive for the peasants to grow the cash crop. New products for capital intensification may be available, but there are no credit facilities with low enough interest rates to make the purchases worthwhile. Corrupt government officials or monopolistic wholesalers or suppliers may negate many of the profits the peasant feels he would otherwise be able to gain. The new network within which the peasant operates is not yet a "social whole" but rather still has many "imperfectly linked" component parts.[32]

Initial responsiveness of peasants to organizers, it seems, is not to what organizers say or promise in terms of long-term changes, since peasants have had experience with outsiders and have learned to be distrustful and suspicious of them. Instead, they respond to the immediate material trade-offs they can garner in exchange for their organizational membership, *trade-offs that overcome some of the shortcomings of the institutional network* that peasants have faced with increasing outside market participation. The initial political organization of peasants is most often not in terms of their overarching goals but must be seen in light of the changes that have occurred in their daily relations and the problems such changes have brought. Peasants seek immediate solutions to solve problems.

The trade-off can be on various levels, but in each case what the peasant gives is commensurate with what he receives. On the simplest level, there is the single action by the peasant. In Hsin Hsing, Taiwan, for example, villagers received a few packs of cigarettes or some bath towels and soap in 1957-1958 in exchange for their votes for a particular candidate for the *hsien* (county) assembly.[33] On more complex

[32] F. G. Bailey, *Politics and Social Change: Orissa in 1959* (Berkeley: University of California Press, 1963), p. 219, speaks of Orissa, India, in these terms.

[33] Bernard Gallin, "Political Factionalism and its Impact on Chinese Village Social Organization in Taiwan," in *Local-Level Politics*, ed. Swartz, p. 386. Such buying of votes is the most common trade-off in a number of other countries, as well. Bailey (*Politics and Social Change*, pp. 32-35) speaks of bribes for votes being accepted as a legitimate form of behavior in Bisipara (Orissa, India).

211

levels, as we shall see below, continuing benefits of various kinds are traded off for sustained and active participation in various political organizations. The ability to draw upon the participation of many peasants in the political arena is the inducement to the political organizations to offer peasants material incentives.

Peasants join when there is something tangible to be had which they desire, and these desires stem, for the most part, from the structurally incomplete, corrupt, and monopolistic networks within which they operate. Their initial aims in joining are not to implement a particular ideology. They do not even have such high hopes as to expect an influential role with the critical decision-makers at the locus of the new politics. Instead they seek immediately useful concessions that will aid them in navigating their social and economic environment.

Peasants' political actions in this century have been characterized all the way from reactionary to radically revolutionary. The same Mexican peasants have supported one of the major progressive revolutions in history under the leadership of Zapata and later Cardenas, and they have also supported the highly repressive regime of the last twenty years. The point here is that it is fruitless to begin one's investigation of peasant organizational support with the content of the programs and the ideology of those they have followed. Politics for peasants starts at the level at which they can trust outsiders: suspicion of long-term promises and acceptance only of the more immediate benefits that can be provided. Increases in market participation have taught peasants that outsiders are willing to fill certain needs, if there is something to be given to them in return.

Evidence to test this hypothesis is scarce since most studies have not related peasant political organization to the increases in market relations. Changes in politics have not often been tied by scholars to peasant economic crises nor to the structurally incomplete and poorly regulated economic network within which peasants must now regularly act, yet bits and pieces of evidence do exist.

One of the most pressing needs of a peasantry which is in the process of increasing its market involvement is credit. In La Laguna, Mexico, all three regional political organizations deal with the supply of credit to the peasants. When a villager receives official credit, unless he indicates otherwise, he is automatically enrolled as a member of the Regional Committee which is tied into the ruling PRI. The Committees, in turn, deliver support to the government. Many peasants also joined because they felt such membership would help in processing their petitions involving government agencies, but this has not been the case.

In fact, the failure of the Regional Committees to give their members special consideration in government offices has enabled the other two regional organizations to offer specific incentives for joining besides that of receiving credit. Since they are not dependent on government subsidies for their credit, they can present demands and petitions without fear of being cut off, and peasants feel that they have been more effective than the Regional Committees in this respect. For these organizations, political survival depends on enrolling members through these "extra" services in order to combat the dominant position and the concentration of resources of the PRI.[34]

In the *municipio* of Taretan in Michoacan, Mexico, credit plays a central role in the formation of a whole set of organizations. This has been so since 1937 and even more effectively since the establishment of a nearby sugar mill in 1946. The *Banco Nacional de Credito Ejidal* gives credit only

[34] Henry A. Landsberger and Cynthia Hewitt de Alcantara, "Peasant Organizations in La Laguna, Mexico: History, Structure, Member Participation and Effectiveness," Research Papers on Land Tenure and Agrarian Reform, no. 17, Inter-American Committee for Agricultural Development (CIDA) (Washington: General Secretariat of American States, November 1970), pp. 82 and 105-106.

through the credit societies associated with the sugar mill. Every week, the credit societies dispense the bank's money to the cane growers. In addition, they are involved in such projects as repairing schools and installing a system of potable water. Through the bank and the link to the credit societies, then, the government is able to ensure itself the support of the peasants by the dependency it engenders.

Besides the credit societies, there are also organizations of *ejidos* (villages with communal lands) and cattlemen's and smallholders' associations. Cattlemen must pay a double tax on each cow sold if they are not members of the cattlemen's association. The peasants can use their organization's relation to the larger *Liga de Comunidades Agrarias* in order to get special favors, such as strategic phone calls or letters when they need to deal with the *Departmento Agrario*.[35]

This latter pattern of giving peasants special favors in their dealings with government offices in exchange for support is a common type of trade-off. Leaders of peasant organizations in Venezuela, for example, are expected to use their contacts with the political party, local government officials, and higher officers of the Peasant Federation in order to gain support for local community projects and to solve local problems.[36] The local Member of the Legislative Assembly in Orissa, India, is similarly expected to help the peasants get what they want out of the Administration and to assist them when they are in trouble.[37] In exchange for credit, special favors, breaks on taxes, etc., the organizers get several benefits. They can utilize peasant votes in elections, peasants' presence in rallies and demonstrations, and the threat of peasant mobilization in their dealings with other opposing groups. In the case of an organizer like the Mexican PRI, the threat of a withdrawal of bene-

[35] Henry A. Landsberger and Cynthia N. Hewitt, "Preliminary Report on a Case Study of Mexican Peasant Organization" (Ithaca, N.Y.: New York State School of Industrial and Labor Relations, Cornell University), mimeo, pp. 8-9 and 45-46.

[36] Powell, *Political Mobilization of the Venezuelan Peasant*, p. 143.

[37] Bailey, *Politics and Social Change*, p. 25.

214

fits to the peasants can be used to insure a lack of peasant opposition to the government. A network of pyramidal organizations, then, becomes a potent means of political and social control.

Credit is an effective means of gaining sustained support because it can be given regularly, as the Banco does by doling it out weekly. Land reform, on the other hand, is much less likely to present the same possibilities to the organizer. It can be used for an initial swelling of the ranks of organizations, as in Italy and Venezuela.[38] Soon, however, the peasant asks "what-have-you-done-for-me-lately?" before participating in the organization any more. The successful organizer follows up land reform with credit, agricultural extension services, pure water, electricity, improved marketing services, a source for favors, etc.[39]

The relationships within the organization can be patron-client in nature if there is paternalism and the supply of a large number of the peasants' needs. On the other hand, the transactions may be very businesslike, and the peasant may divide his support among a number of organizations. As in lord-peasant relationships discussed in Chapter II, however, the degree to which organizers can gain peasant support depends on the scope of the services they provide, the primacy of those services, and their degree of monopoly over the provision of the services.

Such trade-offs within organizations often come after the decline in the lord's control. Patron withdrawal is followed by an expansion of outside involvement by peasants. This is accompanied by a willingness to substitute some of their former loyalty they gave to the lord to groups that can overcome some of the shortcomings of outside institutions and can protect them against monopolistic exploitation. In the Peruvian Sierra, for example, the growth of peasant organizations fol-

[38] John Duncan Powell, "Peasant Society and Clientilist Politics," *American Political Science Review* 64 (June 1970), 418.
[39] *Ibid.*, 420.

lowed the dual process of decline in the lords' powers and a growth of new economic enterprises. With the loss of total control by the lords, the implicit alliance of lord and government declined (the government had kept hands off as long as the lords had maintained complete control) and outside politicians moved in to organize the peasantry.[40]

Brazil's experience was somewhat similar.[41] There had been a hierarchical nature to politics with the landowner of each fazeda (hacienda) granting favors, such as fiestas, credit, land, protection, and medicine, to peasants in exchange for labor, service in his private army, and (after 1891) the control of their vote. In turn, the landowner delivered the votes to a political boss (perhaps a larger landowner). In exchange for this support, the boss gave the landowner patronage jobs, public works (roads or bridges) near his land or on it, credit, and so forth. Also, the landowners could be assured of a lack of outside harassment and use of army troops or police if needed to maintain order.

With patron withdrawal, increased seasonal migration of peasants, and economic growth sparked by a new middle class, there was a rapid rise of peasant organizations in Brazil. The *Ligas Camponesas* (from 1955) and the rural syndicates (from 1962) have been gaining in strength, yet the hierarchical nature of Brazilian politics did not change considerably. These organizations responded to the insecure environment within which peasants had to act.[42]

> We are inclined to see the Ligas Camponesas and the rural syndicates as the transformation of the old following of the landowner into the following of a politician or a government. This explains why two Ligas or syndicates can be adversaries if their leaders are political opponents. It also

[40] Borque, "Cholification and the Campesino," pp. 34-37.

[41] The account of Brazil is taken principally from Benno Galjart, "Class and 'Following' in Rural Brazil," *América Latina* 7 (July-September 1964), 5-22.

[42] Bertram Hutchinson, "The Patron-Dependant Relationship in Brazil: A Preliminary Examination," *Sociologia Ruralis* 6 (1966), 18.

explains why certain favours are granted to one group and not to another, yet similar one, in one place and not in another, although similar, place: the politician, the government, grants favours to his following, not to that of others.[43]

Increased market participation makes peasants aware of different kinds of "favors" they want from the political hierarchy, but their relationship to the hierarchy remains one of dependence and subordination. The content of exchange may now differ but the form remains the same.[44] Only for a very few do the expanding resources of the outside open great opportunities for mobility and possible escape from such domination.

Peasants who have greatly expanded the scope of their economic activity have found inadequacies in the components of the infrastructure within which they must act. The strength of political organizers lies in their connections with the government or some other supplier of resources to fill the gaps, to make those components more equitable to particular peasants. These organizers respond to the peasants' attempts to penetrate the market fully, to gain added value through expanded outside relations. Such organizers can offer jobs or elements to make cash cropping more profitable. The process is self-reinforcing. Once the peasants are organized (which remains a rare phenomenon) the politician has a greater lever for extracting more resources to use as inducements to peasant political participation. Peasants, in turn, participate in proportion to what they receive from the organizers. The ends of the organizers can be reformist, or they can be conservative (designed to bring the peasantry under control).[45] Organ-

[43] Galjart, "Class and 'Following' in Rural Brazil," p. 21.

[44] Andrew Pearse, "Metropolis and Peasant: The Expansion of the Urban-Industrial Complex and the Changing Rural Structure" in *Peasants and Peasant Societies: Selected Readings,* ed. Teodor Shanin (Baltimore: Penguin Books, 1971), p. 79.

[45] Landsberger and Hewitt, "Peasant Organizations in La Laguna," p. 37, refer to this as a "policy of absorption."

217

izers' goals may stem from being power hungry. Or reformers may be simply morally indignant, seeking a redistribution of power and wealth.[46]

This process of peasant incorporation into political organizations is in many ways analogous to machine politics. In machine politics, there is a process of exchange between the organizers and their constituents, usually involving votes for some type of selective material or social benefit.[47] As F. G. Bailey writes in making this analogy in Orissa, India, "The machine recruits its workers by giving them what they want."[48] This analogy should not be taken too far, however. Machine politics is usually designed to mobilize nothing more than voters on election day, whereas organizers of peasants may seek continuous active participation in exchange for a continuous flow of benefits. Machine politics involves no larger goal usually than attaining local power, on the part of the organizers, and gaining individual benefits, on the part of the constituents. The incorporation of peasants into political organizations may grow to involve much more. Although peasants are great skeptics about the sincerity of outsiders, their confidence grows as exchanges become institutionalized. In fact, we may identify four analytically distinct levels of peasant political action, each with its own goals.

1. *Peasants without any political organization accommodate to demands of outside political institutions wherever necessary.* They attempt passively to avoid complying when they can but they do not attempt to influence or manipulate the institutions in their interests. A great percentage of world peasantry is still in this passive political condition.

The next three levels all involve participation in political organizations or institutions, but each demands different degrees and kinds of activities on the part of the peasants. It is

[46] Galjart, "Class and 'Following' in Rural Brazil," p. 20.

[47] See James C. Scott, "Corruption, Machine Politics, and Political Change," *American Political Science Review* 63 (December 1969), 1144.

[48] Bailey, *Politics and Social Change*, p. 142.

hypothesized that participation is sequential. Peasants will not participate on Level 3 until they have achieved a history of success (rewards) on Level 2, and, similarly, they will not participate on Level 4 until there has been a history of success on Level 3.

2. *Peasants seek individual material or social gains.* This is the type of action of which we have spoken and which is tied to a desire for economic gain that is otherwise blocked by corruption, monopolistic practices, or a structurally incomplete market network. It is hypothesized here that initial involvement in politics by peasants is on this basis and that their operative behavior in organizations is limited, at first, in intensity, frequency, and scope proportionately to the individual rewards they can garner. The possibility of peasants engaging in action which would not bring individual rewards but is designed to achieve other, larger goals is dependent upon a positive experience within the organization in achieving this simple set of goals. Most Indian peasants, for example, probably still limit their political behavior outside the village to Level 2.

3. *Peasants seek gains for their particular group or segment within the community or for their entire community.* Their desire here is to seek gains for a small cluster of people (larger than just the household) relative to all other groups in the society, including other groups of peasants.[49] The rewards here are collective but still quite selective. In the exchange of support for such gains as a road to a particular village, for example, the organizers' willingness to provide the collective good is not dependent on any one individual's support. Thus, any peasant could think that he will let the others expend the effort but he will reap the benefits with them. Prior action with others in the group which was successful

[49] See the discussion on subgroup mobility and "limited concern" in Henry A. Landsberger and Cynthia N. Hewitt, "Ten Sources of Weakness and Cleavage in Latin American Peasant Movements," in *Agrarian Problems and Peasant Movements in Latin America,* ed. Rodolfo Stavenhagen (Garden City, N.Y.: Doubleday, 1970), pp. 573-575.

in getting him individual benefits, however, gives him the needed experience of success to gain confidence in achieving larger goals. Previous cooperation with others within the organization gives the peasant stable expectations of others' performance in achieving larger goals, as well. Many segments and communities of Mexican peasants, for example, act on the basis of Level 3 goals. When, however, there is a widespread belief, as in Orissa, India, that middlemen are siphoning off the benefits, there is little reason to seek more complex goals within that organization,[50] and peasants, in that case, will probably remain on Level 2.

4. *Peasants seek gains for their entire class*, that is, class mobility relative to other classes in the society. This, of course, is the most complex of goals, for it seeks from the peasants' organizational involvement a far-reaching redistribution of the state's economic and political power. As they achieve immediate ends time and again and as they win local collective benefits, the peasants become less suspicious of the organization and begin to support it on the basis of its larger program and ideology.[51] On Level 4, they are willing to engage in operative action to achieve these ultimate goals, self-sacrificing action with few or no immediate individual or local benefits. This level can be only achieved when some organization has, in fact, brought a large segment of the peasantry together, without dividing peasants in competition for scarce resources.

Rarely do peasants engage in complex Level 4 political action. We shall leave a discussion of such limited cases to the following chapter on revolution. Most often, however, peasant political participation has been a discouraging process and has not gone significantly beyond mere accommodation (Level 1), action designed to achieve individual material or

[50] Bailey, *Politics and Social Change*, pp. 155-156.

[51] Powell, *Political Mobilization of the Venezuelan Peasant*, pp. 56-58, talks of this as distinction between ultimate and intermediate goals. My point is that for peasants to act as if the ultimate goals are operative, the intermediate rewards must come first.

social rewards (Level 2), or, at most, participation to achieve local collective rewards (Level 3).

THE TRADEGY OF PEASANT POLITICAL INVOLVEMENT IN THE NEW POLITICAL COMMUNITY

Expanded market relations thrust peasants into the outside economic hierarchy and left them on the bottom of that hierarchy. Similarly, the new politics is increasingly organizationally based.[52] The desirable positions in the hierarchy demand resources and skills[53] which peasants generally do not possess.[54]

Teodor Shanin has noted that at the same time peasants are increasing their degree of external relations, often their national importance declines as their "food-monopoly" is broken through the state's increasing international trade. "Once again, the course of historical development seems to weaken peasants' political influence."[55] With a low sense of political efficacy[56] and increasing differentiation within the village undermining a high degree of total class solidarity, "the probability of achieving significant collective benefits through the existing political system is also of a modest, and

[52] A number of theorists of political development have focused on the organizational basis of politics. See, for example, Samuel P. Huntington, *Political Order in Changing Societies* (New Haven: Yale University Press, 1968); Lucian W. Pye, *Politics, Personality, and Nation Building: Burma's Search for Identity* (New Haven: Yale University Press, 1962); and Edward C. Banfield, *The Moral Basis of a Backward Society* (New York: The Free Press, 1958).

[53] See Pearse, "Metropolis and Peasant," p. 79.

[54] Robert Presthus, *The Organizational Society: An Analysis and a Theory* (New York: Alfred A. Knopf, 1962), p. 35, notes that organizational authority is based on a hierarchy of unequals in which scarce values are most scarce at the bottom.

[55] Teodor Shanin, "Peasantry as a Political Factor," in *Peasants and Peasant Societies*, ed. Shanin, p. 256.

[56] See, for example, Borque, "Cholification and the Campesino," p. 201.

declining, magnitude."[57] The most that peasants have achieved, in many cases, is a low level of material concessions in exchange for specific support. With numbers being their most valuable resource, any success that those above have in dividing peasants and robbing them of the strength of their numbers leaves them without highly valued resources for participation in national politics. The scarcity of sufficient resources in many third world countries and the competition for those resources often means there is no group having enough resources to keep up a steady flow in order to gain peasant support for more complex goals. Competition among outside organizers vying for peasant support or votes creates increased factionalism within the village.[58] Each organizer who comes uses his inducements to divide some peasants from the constituencies of other organizers.

The more divided the peasants, the less they can expect to have a class impact on state policy in return for their support. Peasants have been most effective when for short periods they have achieved unity of numbers and have engaged in fully spontaneous, amorphous political action.[59] But this is a far cry from the organizational politics needed for sustained pressure on the top. One of the primary difficulties the peasantry has had in building strong, independent organizations which could have a marked impact on national politics is the continuous disappearance of its leadership. That is, those with the resources which most likely would lead to political efficacy move upward out of the peasant class as soon as possible. The skills associated with political efficacy are also highly correlated with movement up the national status hierarchy—in effect, individual mobility into another class. Prior to peasants' expansion of external relations, the most resourceful peasants often moved into the gentry or became small landlords. These

[57] John Duncan Powell, "Venezuelan Agrarian Problems in Comparative Perspective," *Comparative Studies in Society and History* 13 (July 1971), 299.

[58] Powell, "Peasant Society and Clientilist Politics," p. 416.

[59] Shanin, "Peasantry as a Political Factor," p. 258.

men were often simultaneously exploiters of the peasantry and brokers for the villagers to the outside world.

In more recent times, there has been a shift so that upwardly mobile peasants have often become entrepreneurs, bureaucrats, party officials, and so forth. Where political opportunities are high compared to those gained solely through market relations, innovators often use politics as their means of upward mobility.[60] For example, peasants in La Laguna, Mexico, who do political work for the Regional Committees aspire to movement up a ladder through the posts of "peasant representative," secretary-general of a Regional Committee, city councilman, municipal president, and finally a post in the State League. Very rarely some even become federal deputies. The Regional Committees, in effect, "provide a route of socioeconomic mobility for local peasant leaders whose goal is to *escape* from the peasant class, not to fight for it."[61]

Peasants who work actively in peasant organizations are the ones with the resources needed for effectiveness in the political world: urban experience,[62] education, and sufficient wealth to make the proper payments where needed.[63] Only rarely do they remain living within the village in order to provide an indigenous leadership necessary for independent organization and initiative in the larger political system. And even in cases when those with significant resources for making political alliances outside do remain in the village, their lead-

---

[60] Landsberger and Hewitt enumerate five alternatives such leaders have rather than battling on behalf of all peasants. Three of these involve leadership as a means directed toward personal mobility. "Ten Sources of Weakness," pp. 566-577.

[61] Landsberger and Hewitt, "Peasant Organizations in La Laguna," p. 82.

[62] John Duncan Powell, "Venezuela: The Peasant Union Movement," in *Latin American Peasant Movements*, ed. Landsberger, p. 83, found that 34.5% of local leaders had previously lived in a city for up to ten years, and 12.7% had for more than ten years.

[63] See Henry A. Landsberger, "The Role of Peasant Movements and Revolts in Development," in *Latin American Peasant Movements*, ed. Landsberger, p. 41.

ership effectiveness is somewhat limited because of the distrust other villagers have for them.[64] As a result, peasant politics has been most often characterized by factionalism and manipulation from above, rather than any class solidarity.

SUMMARY

The greater the degree of outside social and economic participation by peasants, the more likely are political changes to occur in two areas. First, the introduction of new bases of resources and increasing differentiation of work experiences are likely to have profound effects on the distribution of power within the village. Challenge to the old leadership and formation of different types of associations are two responses to such changes. Second, the peasants' perception of the locus of crucial decision-making—that is, from where he sees most constraints and demands on his individual behavior coming and where he believes the potential for problem solving lies—shifts to outside the village. The importance of the community as a political unit diminishes.

In most cases, peasants have had only minimal influence on outsiders making critical decisions. The shift in locus has meant only accommodations to the forces restricting their behavior or perhaps low-level participation based on exchange for material inducements. These inducements come from outside organizers who build power by responding to specific difficulties peasants face as they move to an outward-orientation.

Rarely, however, is politics an avenue for solving the deep-rooted, intrinsic problems which peasants face as a class. Only a very few find in politics an escape from their most pressing problems. For the majority of peasants, the same vulnerability and corruption that plagues them in the economic sphere, affects them in the political, as well. Their influence on low bureaucrats remains minimal, let alone their capabilities of influencing those making major policy decisions. When asked

[64] Bailey, *Politics and Social Change*, pp. 58-59.

if they continue to feel discrimination from their former Zam-indars (landlords), the untouchables of Bagerawan (Uttar Pradesh, India) said yes, that they are teased, their animals are kicked, and they are occasionally beaten. When further pressed as to why they did not summon the police when they were beaten, they smiled in a resigned way and stated, "They have more money than we to pay off the police. If we sum-moned the police, it would be we who ended up in jail."

CHAPTER X

Peasant Revolution

INTRODUCTION

THE TWENTIETH CENTURY has been the century of peasant revolution.[1] In the last fifty years, peasants in certain areas have engaged in prolonged national struggles to change the system of government and the distribution of power. These movements have not been based on a sudden burst of violence after frustration has built as was often true of the spasmodic, anomic peasant rebellions of past centuries. Rather, peasants in these cases have engaged in long drawn-out revolutions in a variety of institutionalized ways—as political cadres, as disciplined soldiers, as loyal suppliers of food, money, and shelter, and as active and passive members of a host of revolutionary organizations and groups. With the success of the Chinese Communists and the Viet Minh, with the prolonged struggle of the National Liberation Front (NLF) in Vietnam, and with numerous other attempts at revolution by

[1] The meaning of revolution used here is that of Meusel quoted by George I. Blanksten, "Revolutions," in *Government and Politics in Latin America*, ed. Harold E. Davis (New York: Ronald, 1958), p. 121. "A major change in the political order—not merely a shift in the personnel of the government or a reorientation of its concrete policies—must be preceded or accompanied by a drastic change in the relation among the different groups and classes in society." Also, there is violence used in achieving this change.

226

guerrilla fighters,[2] peasants have become the focal point for major political upheaval in the third world. In the Chinese and Vietnamese cases, they have acted as a class and made up the majority of the revolutionary movements dedicated to the overthrow of the existing political institutions—movements with formal, hierarchical structures and well-articulated political goals.

There has been a lag, however, in the development of social and political theories which could explain the complexity of peasant participation in institutionalized revolutionary struggles. Numerous questions remain unanswered. Why have peasants emerged as such decisive political figures? Why now, in the twentieth century? Why has the character of their participation changed from the more eruptive, anomic qualities of the French Revolution, the Taiping Rebellion, and the Russian Revolution to the organized aspects of the Chinese and Vietnamese Revolutions?

Previously existing theories have been stretched and adapted in all sorts of ways to incorporate the novel events of peasants' participation in revolutionary institutions since the 1920s. Marxist theorists have been at pains to analyze the new events in orthodox terms. They have referred to peasants as allies of the proletariat in revolution—at times when the presence of any industrial workers was negligible. Or else they have spoken of the transformation of the peasantry into a segment of the proletariat.[3]

---

[2] For an account of the Latin American situation, see Richard Gott, *Guerrilla Movements in Latin America* (London: Nelson, 1970).

[3] William Hinton, *Fanshen: A Documentary of Revolution in a Chinese Village* (New York: Monthly Review Press, 1966), p. 184, writes of the Chinese Revolution: "The Party remained a working class Party which *transformed* its non-working class recruits rather than allowing them to transform it." Hinton quotes Liu Shao-ch'i, Mao Tse-tung's former comrade-in-arms, as saying that the peasants and intellectuals studied and accepted Marxism-Leninism and Mao's

In the United States, much social scientific effort followed the government lead and resulted in a largely useless, if not pernicious, body of tactical recipes for counterinsurgency.[4] But serious American social and political theorists, as well, have had difficulty incorporating peasant revolutions into existing theories. As we shall see in the Conclusion, their theories have most often simply made such revolutions the end point of a spectrum of all rebellious violence, from riots to coups d'état. The same sociological and social psychological concepts are used to explain all these types of rebellious violence.

This chapter rejects the view that long-term participation by peasants in revolutionary institutions can be understood in the same terms as more eruptive, anomic forms of collective violence. A more cogent explanation can be built upon the theory developed in the first nine chapters of this book on social and political change in peasant communities.[5] The hypothesis here is that peasants' participation in institutionalized revolutionary movements is initially an attempt on their part

---

theories. "In the course of doing this they changed their original character and became Marxist-Leninist fighters of the *proletariat*" (p. 179; my emphasis).

[4] Topping the list is Charles Wolf, Jr., *United States Policy and the Third World* (Boston: Little, Brown, 1967). Also see Nathan Leites and Charles Wolf, Jr., *Rebellion and Authority: An Analytic Essay on Insurgent Conflicts* (Chicago: Markham, 1970); T. N. Greene ed., *The Guerrilla—And How to Fight Him: Selections from the Marine Corps Gazette* (New York: Praeger, 1962); and David Galula, *Counterinsurgency Warfare: Theory and Practice* (New York: Praeger, 1964). The British have also produced some works in this vein. Perhaps the most simplistic of this list is Douglas Hyde, *The Peaceful Assault: The Pattern of Subversion* (London: The Bodley Head, 1963).

[5] The explanation offered in this chapter is not a comprehensive theory of peasant revolution. The best start in developing such a theory has been made by Barrington Moore, Jr., *Social Origins of Dictatorship and Democracy: Lord and Peasant in the Making of the Modern World* (Boston: Beacon Press, 1966).

to solve certain individual and local problems through the immediate selective incentives offered by the revolutionary organizations.

These problems stem from household economic crises and from subsequent involvement in the national market. Central to the analysis of peasant revolutions are the changes which induced increased participation in an institutionalized network that is often structurally incomplete, corrupt, and monopolistic. Revolutionary participation, it is hypothesized, is initially a type of Level 2 political action. In other words, it is a political response to the continuing difficulties peasants face because of their increased outside participation, involving a trade-off in which peasants give organized support and receive individual means to overcome the shortcomings in the network of economic institutions.

The explanation presented here for peasants' participation in organized revolutionary movements is a deglamorizing one. It does not account for such revolutionary participation in terms of an explosive reaction from the growing frustration which arises from deprivation. Nor does this book view peasants as so free from poverty or so naive about the sincerity of outsiders that they would commit themselves to a long and highly dangerous struggle based simply on broad altruistic goals. Rather, outside revolutionaries initially must address themselves to the changes in outside participation which peasants have undergone and the mundane structural problems such changes have wrought for individuals, households, and communities.

PREREQUISITES OF REVOLUTION: ECONOMIC NEEDS AND INTENSITY OF LEADERSHIP

The probability of peasants' participation in institutionalized revolutionary movements depends on three factors. First, there must have been increased market participation by peasants stemming from economic crises. For example, the autarchic village in Vietnam, as John McAlister and Paul Mus call it, became a thing of the past as increasing external demands were put on individual peasants instead of the village as a whole. Under the French colonial rule, the control of the central administration began to reach down to the individual level as household taxes in money, rather than village taxes in kind, were demanded. Increased involvement in the cash economy resulted in a new social stratification among the Vietnamese as more usurious loans resulted in an increasing consolidation of land in larger estates.[6] This crisis for the impoverished peasant was compounded by a rapidly growing population.

Those limited areas where peasants have managed to maintain a severely limited degree of external relations, subsistence-oriented areas (e.g., certain mountainous areas of China),[7] will prove much more difficult to penetrate by revolutionary organizers.[8] The same is true where strong and vigilant lords continue to provide a wide scope of high primacy resources.

Second, this market participation must be fraught with the dangers and unprofitability associated with corruption, monopoly, and structural incompleteness. Where the government has failed in creating viable, well-regulated institutions and where powerful lords make peasant participation unprofitable, peasants are more likely to welcome other institutional arrangements.

Returning to our example of Vietnam, as the economic crisis developed, the peasants found no adequate network of national institutions through which they could alleviate the

[6] John T. McAlister, Jr. and Paul Mus, *The Vietnamese and Their Revolution*, Harper Torchbooks (New York: Harper and Row, 1970), p. 41.

[7] See John W. Lewis, "The Study of Chinese Political Culture," *World Politics* 18 (April 1966), 509.

[8] See Maurice Zeitlin, *Revolutionary Politics and the Cuban Working Class* (Princeton, N.J.: Princeton University Press, 1967), pp. 60-61 and 144-145.

230

stress.[9] McAlister and Mus state that the peasantry was reduced to a social infrastructure under French policy: "However, it was lacking a superstructure that might have linked
the infrastructure to a new age."[10] Even after the French
departed, the same problems continued to affect South Vietnam. The all-important land question, Samuel Popkin writes,
was handled through government promises of rent ceilings, a
government loan program, providing for displaced persons,
etc. Yet the lack of organizational components and political
commitment to bring Diem's promises to fruition on the village level meant that little was actually accomplished to relieve the stress.[11] Local lords continued to disrupt weak peasants' attempts to gain income through outside marketing
institutions. Insecurity of outside economic involvement for
peasants stemmed also from the monopolistic rice merchants
who dominated much of the marketing system.[12]

Conditions of monopoly, corruption, and structural incompleteness are most likely to exist in marginal and frontier
areas. The stratification patterns are most likely to be those
of the second pattern (see Chapter VIII), that is, where the
peasants have not been driven from the land by extensive,
mechanized farming.

The third factor determining the probability of peasants'

[9] An interesting parallel in Europe can be found in Spain. See
Éléna de la Souchère, *An Explanation of Spain* (New York: Random
House, 1964), p. 98.

[10] McAlister and Mus, *The Vietnamese and Their Revolution*, p.
102.

[11] Samuel L. Popkin, "South Vietnam," in *Conflict in World
Politics*, ed. Steven L. Spiegel and Kenneth N. Waltz (Cambridge,
Mass.: Winthrop, 1971), p. 268. Jeffrey R. Race writes that the
striking fact about the land program in the province of Long An
was that "the maximum impact of the program was limited, even
on paper." *War Comes to Long An: Revolutionary Conflict in a
Vietnamese Province* (Berkeley: University of California Press,
1972), p. 60, and see his whole discussion, pp. 56-61.

[12] Robert L. Sansom, *The Economics of Insurgency in the Mekong
Delta of Vietnam* (Cambridge, Mass.: The M.I.T. Press, 1970),
p. 103.

participation in revolutionary movements is the degree to which revolutionary leadership appears, with an organizational framework capable of absorbing peasants and then expanding power through their recruitment. As in other cases of national political organizations, revolutionary movements are created by the impetus of those from outside the peasant class. Although increasing work and commercial interdependencies give peasants the basis for similar role-playing in a formal, voluntary political organization, they are still relatively weak in organizational ability compared to other classes in the society. Also they generally possess relatively little of the resources, such as expertise and education, associated with organization building. As a result, the participation of peasants in revolutionary organizations is preceded by the development of an organizational superstructure by students, intellectuals, and disaffected members of the middle class.

This view of peasants as capable of being organized, but needing outside leadership and direction, is put forth by Camilo Torres, the former Catholic priest who led guerrillas in the mountains of Colombia: "For many years the poor of our country have been waiting for the word of command to throw themselves into the final struggle against the oligarchy. . . . The people are waiting for their leaders, who by their example and their presence will sound the call to arms."[13]

Like many others who aspire to lead peasants in revolution, Camilo Torres made the mistake of taking such rhetoric too seriously. He actually seemed to believe that large numbers of peasants would accept with open arms any revolutionary outside "leadership" that might appear. The peasants' numerous encounters with outsiders of other classes has taught them more than simply to await "the call to arms." Self-sacrificing action, action that offers no immediate return in benefits, is shunned by peasants. The revolutionary looks no different

---

[13] Quoted in Luis Mercier Vega, *Guerrillas in Latin America: The Technique of the Counter-State* (New York: Frederick A. Praeger, 1969), pp. 11-12.

from all the other city folk who have taken advantage of the peasants' weaknesses.

Like the other types of political organizations that peasants join, revolutionary movements must trade off inducements to individual peasants in return for their participation and support. They must demonstrate to peasants that their organization can supply villagers' particular needs, which have arisen as communities have moved from an inward- to an outward-orientation. In the Balkans, Fischer-Galati writes, "outside leadership, unless forced upon him, was acceptable only when trusted, when guaranteeing the realization of his pragmatic aims, and above all, when providing adequate military protection."[14]

Yet, in offering material inducements to overcome corruption, monopoly, and structural incompleteness, revolutionary organizations must be even more attractive than other types of political organizations because the risks of involvement are much greater for peasants.[15] Peasants are quite aware that there are costs involved in any kind of political participation, ranging from losses of valuable time to incurring the wrath of local lords. Involvement in revolutionary movements, directed against specific classes, however, can bring severe retaliation, and organizers must overcome the fear that peasants have of that retaliation.

Revolutionary organizers differ from other political organizers in another respect as well. Revolutionaries do not aim merely to ameliorate individual and local conditions in the network of economic and political institutions in order to gain initial peasant support on their behalf. Instead, they seek to supply an increasing number of components leading to the development of a new network, autonomous from the existing national system.

[14] Stephen Fischer-Galati, "The Peasantry as a Revolutionary Force in the Balkans," *Journal of Central European Affairs* 23 (April 1963), 22.

[15] Race, *War Comes to Long An*, p. 183, mentions accepting the risks of involvement as an important calculation for the peasant.

In Vietnam, the Viet Minh and later the NLF first responded to the situation in which there was a network of institutions lacking essential components and being monopolized by large merchants and landlords. Although we will discuss below more specifically the types of inducements they used, we can say here that support for the revolution was gained by a dual policy. The revolutionary leadership sought to make the existing political and economic institutions even more incomplete by disrupting their workings. Simultaneously, the revolutionaries sought to supply the missing and disrupted components of those institutions through their own network. Their goals at first entailed seeking to provide selected services and then increasingly to develop a totally autonomous network.[16] Their policies were designed to attract first the innovators who would use the economic crises to expand outside participation if the environment were secure enough. And then the revolutionaries sought mass support from poorer peasants who moved to obtain relief from the crises only after the innovators paved the way.

Structural incompleteness, monopolies, and corruption are almost universal factors, in varying degrees of intensity, in Latin America and Asia today. The need for components and adequate regulation, and removal of powerful monopolists to allow greater penetration of the market on a more profitable basis is great almost everywhere in the third world, yet significant numbers of peasants have participated in long-term revolutions in only a smattering of countries. The key to this paradox lies not in a scale of "revolutionary readiness"[17] of peasants but in an understanding of crucial external variables. Most important of these is the degree of revolution-

[16] Douglas Pike, *Viet Cong: The Organization and Techniques of the National Liberation Front of South Vietnam* (Cambridge, Mass.: The M.I.T. Press, 1966), pp. 298, 303.

[17] See, for example, Lewis, "The Study of Chinese Political Culture," pp. 510-511.

ary leadership to which the peasants of an area are exposed. In other words, peasants are most likely to participate in the complex organizations of revolutionary movements where outside leadership presents them with capable institutions, offering the inducements for which peasants are willing to trade support.

As we have said, the intensity of leadership must be greater than for other cases of political organizing because of the risks involved in peasant complicity with the revolutionaries. No peasants would accept merely a pack of cigarettes for some act of support as they occasionally do in committing their vote. Once the risk factor is weighed, however, the greater the benefits offered the more support the peasants are willing to give both in frequency and intensity. They can be only passive supporters of the revolution, e.g., by not divulging the leaders' whereabouts to the authorities, or they can be involved in various degrees of active participation as supporters, political cadres, or soldiers.

In China, the very presence of the Chinese Communist movement was a key factor in determining which areas became revolutionary. Their organizational presence, their vitality, and their capacity to expand, all acted to combine with the shortcomings and injustices peasants faced to result in a large, strong movement.[18] Various exogenous factors (outside the scope of this study) determine in which countries such outside revolutionaries will appear and where they will provide a high degree of revolutionary leadership in those countries in which they do appear.

Certainly, one crucial factor is the degree to which the area can provide freedom from repression and destruction by the state's force, especially while the movement is small and vulnerable. These areas seem to correlate with ones where struc-

[18] Roy Hofheinz, Jr., "The Ecology of Chinese Communist Success: Rural Influence Patterns, 1923-45," in *Chinese Communist Politics in Action*, ed. A. Doak Barnett (Seattle: University of Washington Press, 1969), p. 77.

tural incompleteness of the market is likely to exist, i.e., areas of poor administration, communication, and transportation.[19] That is, areas where the state's armed forces are relatively weak are also likely to have little penetration by the state's political and economic institutions. In China, the revolutionaries were successful in border areas and the great rear area[20] and were notably unsuccessful where advance communications and concentrated economic power made the state's security forces a greater threat.[21]

Where all these conditions—increased market participation, a flawed network, and revolutionary leadership—do not exist, even the most severe peasant deprivation, relative or absolute, can lead to passivity. In colonial Indonesia, for example, the lucrative coffee- and sugar-growing enterprises were entirely in the hands of the Dutch, who used forced, imported labor on their huge plantations. Upward mobility and capital intensification of agriculture were closed to the Javanese peasants, as the two halves of the dual economy operated almost totally exclusive of each other. The crisis of a rapidly growing population, then, was handled by what Clifford Geertz calls "shared poverty." Land fragmentation increased, and a falling per capita income came to be expected. No revolutionaries appeared, and little opportunity to move away from primarily subsistence production developed. Rather, the Javanese peasants kept themselves alive through "agricultural involution" of

[19] Robert W. McColl, "A Political Geography of Revolution: China, Vietnam, and Thailand," *The Journal of Conflict Resolution* 11 (June 1967), 155, calls these areas in China ones of weak or confused political control. Also see Eric R. Wolf, "Peasant Rebellion and Revolution," in *National Liberation: Revolution in the Third World*, ed. Norman Miller and Roderick Aya (New York: The Free Press, 1971), p. 57. In such areas, the application of military force by the government without penetration of its economic and political institutions can lead to counterproductive violence, that is, violence which aids the revolutionaries. For example, see Race, *War Comes to Long An*, p. 152.

[20] Hofheinz, "The Ecology of Chinese Communist Success," pp. 73-76.

[21] Lewis, "The Study of Chinese Political Culture," pp. 509-510.

236

wet rice, that is, a phenomenally labor-intensive type of agriculture.[22] A market closed to more complete peasant penetration and increasing poverty became expected aspects of life.

A Theory of Peasant Participation in Institutionalized Revolutionary Movements

We thus have seen that there are three prerequisites for the institutionalization of sustained peasant participation in a revolutionary movement: (1) a peasantry that has been driven to increased outside participation, (2) in an economic network full of shortcomings and injustices, and (3) an outside revolutionary leadership willing and able to invest organizational effort to build a new network of economic and political institutions to challenge the old. The goal of the revolutionaries is to build new institutions by mobilizing the peasantry (and perhaps other formerly dormant groups) into politics and to then use those institutions to destroy the existing political institutions.[23]

The key question that remains is, what is the specific basis for the creation of political and economic institutions strong enough to challenge the state's existing ones? What is the process in which the three prerequisites interact so that large numbers of politically inactive peasants become parts of powerful institutions challenging the very existence of the state which has long affected their lives? All too often these critical questions are glossed over by reference to the revolutionaries' propaganda, organization, or symbol manipulation and to the peasants' readiness to heed any call to arms.

There are one of two assumptions in such explanations. First, the peasants may be viewed as an undifferentiated mass,

[22] Clifford Geertz, *Agricultural Involution: The Process of Ecological Change in Indonesia* (Berkeley: University of California Press, 1966), p. 100.

[23] This is what Samuel P. Huntington labels the "Eastern Revolution." *Political Order in Changing Societies* (New Haven: Yale University Press, 1968), p. 266.

utterly malleable or else totally gullible to any messianic appeals. In this assumption, peasants are not seen as having revolutionary tendencies prior to the coming of the outside leaders, but neither are they resistant. Instead, they are seen completely as a dependent variable who bend to the cajoling or coercion of outsiders. Second, the assumption may be that peasants are so impatient or frustrated with the current state of events that the mere appeal to revolution will spark loyalty and support. In this view, peasants are understood to have a definite revolutionary tendency, being highly dissatisfied with society's total array of institutions.

The thrust of this study has been to reject such assumptions and point instead to the specific patterns of interaction and accommodation between peasants and those from other classes. The following analysis is an explanation of initial peasant revolutionary behavior which views the peasants neither as totally manipulable nor as opponents of the entire political system just waiting for the call to arms. Instead, it focuses on the specifics of the interaction of outside forces and peasant needs. It sees various segments of the peasantry seeking to solve certain very specific problems that arise as villages move from an inward- to an outward-orientation. These problems stem from the conditions of monopoly, corruption, and structural incompleteness peasants face in their expanded outside involvement.

Social exchange lies at the heart of the creation of any institution or organization. Peter Blau has written of social exchange: "An individual who supplies rewarding services to another obligates him. To discharge this obligation, the second must furnish benefits to the first in turn."[24] The same is true within institutions. A peasant who furnishes support, i.e., adapts his behavior to the demands of the organizational role he plays expects that organization to give him benefits in turn, benefits he would otherwise not get.

What is the specific process of social exchange in the mo-

[24] Peter M. Blau, *Exchange and Power in Social Life* (New York: John Wiley and Sons, 1964), p. 89.

238

bilization of peasants into revolutionary organizations? The revolutionaries, for their part, seek power to overthrow the existing political system. They build institutions to accomplish their goals because, as Kalman Silvert says, institutions are the power train of politics: "Through institutions power is made manifest, and the raw power of individuals and of groups is turned into applied power."[25] Institutions and organizations can accomplish the harnessing of power for the simple reason that they make the behavior of large numbers of people predictable.[26] By assigning varying tasks, the leaders know that a predictable division of labor can be assured for the actualization of complex and broad goals.

Consequently, revolutionaries must no longer wait for the collapse of the state through an instantaneous mobilization of large numbers into violent action. Rather, by painstakingly building institutions, which are merely sets of routinized behavior patterns that cluster around certain specific functions,[27] they can increasingly gain control over the political environment. Frustration may spur riots and rebellions in the streets, but it is very doubtful that it can motivate people to perform highly specific, demanding tasks within organizations over a prolonged period.

What, then, is the other half of the social exchange? Why are peasant members willing to perform tasks within institutions? This question, although seemingly straightforward and simple—and certainly a basic question in organization theory —for some reason is not generally asked in the literature on peasant revolution. Although theorists speak of the organizational ability of the revolutionaries, they only see that as a means of the leaders' creating power.[28] The corollary ques-

[25] Kalman H. Silvert, *Man's Power: A Biased Guide to Political Thought and Action* (New York: The Viking Press, 1970), p. 28.

[26] See James G. March and Herbert A. Simon, *Organizations* (New York: Wiley, 1958), p. 4.

[27] *Ibid.*, pp. 28-29.

[28] Chalmers A. Johnson, *Peasant Nationalism and Communist Power: The Emergence of Revolutionary China 1937-1945* (Stanford: Stanford University Press, 1962), pp. 11-12, writes that many have

tion of why peasants participate in the organization is either not asked or is answered by reference to diffuse popular support (peasants' revolutionary tendencies) or else to the coercive elements of the revolutionaries (the ease of manipulating peasants).[29]

Organizational theory has long accepted that people are recruited into institutions and give the leadership power only if they receive benefits.[30] Each member receives inducements to join and continues to participate as long as those inducements outweigh his contributions[31] and outweigh the risks (the probability of other losses) involved in joining. The benefits and inducements are both positive and negative, coming as rewards and sanctions. Thus inducements may be in the form of material rewards or sanctions, social rewards or sanctions (gaining or losing status), or coercive sanctions. "Social sanctions and social rewards," Mancur Olson writes, "are 'selective incentives'; that is, they are among the kinds of incentives that may be used to mobilize a latent group."[32] In other words, people join specific organizations because of immediate, *personal* benefits or sanctions, rather than for benefits that they would receive whether they personally joined or not.

---

elevated "organization" to the level of a sociological secret weapon and others too readily accept a theory that revolutionaries only manipulate peasants. "Analyses of Communist methods that make much of organizational technique at the expense of operational context are erroneous" (p. 72).

[29] Sansom, *The Economics of Insurgency*, p. 242; and for one who believes in the power of pure coercion, see Charles Wolf, Jr., "Insurgency and Counterinsurgency: New Myths and Old Realities," *Yale Review* 56 (Winter 1967), 225-241. Similarly, for all Pike's talk of organization, he assumes the corollary question to be nonexistent. Pike, *Viet Cong.*

[30] Blau, *Exchange and Power*, p. 29.

[31] March and Simon, *Organizations*, p. 84.

[32] Mancur Olson, Jr., *The Logic of Collective Action: Public Goods and the Theory of Groups* (Cambridge, Mass.: Harvard University Press, 1965), p. 61.

Sanctions alone are inadequate in gaining the kind of substantial regularized changes in behavior demanded by institutions. A person may perform a single act or even a series of acts solely because of the threat of sanctions, particularly coercive ones. An organization building a power base, however, demands a continuous performance of varying tasks by many members. No organization can function long if behavior is not routinized, and behavior is not routinized if someone performs only with a gun at his head. Incidentally, the revolutionaries' use of sanctions in certain situations should not be taken as proof of their autocratic designs and lack of "popular support." All institutions, and particularly those of governments, depend on a mix of sanctions and benefits in order to achieve their goals.

By decentralizing control, revolutionaries can use an effective combination of benefits and sanctions to recruit peasants to their institutions and organizations. For *particular* villages and areas, they can buy or market crops, redistribute land, provide harvest labor, build roads, supply communication facilities and, most importantly, break the power of the exploiters of the peasantry—the corrupt officials and the monopolistic lords and merchants.

Of course, some of these benefits are not truly selective incentives since they are enjoyed by entire villages or locales. Nevertheless, a collective benefit such as a road provides an added inducement to peasants to participate when combined with highly effective individual incentives and sanctions. Revolutionaries can buy rice only from those who join one of the revolutionary organizations or they can supply educational and medical facilities selectively. Their early success depends on applying that which peasants feel they need but the state has not provided. As Ted Gurr states, "Dissidents can increase the scope of their support and their effectiveness by creating the rewarding patterns of action that regimes fail to provide."[33] Once it has grown somewhat in size and capabili-

[33] Ted Robert Gurr, *Why Men Rebel* (Princeton, N.J.: Princeton University Press, 1970), p. 274.

ties through the use of such inducements, the revolutionary organization can then disrupt government operations, create more needs, and step in to supply those services itself. Over time, its hope is to build a practically autonomous political and economic network upon which the peasants would be dependent.

There are two distinct types of rewards in the process of social exchange which result in strong and autonomous revolutionary institutional networks. Each type draws upon a different segment of the peasantry. The first involves the expansion of the two primary institutions of the revolutionaries, their major political apparatus (e.g., the party) and their army. It also consists of the development of a leadership and skeleton for the host of other organizations that will arise. In this pattern, the primary selective incentive the revolutionaries can use is upward social mobility where other paths for such mobility are blocked.

In South Vietnam, the government recruited the urban middle and upper classes and the rural landlords and rich peasants into its civil service. "By contrast," Jeffrey Race writes, "the social basis of recruitment and promotion within the [Communist] Party was entirely different. Class origin was the key criterion, outweighing even technical skills of education in importance."[34] That is, peasants were selected before others as political cadres. Similarly, the equivalent of an officer's position in the revolutionary army can serve as a vehicle for peasant upward mobility, while the Saigon government continues to draw its officer corps from the elite.

In this first type of reward, upward mobility appeals most to those with sufficient resources and skills (such as educa-

[34] Race, *War Comes to Long An*, p. 168. Race goes on to write, "No matter how hard a government village chief worked, he could never hope to be more than a village chief, whereas a poor peasant [in the revolutionary apparatus] could hope to become the village secretary, the district secretary, or even higher—his lack of education and his inability to speak flawless French would not weigh against him. In fact, they would be in his favor" (p. 170). Also see Pike, *Viet Cong*, p. 230.

tion) to make outside alliances but who are unable to do so because of the lack of opportunity. These are the innovators who take advantage of the numerous economic crises in the village. Blocked from upward mobility in both the state's economic and political institutions, these peasants are attracted by the political opportunities offered by the revolutionaries. They use the new organizations' resources as the basis for a new stratification of the village.

These innovators often are the young of the village. Frequently, they feel frustrated by the concentration of power among the elders and are resentful that the distribution of economic and political power within the village has not changed as rapidly as changes in external relations. In short, opportunities for mobility are blocked within the village as well as on the outside. In the Chinese village of Long Bow, the members of the nucleus of the revolutionary organization were all under 25 years old.[35] The NLF consciously sought the young, recruiting 16- to 20-year-olds first, then 21 to 25, and finally people over 25 if they had some special talent.[36]

The second and much broader type of rewards in the process of exchange goes to the large number of peasants recruited for membership in the various institutions that the revolutionaries are building. As in other cases of stratification discussed in Chapter VIII, the opportunities for the mass of the peasants are determined, in large part, by the prior actions of the innovators. The revolutionary organization becomes the vehicle for solving material problems. Here the selective incentives that the revolutionary organization offers relate to the existing work experiences of the peasants. It does not create new jobs as it did for the innovators.

To succeed in this realm, the revolutionaries must assess and address themselves to the very mundane grievances of each particular village and even each stratum within the village. This is a slow and painstaking process. In the village

[35] Hinton, *Fanshen*, p. 90.
[36] Pike, *Viet Cong*, p. 287.

of Ai Ngai, for example, it took the NLF over two years of continuous political work to convince seventy people that joining the revolutionary movement would be of personal benefit.[37] McAlister and Mus conclude that the revolutionary organizations in Vietnam gave peasants the opportunity to become part of the world outside the village and to gain access to the attributes of that world.[38] Certainly, the supply by the NLF of education, medical care, drugs,[39] and transportation and communication facilities were important selective incentives to induce peasants to joint the second Vietnamese Revolution.

At times the NLF merely carried out the promises of rent ceilings and other programs made by a weak government.[40] Rent ceilings coupled with interest reductions and land redistribution,[41] enabled peasants to retain a greater share of what they produced. In other words, by breaking the power of the local lords, the NLF ensured that less was siphoned off for those who gave few or no services in exchange. Also by forcing the large merchants to withdraw from the market, the NLF destroyed the monopolistic and exploitative marketing system. This provided opportunities for the peasants to make new alliances through marketing.[42]

Sansom notes that consumption levels of rice in Vietnam rose in 1950-1952 for the first time since the Depression, indicating that the Viet Minh's distribution policies had the same effect as that of the NLF a decade later: "It appears that

[37] Race, *War Comes to Long An*, p. 189.

[38] McAlister and Mus, *The Vietnamese and Their Revolution*, p. 138.

[39] Pike, *Viet Cong*, pp. 281-283, 294.

[40] Popkin, "South Vietnam," p. 268.

[41] Land redistribution gained continuing support for the revolutionaries even though it was a single act on their part. This was accomplished because "each beneficiary of land redistribution retained his land only as long as he did not oppose the revolutionary movement, and indeed only as long as he assisted it in required ways." Race, *War Comes to Long An*, p. 174.

[42] Sansom, *The Economics of Insurgency*, p. 103.

the landlord's flight from the countryside in 1945-1946 and the related institutional controls enforced by the Viet Minh denied the landlord his one-half share of the crop in rents—leaving that share to the tenant, who consumed a portion of it."[43]

Besides supplying selective and collective rewards through new patterns of distribution, the NLF in the 1960s also gave the peasants the organizational framework (within the revolutionary movement, of course) to accomplish goals themselves. This enabled peasants to achieve increases in the level of production. Mutual aid teams were organized, for example, that could dig drainage and irrigation ditches. In one six-month period, the leaders claimed that 200,000 yards of canals were dug.[44] One of the revolutionaries' primary goals was to enable peasants to achieve an increase in food production. A 1962 NLF document stated: "The purpose of financial activities is to increase income, economize, and improve financial management."[45]

A similar pattern of social exchange developed in the latter part of the Chinese Revolution. Mao Tse-tung delineated in the 1920s some of the types of benefits that the revolutionaries would have to use to gain support and create power:

> If we do no other work than simply mobilizing the people to carry out the war, can we achieve the aim of defeating the enemy? Of course not. If we want to win, we still have a great deal of work. Leading the peasants in agrarian struggles and distributing land to them; arousing their labour enthusiasm so as to increase agricultural production; safeguarding the interests of the workers; establishing co-operatives; developing trade with outside areas; solving the problems that face the masses, problems of clothing, food, and shelter, of fuel, rice, cooking oil, and salt, of health and hygiene, and of marriage. In short, all problems facing the masses in their actual life should claim our attention. If we

[43] *Ibid.*, p. 39.   [44] Pike, *Viet Cong*, p. 270.
[45] Quoted in *ibid.*, p. 298.

245

have these problems at heart and solve them to the satisfaction of the masses, we shall really become the organizers of the life of the masses. . . .[46]

Mao addressed himself to the shortcomings of the market network: the hoarding of salt, the shortage and high price of rice, an inadequate wooden bridge. These are problems that peasants feel more acutely as they move from self-sufficiency to more reliance on the market. Mao also spoke of other mundane needs, such as primary schools,[47] and he noted the peasants' desire for roads and their inability to organize to build them.[48]

Years later, the success of the Chinese Communist Party hinged on the translation of these insights into strategies for the solution of peasant needs. There was no eruptive mobilization of the peasantry in the Chinese Revolution but sustained recruitment and participation. In the final years of the struggle, cooperatives spread throughout the base areas, stimulating higher agricultural production.[49] The "to the village" movement which began in 1941 sent students and intellectuals to aid in the harvest and moved trained cadres to the most local levels of administration[50] so benefits could be even more selective. By 1943, all revolutionary organizations, including the army, were involved in agricultural production. The goal was an autonomous network of economic institutions in North China.

As peasants participated in institutions that stretched far beyond the village, other needs and desires developed. The

[46] Mao Tse-tung, *Mind the Living Conditions of the Masses and Attend to the Methods of Work* (Peking: Foreign Languages Press, 1953), p. 2.

[47] *Ibid.*, pp. 3, 5.

[48] Mao Tse-tung, *Report of an Investigation into the Peasant Movement in Hunan* (Peking: Foreign Languages Press, 1953), p. 62.

[49] Mark Selden, "Revolution and Third World Development, People's War and the Transformation of Peasant Society," in *National Liberation*, ed. Miller and Aya, pp. 219-221.

[50] Mark Selden, "The Yenan Legacy: The Mass Line," in *Chinese Communist Politics in Action*, ed. Barnet, pp. 122-124.

246

revolutionaries supplied local literacy teams, newspapers, magazines, schools,[51] and hospitals.[52] "Security from outside attack, protection against internal enemies, the monopoly over trade, business, and travel were all signs of the CCP's increasing ability to command the environment of the village."[53] Once they could supply these services and provide an adequate institutional network, the revolutionaries had even more ability to use their benefits selectively to promote membership and active participation in their organizations.[54]

These mundane rewards are initially most enticing to those who are most frustrated by the inadequacies and injustice of outside institutions. These are usually middle peasants who produce a surplus and seek to penetrate the market more fully but are stymied by obstacles that make such activities unprofitable or impossible.[55] Later, the revolutionary movement

[51] Johnson, *Peasant Nationalism*, pp. 151-154.

[52] Hofheinz, "The Ecology of Chinese Communist Success," pp. 40-47.

[53] *Ibid.*, pp. 36-37.

[54] An interesting counterexample of the Chinese and Vietnamese cases is the revolution and civil war in Spain. There, the anarchists did not build an organization that sustained peasant involvement. The movement depended more upon eruption than organization. See Gabriel Jackson, "The Origins of Spanish Anarchism," *The South-western Social Science Quarterly* 36 (September 1955), 136.

[55] The more secure peasants have enough leeway to revolt since they would be less subject to the force of traditional sanctions should the revolutionaries fail. See Henry A. Landsberger, "The Role of Peasant Movements and Revolts in Development," in *Latin American Peasant Movements*, ed. Landsberger (Ithaca, N.Y.: Cornell University Press, 1969), p. 39; Kathleen Gough, "Peasant Resistance and Revolt in South India," *Pacific Affairs* 41 (Winter 1968-1969), 529-530, on Communist struggles in Kerala and Tanjore; Robert A. White, S.J., "Mexico: The Zapata Movement and the Revolution," in *Latin American Peasant Movements*, ed. Landsberger, p. 17, found the same in the Mexican Revolution. He wrote that it was not the lowest peons who joined the peasant movement but those who were in the process of losing the most. James C. Davies, "Toward a Theory of Revolution," *American Sociological Review* 27 (February 1962), 7, writes, "It is when the chains have been loosened somewhat, so

addresses itself to the problems of poorer peasants. Through its network of institutions, it disrupts the existing institutions and induces participation by the very poorest with programs such as land redistribution. In this manner, it gains the support of those who were subject to the severest exploitation and to sanctions by lords for engaging in deviant behavior.[56]

It is the institutionalization of this process of social exchange which results in a revolutionary peasantry. Prior to the coming of outside leaders, the peasants are not necessarily revolutionary in spirit, in the sense of wanting to overthrow the state's institutions. They are not simply awaiting the call to arms and the organizational ability of an outside revolutionary leadership. They are, however, aware of the glaring deficiencies in the broader network within which they interact, shortcomings which prevent an easy integration into the new world to which they have turned in order to solve their economic crises.

These peasants seek, as best they can, to eliminate, or at least minimize, those deficiencies. Thus, peasants' dissatisfaction is with very specific aspects of their immediate environment, and they usually do not have a vision of the overthrow of the entire system with which they are still relatively unfamiliar. There may be cases where outside revolutionaries take advantage of peasant eruptions against local conditions, but these revolutionaries still must institutionalize organizations and procedures for peasant participation in order to achieve their own long-term, far-reaching goals. Does this mean that peasants can never gain self-awareness as a class

that they can be cast off without a high probability of losing life, that people are put in a condition of proto-rebelliousness." Also, see E. Wolf, "Peasant Rebellion and Revolution," pp. 55-56, and *Peasant Wars of the Twentieth Century* (New York: Harper and Row, 1969), pp. 290-291.

[56] See Isabel and David Crook, *Revolution in a Chinese Village: Ten Mile Inn* (London: Routledge and Kegan Paul, 1959), p. 114; and Hamza Alavi, "Peasants and Revolution," in *The Socialist Register 1965*, ed. Ralph Miliband and John Saville (New York: Monthly Review Press, 1965), pp. 274-275.

and act on that basis? Not necessarily, for participation in revolutionary institutions gives peasants the experience which they lacked previously. Through their effective participation in the revolutionary movement, peasants gain confidence in their ability to achieve larger goals. And, just as significantly, they gain confidence in their ability to cooperate with others in order to achieve these goals.

Class consciousness does not develop from exploitation alone. Instead, such collective self-awareness develops out of a history of extensive interaction and interdependency—exactly the kind of relationship peasants have always lacked. The revolutionary organization can provide these opportunities. As in other cases of incorporation into political organizations (see Chapter IX), there are four analytic levels of revolutionary actions and goals by peasants, ending with the development of an orientation to seek gains for the entire peasant class.

1) *Peasants accommodate to revolutionary institutions.* Although this is the most passive level, for the revolutionaries it is crucial. Especially in the early stages of revolution, revolutionaries stake their lives on the hope that peasants will not expose them to the authorities. In such cases, the revolutionaries depend upon the peasants' lack of commitment to the existing political order. This level may be bypassed if revolutionaries are able to offer an immediate apparatus to deal with peasants' grievances against *local* injustices and are able to apply sanctions against recalcitrant peasants. This could occur if the organization has been established in one area and is brought intact to another part of the country.

2) *Peasants seek individual material and social gains from the revolutionaries.* This comes in the initial process of social exchange of which we have been speaking.

3) *Peasants seek collective gains for their particular group, segment, or village.* Usually, only with the successful history of a process of social exchange in which they get individual benefits in return for their active support and only with the continuation of this process are peasants willing to expand the

249

nature of their revolutionary action to engage in projects for which there is no immediate personal gain but in which collective, local goals are achieved.

There is another manner in which revolutionaries can stimulate action oriented toward collective, local goals. In cases where some aspects of the village social organization are still viable despite the increases in outside relations, the revolutionaries can win the village over as a whole. They can then take advantage of the old patterns of authority which have not yet lost their hold entirely to spur collectively oriented political action. The lack of selective material benefits, in such cases, may mean that the commitment of individuals to the revolutionaries is not very deep. Because Level 2 has been omitted, the revolutionaries cannot gain the same confidence as they can with peasants who first had a history of success on Level 2. At times, then, whole villages may switch their support away from the revolutionaries.

4) *Peasants seek an overthrow of the present political order to be replaced by the personnel, institutions, and programs of the revolutionary movement.* The internalization of such broad goals and the willingness to engage in self-sacrificing action comes only after success has been achieved in numerous other instances where personal and local interests are involved. Commitment to revolutionary ideals grows out of previous success. Repeated social action within the revolutionary organization produces a political commitment to the survival of that organization and to the actualization of its goals. Such commitment comes first and most often from the innovators whose material and social standing as leaders of local, revolutionary organizations is dependent on the success of the movement.

In his fascinating book, *Fanshen*, William Hinton recounts some of the motives for various peasants' joining the Communist Party in the Chinese village of Long Bow. The reasons included a desire to gain land from a redistribution of landlords' property, an attempt to protect one's family from possible recriminations, an effort to become influential and to gain glory, and a wish to strike down local despots.[57] Even among the most revolutionary of peasants, there was no vision of social and political revolution but rather the desire for personal upward mobility and for the landlords' fields. At its most political level, the desire was to achieve relief by eliminating local despots. As a result of the effectiveness[58] of the Long Bow revolutionary organization, these Party members became dedicated to the principles and goals of the Party, and their fellow peasants also became committed to the success of the revolution.

Kao Pin-ying lived in Yulin hsien (China) with his parents and uncle. Without land they survived as day laborers until 1942 when Kao's parents died. Having heard that in Yenan the Communists were letting people have land and freedom from taxes for three years, he migrated to the village of Liu Ling with just a pack on his back. Kao was far from a revolutionary. In fact, he did not join the revolutionaries' organization until *five* years later after he received a beating for being a suspected guerrilla. In 1942 his goal was simply to escape his landless condition by living in a Communist administered area and taking the benefits offered there.[59] The machinations of national politics and the overthrow of the political system are usually thoughts far from the minds of peasants such as Kao. It is only after recurrent experience within the revolutionary framework that the individual accepts the revolution's goals as his own.

This change from revolutionary action for personal gain (Level 2) to action for broader social and political goals (Level 4) presents an instructive analytic lesson. When peasants were inward-oriented, in most cases the most appropriate levels of analysis to explain social and political action were the household and the community. With the great expansion of outside involvement, the village social and political organi-

[57] Hinton, *Fanshen*, p. 181.

[58] *Ibid.*, pp. 118, 125.

[59] Jan Myrdal, *Report from a Chinese Village* (New York: Pantheon, 1965), p. 102.

zation and the household have a diminished effect upon such action, and the individual increasingly becomes the appropriate level of analysis. But once new forms of institutionalized social exchange emerge in a coherent network of institutions, then again social and political organization becomes an increasingly important component of social and political action. The new social and political organization, however, has a much wider scope than just the village and has individuals, rather than households, as building blocks. Once institutionalized into a wider social and political system, peasants more often see goals in individual *and* class or group terms, rather than in terms of the household and the village.

WAR AND REVOLUTION

Many peasants who are not directly exposed to revolutionary leadership often adapt to slowly increasing poverty, as occurred in Java. Revolutionaries, in fact, are likely to be more successful among peasants who find their normal social patterns suddenly disrupted than among those who have had years to develop means of coping with an insecure environment. In both Jan Myrdal's and Isabel and David Crook's accounts of Chinese villages, one is struck by the number of peasants, like Kao, who had their routines upset through the death of their kin before they joined revolutionary organizations. Also, in Long Bow (China), one finds that T'ien-ming, for example, one of the first to join the Communists, was an orphan and also a bachelor at the relatively late age of 20.[60]

The disruption of their normal means of livelihood, as well as their responsibilities, meant they were free to engage in new types of social exchange. We can hypothesize that the faster the *rate* of the disruption of peasants' economic patterns

[60] Hinton, *Fanshen*, p. 89.

252

and of the creation of an economic crisis, the more likely will peasants be open to the efforts of outside revolutionary organizers. Conversely, the slower the rate and the greater time peasants have to develop adaptive mechanisms to increasing poverty, the more difficult will revolutionaries find the process of organization.

War is one event which affects large numbers of peasants and which often occurs in such a short span that there is no time for development of adaptive mechanisms. The rate of disruption is conducive to revolutionary organization. The failure of the state to provide protection and the disruption of various components of the institutional environment point out to peasants how little they are receiving in their social exchanges.

In such cases, economic crises intensify greatly in months instead of decades. Mechanisms allowing for shared poverty that are able to deal with a single crop failure or a population growing over time cannot cope with two, three, or four consecutive crop losses. Adaptation in such a telescoped time period is almost impossible, and, as a result, peasants are more willing than usual to risk loss of the minimal benefits they receive in their current institutional exchanges for other institutional arrangements. This is especially true since one of the major benefits of their usual social exchanges, security, and one of the major sanctions, effective policing, are often wholly disrupted.

The Chinese Communists learned much about the need for military protection for their supporters and themselves during the repression they suffered in the 1920s. Thus in the late 1930s and early 1940s, they could take advantage of the disruption caused by the Japanese War.[61] The dislocation of the Sino-Japanese War was extremely severe because of

[61] Roy Mark Hofheinz, Jr., "The Peasant Movement and Rural Revolution: Chinese Communists in the Countryside (1923-7)" (unpublished Ph.D. Dissertation, Harvard University, 1966), pp. 362-366.

Japan's indiscriminate mopping-up campaigns and mass civilian reprisals in areas it controlled.[62] This was reinforced by the flight of many of the traditional rural elites, including those of the higher levels of the Kuomintang.[63]

Providing more security than the Kuomintang in certain areas and developing the organizational capacity to deliver benefits in exchange for participation, the Chinese Communists offered peasants some relief from the disruptions created by the war. At first, this may have meant aiding the peasants in harvesting what was left of their crops. Later the revolutionaries' organizational capacities increased so they could deal with more than just the dislocation of war; they developed social exchanges that addressed many of the deficiencies from which the peasants had suffered even before the war.

SUMMARY

For revolutionaries to succeed in building a powerful movement, they must routinize peasant action so that powerful, complex organizations are built. This comes about in a process of social exchange, in which peasant support and participation are traded off initially for individual rewards. Peasant willingness to engage in these trade-offs stems from the crises that have occurred as they have moved from an inward- to an outward-orientation and have found an external environment that simply does not meet their needs. Even more than other political organizers, revolutionaries must provide rewards and sanctions that can overcome the costs and risks to the peasant of participating.

Only with a successful history of exchange of their efforts for personal and then local, collective goals do some peasants begin to take on the goals of a nationwide revolution. Peasants do not start with the goal of changing a whole national political and economic system, at a high cost to themselves when

[62] Johnson, *Peasant Nationalism*, p. 31.
[63] *Ibid.*, p. 70; and Hinton, *Fanshen*, p. 84.

they are not even integrated into that system. It is only after the revolutionaries have successfully integrated peasants into an autonomous economic and political network that villagers develop a sense of commitment to that network.

A very small minority of Latin America's and Asia's peasants have been involved in revolutions and have become committed to a nationwide class struggle. This participation has come only during the last half century, yet this change signals the new political possibilities arising out of the crucial change from an inward- to an outward-orientation.

The Chinese revolutionaries served as a catalyst in a change in the historical character of peasant participation in revolution.[64] It was no longer eruptive participation[65] but sustained involvement in an institutionalized movement. The Chinese Communists took advantage of the increased organizational capacity of peasants stemming from increased differentiation and specialization which came with greater external relations. They offered the organizational leadership peasants had never had before. Their inducements to the peasants were the necessary links to integrate into a community larger than the village.

Mao's theory was not just tactically different from Lenin's dictates to establish small, disciplined organizations to carry on the revolutionary struggle.[66] Rather, through a method of

[64] Hofheinz, "The Ecology of Chinese Communist Success," p. 6, discusses some of the similarities and differences between the Chinese Communists and such movements as the Taipings, the Nien, and the Boxers.

[65] The past character of peasant revolutions or rebellions can be seen in a quote by Bakunin in which he states that peasant revolutions are anarchic by their very nature. This is quoted in the Introduction of Frederick Engels, *The Peasant War in Germany* (New York: International Publishers, 1966), p. 8.

[66] This takes issue with the argument of Andrew C. Janos, "The Communist Theory of the State and Revolution," in *Communism and Revolution: The Strategic Uses of Political Violence*, ed. Cyril E. Black and Thomas P. Thornton (Princeton, N.J.: Princeton University Press, 1964), pp. 36-37. Alavi has spelled out much more clearly the evolution of Mao's thinking from its Leninist starting point. Alavi, "Peasants and Revolution," pp. 252-262, *passim*.

255

social exchange that applied both benefits and sanctions selectively, Mao established an entire institutional network—a network which responded to the past micro-economic changes among Chinese peasants and which could count on *mass* performance of complex tasks.[67] The Chinese revolutionaries were not organizing themselves to induce the cataclysmic uprising of the masses but were organizing the masses in order to create systematically institutions more powerful than those of their opponents'.

[67] For a discussion of Marx and Lenin in this respect, see Olson, *The Logic of Collective Action*, p. 105.

CHAPTER XI

Conclusion: The Shrinking World

THE END OF ISOLATION

THE OLD, autarchic village is now almost entirely extinct. Over the course of the nineteenth and twentieth centuries, peasants have greatly increased involvement outside their little communities. Vigilant lords and community organization now only infrequently apply effective sanctions against peasants' widening the scope of their external participation. Rapid and socially destabilizing changes have affected all types of peasant villages, ranging from those which were freeholding to those with powerful lords.

One reason for these changes stems from outside classes which have overwhelmed the peasantry. This is not unprecedented in peasant experience. Freeholding cultivators were reduced to peonage many times in the past by strong lords from the outside. At times, only brute force was used. In recent centuries, however, more subtle methods have been added. Changes in land tenure systems in the Middle East, South Asia, and Latin America, for example, enabled opportunistic outsiders to gain control of huge tracts of cultivable land.

In many areas in the nineteenth and twentieth centuries, those from other classes who have overwhelmed weak peasants have brought even greater dislocation than those in the past who had used brute force. There has been a shift in motivation from controlling land and people to garnering ever-growing profits. The result has been a search for more productive methods of cultivation. In some cases, this has resulted in a displacement of the peasantry for a cheap or slave labor force which could carry on plantation farming. Other areas have seen the demise of the peasantry through the introduction of a highly capital-intensive agriculture. Both of these occurred most prominently in areas ecologically suited for such extensive cultivation. In short, new land tenure laws have made peasants defenseless. New techniques have made them uncompetitive.

Besides being directly overwhelmed by those from other classes, a second set of factors has been responsible for villages' move from an inward- to an outward-orientation as well. These factors have had a dual effect: they have weakened the personalistic bonds between lord and peasant, and they have undermined the stability of peasants' incomes and expenditures, causing household economic crises. Eric Wolf has subsumed this set of factors under the heading of capitalism.[1] Certainly, capitalism has been in the forefront in introducing disequilibrating changes, but the causes go beyond capitalism alone.

More generally, peasants have been the victims of a rapidly shrinking globe. Imperialism, especially during the nineteenth century, was the most prominent force which accelerated this shrinking process. Peasant incomes declined as cheap manufactured goods cut into the handicraft market. Improved administration enabled governments to make demands for money taxes. Lords' private domains were challenged by enterprising businessmen and political leaders, and the lords themselves were drawn to the profit-making techniques of the outside. Imperialism introduced capitalism's new forces of

---

[1] Actually, Wolf's use of the word capitalism is somewhat broader, for he also includes land tenure changes. See Eric R. Wolf, *Peasant Wars of the Twentieth Century* (New York: Harper and Row, 1969), pp. 279-280. Tilly identifies these factors under the rubric of "urbanization," quite a misleading word, given the factors we (and he) have identified. Charles Tilly, *The Vendée*, Science Editions (New York: John Wiley and Sons, 1967), pp. 10-12.

production. Simultaneously, however, it offered a second strand of technological improvement. New health techniques resulted in a growth of population. Families and villages grew so that the old methods of farming were simply inadequate to deal with their larger numbers.

These factors, which have caused a decline in peasants' isolation, have remained in effect even though the colonial era has drawn to a close. The powerful capitalist states of the nineteenth century initiated a process which continues to gain momentum even in noncapitalist areas. Governments in the new states, whether socialistic or capitalistic, have continued to foster programs which undermine a subsistence-orientation and promote peasant entry into a larger social and economic world.

New patterns of distribution of peasant products and, even more important, new patterns of production are demanded as money taxes are collected, as manufactured goods flood the market, and as population continues to soar. Innovative peasants have joined those from other classes in taking advantage of any new opportunities arising from peasants' increased involvement with outside institutions. With each new innovation, they profit. And with each new innovation, the large numbers of peasants who were protected by the old modes of action suffer even more—relatively and often absolutely, as well.

In short, the shrinking globe has meant that actions taken outside the village, which have often seemed tangential to peasants, have forced the peasants into an entirely new world. Large numbers of these villagers were unprepared to cope with the powerful forces and classes which dominated this new world. We have developed a model which identifies the stages of this complex process. (1) At first, lords and villages' social and political organizations were generally able to prevent expanded outside relations by those who had the aspirations and resources to make outside alliances. (2) The low degree of outside involvement resulted in a fairly fixed level of technology and thus in a stability of household income

259

levels. (3) Outside changes stemming from imperialism produced sustained household economic crises. (4) Under the impact of these forces, the effectiveness of restrictions on expanded outside participation decreased. (5) Those who had previously had the resources and aspirations to forge outside alliances were then able to do so.

The shrinking world leads to three new patterns of rural stratification. In the first, the mechanized and extensive agriculture pattern, there is a demise of the peasantry. The long-term result is a great migration to the cities, with those left in the rural areas being divided between a poor rural proletariat and a wealthier set of managers and entrepreneurs. The second pattern, the intensive agriculture pattern, results in a polarization of the peasantry around farming. Some are able to become small capitalist farmers, while others are increasingly relegated to poor tenancies and agricultural day labor. Finally, in the marginal-land agriculture pattern, there is a similar polarization of the peasantry but, usually, centered around nonagricultural work experiences. More innovative peasants use their resources to become businessmen, professionals, or white collar workers. Others remain on the marginal land or join the swelling proletariat.

As the world outside shrinks, the peasants' political world expands. New problems arise that cannot be solved inside the village; the locus for decision-making shifts to the district, province, and state. Simultaneously, the resources crucial for influencing decisions change. Except for the innovators, peasants most often lack those resources. There is little they can do except yield to the demands made upon them. In some instances, however, political organizers can take advantage of peasants' relation to the world outside the village. The new patterns of economic stratification result in increasing single-interest interdependencies between peasants and outsiders and among peasants themselves. Outside organizers can use this social experience to bring peasants into political organizations demanding similar single-interest relationships. In exchange, peasants can gain some individual (and perhaps later, some collective) benefits to make their entry into the wider world a little less painful.

Revolutions are the extreme case of political change, both in rate and degree. The process of peasant recruitment into revolutionary movements can be understood analytically in the same terms as recruitment into other types of political organizations. The goals peasants initially seek to achieve are somewhat similar in both cases. Peasants have been forced into a new social and economic world, but that world does not meet their needs.[2] They are constantly confronted by the corruption, monopoly, and structural incompleteness of the outside institutional network. It is to these problems that revolutionaries must address themselves.

SOCIAL SCIENCE THEORY AND PEASANT REVOLUTION

In recent years, there has been a plethora of social science works on peasant revolution. Pike has rightly criticized many of the analyses dealing with Vietnam for neglecting to incorporate any mention of organizational structure. By any measure, he states, organizational matters "dominated the day-to-day life of both the rank and file and the leadership and dwarfed the military aspects."[3] Yet, in an odd way, Pike has set his own trap, and ultimately his book fails. His stress on organizational *structure* comes at the almost total exclusion of the *process* of organization building. And it is the process of institutionalized exchange which explains the *why* of peasant participation and the *how* of revolutionary creation of power.

[2] Moore has expressed this on a different level by saying that peasants revolt when their institutions are subject to new stresses and strains but they have not been led through a commercial revolution. Barrington Moore, Jr., *Social Origins of Dictatorship and Democracy: Lord and Peasant in the Making of the Modern World* (Boston: Beacon Press, 1966), p. 477.

[3] Douglas Pike, *Viet Cong: The Organization and Techniques of the National Liberation Front of South Vietnam* (Cambridge, Mass.: The M.I.T. Press, 1966), pp. 50-51.

Power results from the creation of institutions, and institutions are built through a process of social exchange. Thus, it is pure folly to state, as Régis Debray does, that the immediate goal of guerrilla revolutionaries is the destruction of the state's military might. He writes: "In every case this objective requires that the guerrilla *foco* [base] be independent of the families residing within the zone of operations."[4] On the contrary, if the goal of the revolutionaries is power, then there must be an institutionalized *interdependence* with the families in that zone.

Peasants have had long experience with outsiders and any call to change induces a weighing of the immediate benefits against the risks and costs, yet Debray states that the primary political work of the revolutionaries is to "convince" the peasants through propaganda that there are valid reasons for rebellion.[5] Peasants are not "convinced" by words but become committed to revolutionary goals through action, through a process of institutionalized social exchange. Eqbal Ahmad notes this when he says: "The major task of the movement is not to outfight but to outadminister the government."[6] This means that revolutionaries cannot depend upon a short-lived, cataclysmic uprising of frustrated peasants but must build organizations capable of executing complex tasks over time.

It also means that administration by a distant, centralized bureaucracy is inadequate. Successful revolutionaries have decentralized administration by placing its cadres within villages and districts. In rural Vietnam, Race estimates, there were five to ten times as many political workers in villages

[4] Régis Debray, *Revolution in the Revolution? Armed Struggle and Political Struggle in Latin America* (New York: Grove Press, 1967), p. 42.

[5] *Ibid.*, p. 47.

[6] Eqbal Ahmad, "Revolutionary Warfare and Counterinsurgency," in *National Liberation*, ed. Miller and Aya, p. 157. He stated this point earlier in an article, as well: "Revolutionary Warfare: How to Tell When the Rebels Have Won," *The Nation*, August 30, 1965, pp. 95-100.

after the NLF wrested control of them away from the government.[7]

As such, violence against the state, although important to the revolutionaries' ultimate success, plays a secondary role to that of the process of creating power. Initially, the revolutionary army is used to protect that process of creation. And such creation of power involves *institutionalization*.[8] Neil Smelser, by placing revolution on a continuum including all types of group violence (or collective behavior, as he calls it) misses this essential point about twentieth century peasant revolutions. He writes that collective behavior is not institutionalized behavior[9] but, rather, collective behavior occurs in order to alleviate strain while omitting a step-by-step process which would deal with the causes of the strain. It is uninstitutionalized mobilization for action, a short-circuiting of the normal specifications, contingencies, and controls. Collective behavior, he says, is the action of the impatient.[10]

Can we put recent peasant revolutions on the end of such a spectrum of collective behavior? Certainly not. The Chinese Communists, the Viet Minh, and the NLF *institutionalized* procedures and organizations for peasant participation in order to gain power to challenge the existing state institutions. Many peasants participated in Chinese Communist, Viet Minh, or NLF organizations for up to a decade. Revolutionaries create power through a painstaking, step-by-step process of social exchange, a process which routinizes behavior, rather than trying to foment unpredictable and unin-

[7] Jeffery Race, *War Comes to Long An: Revolutionary Conflict in a Vietnamese Province* (Berkeley: University of California Press, 1972), p. 160.

[8] Hannah Arendt, "Reflections on Violence," *Journal of International Affairs* 23 (1969), 16-17, distinguishes between violence and power. Power is the support or consent of people needed for a government to act.

[9] Neil J. Smelser, *Theory of Collective Behavior* (New York: The Free Press, 1962), p. 8.

[10] *Ibid.*, pp. 70-72.

263

stitutionalized action. They work among peasants who have undergone critical changes. Economic crises have resulted in attempts by some to expand external relations, but participation in the outside network of economic institutions is fraught with insecurity for them. Governments have been unable or unwilling to deal with the corruption and monopolization which continue and the gaps which remain.

Through an institutionalized process of social exchange, the revolutionaries are able to address the needs of peasants. If institutionalized peasant revolutions were largely unsuccessful in the 1960s, it was not because governments were now dealing with the deficiencies and exploitation peasants face in rural areas but it was because governments' might (often aided by the Green Berets and the United States' military gadgetry) was sufficient to prevent the revolutionaries from institutionalizing ongoing processes of social exchange. Alternatives for mobility of peasants through out-migration also lessened the opportunities for revolutionary organizers to attract the innovative elements of the peasantry.

Another set of theories places recent peasant revolutions on a continuum of collective violence, explaining such behavior in terms of relative deprivation to other classes in the society or to their own past performance. Ted Robert Gurr holds that the properties and processes that distinguish a riot from a revolution are differences in degree, not kind.[11] Thus, political violence of all kinds, whether it be guerrilla wars, coups d'état, rebellions, or riots can be understood through use of the same analytic concepts. The scope and intensity of frustration and anger are, for the most part, what distinguish which type of collective violence will break out.

This theory has been expressed in several different forms. James C. Davies' J-curve variation explains the frustration in terms of a rising set of economic expectations based on past performance which are suddenly unable to be realized because

[11] Ted Robert Gurr, *Why Men Rebel* (Princeton, N.J.: Princeton University Press, 1970), p. 5.

264

of a change in fortunes.[12] Tanter and Midlarsky characterize this syndrome in terms of rising aspirations spurred by rising achievement followed by a drop in achievement and expectations but not in aspirations. The difference between aspirations and expectations is the "revolutionary gap" and its size determines the degree of collective violence that erupts.[13]

Such theories are quite valuable in explaining revolutions based on sudden eruptions of violence, and they also may offer valuable tools for understanding the violent intensity of parts of twentieth century peasant revolutions. The social-psychological variables predominate in these analyses and lead one to focus on frustration and anger. They help us much less in understanding the institutionalized nature of recent peasant revolutions—the hours, months, and years of patient institution-building.

Only the *consequences* of collective violence are viewed as political in these theories. The process, however, is taken completely out of the political realm. In the case of peasant revolutions, however, the movement is, in fact, best understood as the building of power prior to the ultimate confrontation. And the building of such power is a political process. There are incentives, benefits, and sanctions just as most citizens receive from state institutions. There is a growth of commitment to the survival of the network of revolutionary institutions and to the actualization of their goals. Why should the actions that peasants engage in for those institutions be analyzed solely in terms of impulsive collective violence rather than in terms of the same motivating factors which explain why citizens, soldiers, and police act for their country?

Peasant revolution starts with politics, as Mao well knows

[12] James C. Davies, "Toward a Theory of Revolution," *American Sociological Review* 27 (February 1962), p. 6; also, see Carl Leiden and Karl M. Schmitt, *The Politics of Violence: Revolution in the Modern World* (Englewood Cliffs, N.J.: Prentice-Hall, 1968), pp. 42-44.

[13] Raymond Tanter and Manus Midlarsky, "A Theory of Revolution," *The Journal of Conflict Resolution* 11 (September 1967), 270-271.

265

and Che never lived to find out.[14] What begins with nothing more than a commitment by peasants to certain selective benefits becomes a commitment analogous to patriotism. At that point, peasants are not merely directing their energies for specific material gains, nor are they rebelling merely against the distribution of values expressed in the existing institutions. They are rebelling against a system of justice which has failed to provide them with a larger political community adequate to their new economic reality.[15] They are fighting for the links to a new world whose boundaries are far wider than that of the village's bamboo hedge.

[14] See, for example, Che Guevara, *Guerrilla Warfare* (New York: Monthly Review Press, 1961), pp. 28-29, where he emphasizes the moral effect of guerrilla's behavior but neglects the need for political organization.

[15] Chalmers Johnson, *Revolution and the Social System* (Stanford: Stanford University, The Hoover Institution, 1964), p. 6, overemphasizes the *prior* integration of the social system.

The Scale of External Relations

The scale of external relations is constructed on a simple numerical basis. A content analysis of the monographs on the 51 cases was carried out. Three of the categories established were based on degree of external labor involvement, cash involvement, and national market involvement. For each category a village could be awarded from zero to three units (zero meaning no external involvement and three meaning much external involvement). Thus, a village could end with from zero to nine total units. Any total from zero to four was considered low on the scale; any total from five to nine was considered high on the scale.

The following are the criteria for awarding units.

CASH

0—never used
1—rarely used within the village or outside
2—moderately used: moderately both within and outside; or rarely within but frequently outside; or frequently within but rarely outside
3—frequently used both within and outside

MARKETS

0—completely subsistence
1—primarily peasant market or traditional traders

2—primarily middlemen who sell to wholesalers; or middlemen and peasant market or traditional traders; or peasant market or traders combined with more modern markets (3)

3—primarily cooperative, government, or other marketing organizations; direct selling to wholesale houses, factories, or city entrepreneurs

LABOR

0—no external labor

1—very little nonagricultural external labor; any amount of seasonal agricultural labor outside

2—moderate external nonagricultural: any amount of seasonal nonagricultural labor and/or a small amount of daily nonagricultural wage labor

3—large amount of daily external nonagricultural wage labor

Fifteen of the 51 villages ended up on the low end of the scale with less than four units; the 36 others were on the high end with five or more. Here is the distribution.

Total Units	0	1	2	3	4	5[a]	6	7	8	9	Incomplete data[b]
No. Villages	0	0	2	6	6	5	7	13	6	3	3

See Appendix B for the data on where each village falls on the scale.

[a] Two of these borderline cases (Aritama and San Jilotepeque—see Appendix B) are Latin American villages with two distinct groups, Ladinos and Indians. The Indians, despite contact with the Ladinos, usually have far fewer outside relations than the Ladinos and are comparable to peasants in inward-oriented villages.

[b] Though there was insufficient data to assign an exact number of units, two of the villages definitely had more than five units and the third definitely less than five.

A List of the Communities Used

Below is a list of communities used according to geographical location. Following the name of the village are the name of the author and the title of the monograph in which the study appears. (OO) indicates an outward-oriented community and (IO) an inward-oriented one. The letters and numbers in parentheses indicate certain attributes of the community. C, M, and L and the numbers refer to the cash, market, and labor criteria explained in Appendix A. T is the community's total number of points on the scale of external relations.

EAST ASIA

China

(OO) Hang Mei (Hong Kong)—Potter, *Capitalism and the Chinese Peasant* (C = 3; M = 3; L = 3; T = 9)

(OO) Hsin Hsing (Taiwan)—Gallin, *Hsin Hsing, Taiwan* (C = 2; M = 2; L = 2; T = 6)

(OO) Kaihsienkung (East China)—Fei, *Peasant Life in China* (C = 3; M = 3; L = 2; T = 8)

(OO) Liu Ling (Shanshi)—Myrdal, *Report from a Chinese Village* (C = 2; M = 3; L = 2; T = 7)

(OO) Nanching (South China)—Yang, *A Chinese Village*

and its Early Change under Communism (C = 2;
M = 3; L = 2; T = 7)

(OO) Taitou (Shantung)—Yang, *A Chinese Village* (C =
2; M = 2; L = 2; T = 6)

(OO) Ten Mile Inn (North China)—Crook, *Revolution in
a Chinese Village* (C = 3; M = 3; L = 3; T = 9)

SOUTHEAST ASIA

Malaysia

(OO) Jendram Hilir (Malaya)—Wilson, *A Malay Village
and Malaysia* (C = 2; M = 2; L = 2; T = 6)

Thailand

(OO) Bang Chan—Sharp, *Siamese Rice Village* (C = 2;
M = 2; L = 2; T = 6)

(OO) Bangkhuad—Kaufman, *Bangkhuad* (C = 3; M =
2; L = 2; T = 7)

(IO) Ban Ping—Moerman, *Agricultural Change and Peasant Choice in a Thai Village* (C = 1; M = 2; L = 0;
T = 3)

(IO) Ku Daeng—Kingshill, *Ku Daeng—The Red Tomb*
(C = 2; M = 2; L = 0; T = 4)

Vietnam

(OO) Khanh Hau—Hickey, *Village in Vietnam* (C = 2;
M = 2; L = 3; T = 7)

SOUTH ASIA

Burma

(OO) Tadagale—Brant, *Tadagale* (C = 2; M = 2; L = 3;
T = 7)

Ceylon

(OO) Pelpola—Ryan, *Sinhalese Village* (C = 2; M = 2;
L = 3; T = 7)

(IO)   Pul Eliya—Leach, *Pul Eliya* (C = 2; M = 1; L = 0; T = 3)

India

(OO)   Bisipara (Orissa)—Bailey, *Caste and the Economic Frontier* (C = 2; M = 2; L = 3; T = 7)

(OO)   Dalena (Mysore)—Epstein, *Economic Development and Social Change in South India* (C = 3; M = 1; L = 3; T = 7)

(OO)   Gaon (Maharashtra)—Orenstein, *Gaon* (C = 2; M = 3; L = 3; T = 8)

(IO)   Gopalpur (South India)—Beals, *Gopalpur* (C = 1; M = 1; L = 1; T = 3)

(OO)   Mayur (Kerala)—Aiyappan, *Social Revolution in a Kerala Village* (C = 3; M = 3; L = 2; T = 8)

(OO)   Mogri (Gujarat)—Amin, *Mogri* (C = 3; M = 3; L = 3; T = 9)

(OO)   Mohana (Uttar Pradesh)—Majumdar, *Caste and Communication in an Indian Village* (C = 2; M = 2; L = 1; T = 5)

(OO)   Rampur (Delhi State)—Lewis, *Village Life in Northern India* (C = 2; M = N.D.; L = 3; T = 5 +)

(OO)   Ranjana (West Bengal)—Chattopadhyay, *Ranjana* (C = 2; M = 2; L = 2; T = 6)

(OO)   Samiala (Gujarat)—Fukutake, *The Socio-Economic Structure of the Indian Village* (C = 2; M = 3; L = 3; T = 8)

(OO)   Shamirpet (Hyderabad)—Dube, *Indian Village* (C = 2; M = 2; L = 2; T = 6)

(OO)   Shivapur (Mysore)—Ishwaran, *Shivapur* (C =1; M = 3; L = 3; T = 7)

(IO)   Sirkanda (Indian Himalayas)—Berreman, *Hindus of the Himalayas* (C = 1; M = 2; L = 0; T = 3)

(OO)   Supur (West Bengal)—Fukutake, *The Socio-Economic Structure of the Indian Village* (C = 2; M = 2; L = 1; T = 5)

(OO)   Thagasamuthiram (Madras)—Sivertsen, *When Caste Barriers Fall* (C = 2; M = 2; L = 2; T = 6)

(OO)   Wangala (Mysore)—Epstein, *Economic Development and Social Change in South India* (C = 2; M = 3; L = 0; T = 5)

Pakistan

(IO)   Mohla (Punjab)—Eglar, *A Punjabi Village in Pakistan* (C = 2; M = 2; L = 0; T = 4)

ASIAN PACIFIC ISLANDS

Fiji Islands

(IO)   Deuba—Geddes, *Deuba* (C = 1; M = 1; L = 0; T = 2)

Philippines

(IO)   Guinhangdan—Nurge, *Life in a Leyte Village* (C = 1; M = N.D.; L = 0; T = 1 +)

(IO)   Tarong—Nydegger, *Tarong* (C = 1; M = 1; L = 1; T = 3)

LATIN AMERICA

Brazil

(IO)   Buzios Island—Willems, *Buzios Island* (C = 1; M = 2; L = 0; T = 3)

Colombia

(OO)   Saucío—Fals-Borda, *Peasant Society in the Colombian Andes* (C = 3; M = 1; L = 3; T = 7) .

(OO)   Aritama—Reichel-Dolmatoff, *The People of Aritama* (C = 2; M = 2; L = 1; T = 5)

Guatemala

(IO)   Panajachel—Tax, *Penny Capitalism* (C = 2; M = 1; L = 1; T = 4)

272

(OO)   San Jilotepeque—Tumin, *Caste in a Peasant Society*
($C = 3; M = 1; L = 1; T = 5$)

Mexico

(IO)   Chan Kom (Yucatan)—Redfield, Rojas, *Chan Kom*
($C = 1; M = 1; L = 0; T = 2$)

(OO)   Huecorio (Michoacan)—Belshaw, *A Village Economy* ($C = 3; M = 2; L = 3; T = 8$)

(OO)   Tepoztlán (Morelos)—Lewis, *Life in a Mexican Village* and *Tepoztlán* ($C = 2; M = 3; L = 3; T = 8$)

Peru

(IO)   Hualcan—Stein, *Hualcan* ($C = 1; M = 1; L = 2; T = 4$)

MIDDLE EAST

Jordan

(OO)   Baytīn—Lutfiyya, *Baytīn* ($C = 3; M = 1; L = 3; T = 7$)

Lebanon

(IO)   Buarij—Fuller, *Buarij* ($C = 2; M = 1; L = 1; T = 4$)

Turkey

(IO)   Demirciler—Pierce, *Life in a Turkish Village* ($C = 1; M = 3; L = 0; T = 4$)

(OO)   Elbaşi—Stirling, *Turkish Village* ($C = 2; M = 3; L = 2; T = 7$)

(OO)   Hasanoğlan—Yasa, *Hasanoğlan* ($C = 3; M = N.D.; L = 3; T = 6 +$)

(OO)   Sakaltutan—Stirling, *Turkish Village* ($C = 2; M = 3; L = 2; T = 7$)

Works Cited

Abramovitz, Z. and Gelfat Y. *Hameshek Ha'aravi Be' eretz Yisrael U'vartzot Hamizrach Hatichon (The Arab Holding in the Land of Israel and in the Countries of the Middle East).* Palestine: Hakibutz Hameuchad, 1944. (Hebrew).

Adams, Richard N. "Changing Political Relationships in Guatemala." In *Political Changes in Guatemalan Indian Communities: A Symposium,* edited by Adams. New Orleans: Middle American Research Institute, Tulane University, Publication no. 24, 1957.

Ahmad, Eqbal. "Revolutionary Warfare and Counterinsurgency." In *National Liberation, Revolution in the Third World,* edited by Norman Miller and Roderick Aya. New York: The Free Press, 1971.

————. "Revolutionary Warfare, How to Tell When the Rebels Have Won." *The Nation,* August 30, 1965, pp. 95-100.

Aiyappan, A. *Social Revolution in a Kerala Village, A Study in Culture Change.* New York: Asia Publishing House, 1965.

Alavi, Hamza. "Peasants and Revolution." In *The Socialist Register 1965,* edited by Ralph Miliband and John Saville. New York: Monthly Review Press, 1965.

Amin, R. K. *Mogri, Socio-Economic Study of a Charotar*

275

Village. Gujarat, India: Sardar Vallabhai Vidyapeeth Vallabh Vidyanagar, n.d.

Anderson, Robert T. "Studies in Peasant Life." In *Biennial Review of Anthropology, 1965,* edited by Bernard J. Siegel. Stanford: Stanford University Press, 1965.

Apter, David E. *The Politics of Modernization.* Chicago: University of Chicago Press, 1965.

Arendt, Hannah. "Reflections on Violence." *Journal of International Affairs* 23 (1969), 1-35.

Ayoub, Victor F. "Conflict Resolution and Social Reorganization in a Lebanese Village." *Human Organization* 24 (Spring 1965), 11-17.

Bailey, F. G. *Caste and the Economic Frontier, A Village in Highland Orissa.* Manchester: Manchester University Press, 1957.

―――. "Parapolitical Systems." In *Local-Level Politics, Social and Cultural Perspectives,* edited by Marc J. Swartz. Chicago: Aldine, 1968.

―――. "The Peasant View of the Bad Life." *The Advancement of Science* 23 (December 1966), 399-409.

―――. *Politics and Social Change, Orissa in 1959.* Berkeley: University of California Press, 1963.

Balogh, Thomas. *The Economics of Poverty.* London: Weidenfeld and Nicholson, 1966.

Banfield, Edward C. *The Moral Basis of a Backward Society.* New York: The Free Press, 1958.

Barnett, H. G. *Innovation, The Basis of Cultural Change.* New York: McGraw-Hill, 1953.

Beals, Alan R. *Gopalpur, A South Indian Village.* New York: Holt, Rinehart, 1962.

―――. "Leadership in a Mysore Village." In *Leadership and Political Institutions in India,* edited by Richard L. Park and Irene Tinker. Princeton, N.J.: Princeton University Press, 1959.

Befu, Harumi. "Political Complexity and Village Community: Test of an Hypothesis." *Anthropological Quarterly* 39 (April 1966), 43-52.

276

————. "The Political Relation of the Village to the State." *World Politics* 19 (July 1967), 601-20.

Belshaw, Cyril S. *Traditional Exchange and Modern Markets*. Englewood Cliffs, N.J.: Prentice-Hall, 1965.

Belshaw, Michael. *A Village Economy, Land and People of Huecorio*. New York: Columbia University Press, 1967.

Ben-Zvi, Y. *Oclusaynu Ba'aretz (Our Population in the Land)*. Warsaw: Brit Ha'noar, 1932 (Hebrew).

Beqiraj, Mehmet. *Peasantry in Revolution*. Center for International Studies, Cornell University. Cornell Research Papers in International Studies, Vol. v, 1966.

Berreman, Gerald. *Hindus of the Himalayas*. Berkeley: University of California Press, 1963.

Birrell, Robert. "Obstacles to Development in Peasant Societies: An Analysis of India, England, & Japan." In *Peasants in the Modern World*, edited by Philip K. Bock. Albuquerque: University of New Mexico Press, 1969.

Blanksten, George I. "Revolutions." In *Government and Politics in Latin America*, edited by Harold E. Davis. New York: Ronald, 1958.

Blau, Peter M. *Exchange, and Power in Social Life*. New York: John Wiley and Sons, 1964.

Bock, Philip K., ed. *Peasants in the Modern World*. Albuquerque: University of New Mexico Press, 1969.

Boserup, Ester. *The Conditions of Agricultural Growth, The Economics of Agrarian Change under Population Pressure*. Chicago: Aldine, 1965.

Bourque, Susan C. "Cholification and the Campesino: A Study of Three Peruvian Peasant Organizations in the Process of Societal Change." Ithaca, N.Y.: Latin American Studies Program, Dissertation Series, Cornell University, January 1971.

Brant, Charles S. *Tadagale: A Burmese Village in 1950*. Ithaca, N.Y.: Department of Far Eastern Studies, Cornell University, 1954.

Burki, Shahid Javed. "Development of West Pakistan's Agriculture: An Interdisciplinary Explanation." Paper read at the Workshop on Rural Development in Pakistan, Michigan State University, East Lansing, Michigan, July 16, 1971.

Chattopadhyay, Gouranga. *Ranjana, A Village in West Bengal.* Calcutta: Bookland Private, 1964.

Chayanov, A. V. "On the Theory of Non-Capitalist Economic Systems." In *A V. Chayanov on the Theory of Peasant Economy*, edited by Daniel Thorner, Basile Kerbloy, and R.E.F. Smith. Homewood, Ill.: Richard D. Irwin, 1966.

Coleman, Emily R. "Medieval Marriage Characteristics: A Neglected Factor in the History of Medieval Serfdom." *The Journal of Interdisciplinary History* 2 (Autumn 1971), 205-19.

Craig, Wesley W. "Peru: The Peasant Movement of La Convención." In *Latin American Peasant Movements*, edited by Henry A. Landsberger. Ithaca, N.Y.: Cornell University Press, 1969.

Crook, Isabel and David. *Revolution in a Chinese Village, Ten Mile Inn.* London: Routledge and Kegan Paul, 1959.

Dantwala, M. L. "Problems in Countries with Heavy Pressure of Population on Land: The Case of India." In *Land Tenure*, edited by Kenneth H. Parsons, Raymond J. Penn, and Philip M. Raup. Proceedings of the International Conference on Land Tenure and Related Problems in World Agriculture, Madison: The University of Wisconsin Press, 1956.

Davies, James C. "Toward a Theory of Revolution." *American Sociological Review* 27 (February 1962), 5-19.

Debray, Régis. *Revolution in the Revolution? Armed Struggle and Political Struggle in Latin America.* New York: Grove Press, 1967.

Deutsch, Karl. "Social Mobilization and Political Development." *American Political Science Review* 55 (September 1961), 493-514.

Dovring, Folke, "Peasantry, Land Use, and Change, A Re-

278

view Article." *Comparative Studies in Society and History* 4 (April 1962), 364-74.

Driver, Edwin D. *Differential Fertility in Central India.* Princeton, N.J.: Princeton University Press, 1963.

Dube, S. C. *Indian Village.* Harper Colophon Books. New York: Harper and Row, 1967.

Easterlin, Richard A. "On the Relation of Economic Factors to Recent and Projected Fertility Changes." *Demography* 3 (1966), 131-53.

Edel, Matthew. "Innovative Supply: A Weak Point in Economic Development Theory." *Social Science Information* 9 (June 1970), 9-40.

Eglar, Zekiye. *A Punjabi Village in Pakistan.* New York: Columbia University Press, 1960.

Elazari-Volcani, I. *The Fellah's Farm.* Tel Aviv: Jewish Agency for Palestine, 1930.

Engels, Frederick. *The Peasant War in Germany.* New York: International Publishers, 1966.

Epstein, T. S. *Economic Development and Social Change in South India.* Manchester: Manchester University Press, 1962.

Falcon, Walter P. "The Green Revolution: Generations of Problems." Paper presented at the summer meeting of the American Agricultural Economics Association, Columbia, Mo., August 9-12, 1970.

Fals-Borda, Orlando. *Peasant Society in the Colombian Andes: A Sociological Study of Saucío.* Gainesville: University of Florida Press, 1955.

Feder, Ernest. "Societal Opposition to Peasant Movements and Its Effects on Farm People in Latin America." In *Latin American Peasant Movements,* edited by Henry A. Landsberger. Ithaca, N.Y.: Cornell University Press, 1969.

Fei, Hsiao-Tung. *Peasant Life in China, A Field Study of Country Life in the Yangtze Valley.* London: Routledge and Kegan Paul, 1939.

Finn, James. *Stirring Times: Or Records From Jerusalem Consular Chronicles of 1853 to 1856*. Vol. II. London: Kegan Paul, 1878.

Firth, Raymond. "Capital, Saving and Credit in Peasant Societies: A Viewpoint from Economic Anthropology." In *Capital, Saving and Credit in Peasant Societies, Studies from Asia, Oceania, the Caribbean and Middle America*, edited by Firth and B. S. Yamey. Chicago: Aldine, 1964.

———. *Elements of Social Organization*. 3d ed. Boston: Beacon Press, 1963.

Fischer-Galati, Stephen. "The Peasantry as a Revolutionary Force in the Balkans." *Journal of Central European Affairs* 23 (April 1963), 12-22.

Forman, Shepard, and Riegelhaupt, Joyce F. "Market Place and Marketing System: Toward a Theory of Peasant Economic Integration." *Comparative Studies in Society and History* 12 (April 1970), 188-212.

Foster, George M. "Interpersonal Relations in Peasant Society." *Human Organization* 19 (Winter 1960-61), 174-78.

———. "Peasant Society and the Image of Limited Good." *American Anthropologist* 67 (April 1965), 293-315.

———. *Traditional Cultures and the Impact of Technological Change*. New York: Harper & Row, 1962.

———. *Tzintzuntzan, Mexican Peasants in a Changing World*. Boston: Little, Brown, 1967.

Frank, Andre Gunder. "The Development of Underdevelopment." In *Imperialism and Underdevelopment: A Reader*, edited by Robert I. Rhodes. New York: Monthly Review Press, 1970.

Frankel, Francine R., and Vorys, Karl von. "The Political Challenge of the Green Revolution: Shifting Patterns of Peasant Participation in India and Pakistan." Unpublished paper, Department of Political Science, University of Pennsylvania, August 10, 1971.

Frederiksen, Harold. "Determinants and Consequences of

Mortality Trends in Ceylon." *Public Health Reports* 76 (August 1961), 659-63.

—————. "Dynamic Equilibrium of Economic and Demographic Transition." *Economic Development and Cultural Change* 14 (April 1966), 316-22.

Fukutake, Tadashi; Ōuchi, Tsutomu; and Nakane, Chie. *The Socio-Economic Structure of the Indian Village, Surveys of Villages in Gujarat and West Bengal.* Tokyo: The Institute of Asian Economic Affairs, 1964.

Fuller, Anne H. *Buarij, Portrait of a Lebanese Muslim Village.* Cambridge, Mass.: Harvard University Press, 1961.

Galjart, Benno. "Class and 'Following' in Rural Brazil." *América Latina* 7 (July-September 1964), 3-23.

Gallin, Bernard. "Conflict Resolution in Changing Chinese Society: A Taiwanese Study." In *Political Anthropology*, edited by Marc J. Swartz, Victor W. Turner, and Arthur Tuden. Chicago: Aldine, 1966.

—————*Hsin Hsing, Taiwan: A Chinese Village in Change.* Berkeley: University of California Press, 1966.

—————. "Political Factionalism and its Impact on Chinese Village Social Organization in Taiwan." In *Local-Level Politics*, edited by Marc J. Swartz. Chicago: Aldine, 1968.

Galtung, Johan. "A Structural Theory of Imperialism." *Journal of Peace Research* 8 (1971), 81-117.

Galula, David. *Counterinsurgency Warfare, Theory and Practice.* New York: Praeger, 1964.

Geddes, W. R. *Deuba: A Study of a Fijian Village.* Wellington, New Zealand: The Polynesian Society, 1945.

Geertz, Clifford. *Agricultural Involution, The Process of Ecological Change in Indonesia.* Berkeley: University of California Press, 1966.

—————. "The Integrative Revolution: Primordial Sentiments and Civil Politics in the New States." In *Old Societies and New States, The Quest for Modernity in Asia and Africa*, edited by Geertz. Glencoe, Ill.: The Free Press, 1963.

—————. "Studies in Peasant Life: Community and Society."

In *Biennial Review of Anthropology, 1961*, edited by Bernard J. Siegel. Stanford: Stanford University Press, 1962.

Gonzaléz, Alfonso. "Some Effects of Population Growth on America's Economy." In *Population Geography: A Reader*, edited by George J. Demko, Harold M. Rose, and George A. Schnell. New York: McGraw-Hill, 1970.

Gotsch, Carl H. "The Distributive Impact of Agricultural Growth: Low Income Farmers and the 'System' (A Case Study of Sahiwal District, West Pakistan)." Paper presented to the Seminar on Small Farmer Development Strategies, The Agricultural Development Council and the Ohio State University, Columbus, September 13-15, 1971.

Gott, Richard. *Guerrilla Movements in Latin America*. London: Nelson, 1970.

Gough, Kathleen. "Peasant Resistance and Revolt in South India." *Pacific Affairs* 41 (Winter 1968-69), 526-44.

―――. "The Social Structure of a Tanjore Village." In *Village India, Studies in the Little Community*, edited by McKim Marriott. Chicago: University of Chicago Press, 1955.

Gouldner, Alvin M. *The Coming Crisis of Western Sociology*. New York: Basic Books, 1970.

Granott, A. *The Land in Palestine: History and Structure*. London: Eyre and Spottiswoode, 1952.

Grant, James P. "Marginal Men: The Global Unemployment Crisis." *Foreign Affairs* 50 (October 1971), 112-24.

Greene, T. N., ed. *The Guerrilla—And How to Fight Him: Selections from the Marine Corps Gazette*. New York: Praeger, 1962.

Guerra y Sánchez, Ramiro. *Sugar and Society in the Caribbean, An Economic History of Cuban Agriculture*. New Haven: Yale University Press, 1964.

Guevara, Che. *Guerrilla Warfare*. New York: Monthly Review Press, 1961.

Gurr, Ted Robert. *Why Men Rebel*. Princeton, N.J.: Princeton University Press, 1970.

Gusfield, Joseph R. "Tradition and Modernity: Misplaced Polarities in the Study of Social Change." *American Journal of Sociology* 72 (November 1966), 351-62.

Hagen, Everett E. *On the Theory of Social Change: How Economic Growth Begins.* Homewood, Ill.: The Dorsey Press, 1962.

Hallowell, A. Irving. "Sociopsychological Aspects of Acculturation." In *The Science of Man in the World Crises*, edited by Ralph Linton. New York: Columbia University Press, 1945.

Halpern, Joel M. "The Rural Revolution." *Transactions of the New York Academy of Sciences*, ser. II, 28 (November 1965), 73-80.

Hammel, E. A. "The 'Balkan' Peasant: A View from Serbia." In *Peasants in the Modern World*, edited by Philip K. Bock. Albuquerque: University of New Mexico Press, 1969.

Hansen, Börje. "Group Relations of Peasants and Farmers." In *The Peasant: A Symposium Concerning the Peasant Way and View of Life*, edited by F. G. Friedmann. No. 8 (February 1957), mimeo.

Heer, David M., and Smith, Dean O. "Mortality Level, Desired Family Size, and Population Increase." *Demography* 5 (1968), 104-21.

Henry, R. N. "Participation and Initiative of the Local People." In *Social Research and Problems of Rural Development in South-East Asia*, edited by Vu Quôc Thuc. UNESCO, 1963.

Hickey, Gerald Cannon. *Village in Vietnam.* New Haven: Yale University Press, 1964.

Hill, Frances R. "Millenarian Machines in South Vietnam." *Comparative Studies in Society and History* 13 (July 1971), 325-50.

Hinderink, Jan, and Kiray, Mübeccel B. *Social Stratification as an Obstacle to Development, A Study of Four Turkish Villages.* New York: Praeger, 1970.

Hinton, William. *Fanshen: A Documentary of Revolution in*

a Chinese Village. New York: Monthly Review Press, 1966.

Hofheinz, Roy, Jr. "The Ecology of Chinese Communist Success: Rural Influence Patterns, 1923-45." In *Chinese Communist Politics in Action,* edited by A. Doak Barnett. Seattle: University of Washington Press, 1969.

————. "The Peasant Movement and Rural Revolution: Chinese Communists in the Countryside (1923-7)." Unpublished Ph.D. Dissertation, Harvard University, 1966.

Hollnsteiner, Mary R. "Social Structure and Power in a Philippine Municipality." In *Peasant Society, A Reader,* edited by Jack M. Potter, May N. Diaz, and George M. Foster. Boston: Little, Brown, 1966.

Hunter, Guy. *Modernizing Peasant Societies: A Comparative Study in Asia and Africa.* New York: Oxford University Press, 1969.

Huntington, Samuel P. "The Change to Change: Modernization, Development, and Politics." *Comparative Politics* 3 (April 1971), 283-322.

————. *Political Order in Changing Societies.* New Haven: Yale University Press, 1968.

Hutchinson, Bertram. "The Patron-Dependent Relationship in Brazil: A Preliminary Examination." *Sociologia Ruralis* 6 (1966), 3-30.

Hyde, Douglas. *The Peaceful Assault, The Pattern of Subversion.* London: The Bodley Head, 1963.

Ishwaran, K. *Shivapur, A South Indian Village.* London: Routledge and Kegan Paul, 1963.

Jackson, Gabriel. "The Origins of Spanish Anarchism." *The Southwestern Social Science Quarterly* 36 (September 1955), 135-47.

Janos, Andrew C. "The Communist Theory of the State and Revolution." In *Communism and Revolution: The Strategic Uses of Political Violence,* edited by Cyril E. Black and Thomas P. Thornton. Princeton, N.J.: Princeton University Press, 1964.

Johnson, Chalmers A. *Peasant Nationalism and Communist*

Power, The Emergence of Revolutionary China 1937-1945. Stanford: Stanford University Press, 1962.

———. *Revolution and the Social System*. Stanford: Stanford University, The Hoover Institution, 1964.

———. *Revolutionary Change*. Boston: Little, Brown, 1966.

Kaufman, Howard Keva. *Bangkhuad, A Community Study in Thailand*. Locust Valley, N.Y.: J. J. Augustin, 1960.

Kerton, Robert R. "An Economic Analysis of the Extended Family in the West Indies." *The Journal of Development Studies* 7 (July 1971), 423-34.

Kingshill, Konrad. *Ku Daeng—The Red Tomb, A Village Study in Northern Thailand*. Chiangmai, Thailand: The Prince Royal's College, 1960.

Kunkel, John H. "Economic Autonomy and Social Change in Mexican Villages." *Economic Development and Cultural Change* 10 (October 1961), 51-63.

Landsberger, Henry A. "A Framework for the Study of Peasant Movements." Ithaca, N.Y.: New York State School of Industrial and Labor Relations, Cornell University, 1966.

———. "The Role of Peasant Movements and Revolts in Development." In *Latin American Peasant Movements*, edited by Landsberger. Ithaca, N.Y.: Cornell University Press, 1969.

Landsberger, Henry A. and Hewitt, Cynthia N. "Ten Sources of Weakness and Cleavage in Latin American Peasant Movements." In *Agrarian Problems and Peasant Movements in Latin America*, edited by Rodolfo Stavenhagen. Garden City, New York: Doubleday, 1970.

———. "Peasant Organizations in La Laguna, Mexico: History, Structure, Member Participation and Effectiveness." Research Papers on Land Tenure and Agrarian Reform, no. 17, Inter-American Committee for Agricultural Development (CIDA), Washington: General Secretariat of American States, November 1970.

———. "Preliminary Report on a Case Study of Mexican

285

Peasant Organization." Ithaca, N.Y.: New York State School of Industrial and Labor Relations, Cornell University.

Langer, William L. "Europe's Initial Population Explosion." *American Historical Review* 69 (October 1963), 1-17.

Larson, Magali Sarfatti, and Bergman, Arlene Eisen. *Social Stratification in Peru*. Berkeley: Institute of International Studies, University of California, 1969.

La Souchère, Éléna de. *An Explanation of Spain*. New York: Random House, 1964.

Leach, E. R. *Pul Eliya, A Village in Ceylon, A Study of Land Tenure and Kinship*. Cambridge: Cambridge University Press, 1961.

Lee, Shu-ching. "Agrarianism and Social Upheaval in China." *American Journal of Sociology* 56 (May 1951), 511-18.

Leiden, Carl, and Schmitt, Karl M. *The Politics of Violence: Revolution in the Modern World*. Englewood Cliffs, N.J.: Prentice-Hall, 1968.

Leites, Nathan, and Wolf, Charles, Jr. *Rebellion and Authority, An Analytic Essay on Insurgent Conflicts*. Chicago: Markham, 1970.

Lemarchand, René, and Legg, Keith. "Political Clientilism and Development: A Preliminary Analysis." *Comparative Politics* 4 (January 1972), 149-78.

Lerner, Daniel. *The Passing of Traditional Society, Modernizing the Middle East*. New York: The Free Press, 1958.

Lewis, John W. "The Study of Chinese Political Culture." *World Politics* 18 (April 1966), 503-24.

Lewis, Oscar. *Life in a Mexican Village: Tepoztlán Restudied* Urbana, Ill.: University of Illinois Press, 1963.

————. "Peasant Culture in India and Mexico: A Comparative Analysis." In *Village India, Studies in the Little Community*, edited by McKim Marriott. Chicago: University of Chicago Press, 1955.

————. "Some of My Best Friends are Peasants." *Human Organization* 19 (Winter 1960-1961), 178-80.

————. *Tepoztlán, Village in Mexico*. New York: Holt, Rinehart and Winston, 1960.

————. *Village Life in Northern India, Studies in a Delhi Village*. Urbana, Ill.: University of Illinois Press, 1958.

Lijphart, Arend. "Comparative Politics and the Comparative Method." *American Political Science Review* 65 (September 1971), 682-93.

Lord, Peter P. *The Peasantry as an Emerging Political Factor in Mexico, Bolivia, and Venezuela*. Madison: The Land Tenure Center, University of Wisconsin, LTC no. 35, May 1965.

Lutfiyya, Abdulla M. *Baytīn, A Jordanian Village, A Study of Social Institutions and Social Change in a Folk Community*. London: Mouton, 1966.

McAlister, John T., Jr., and Mus, Paul. *The Vietnamese and Their Revolution*. Harper Torchbooks. New York: Harper and Row, 1970.

McColl, Robert W. "A Political Geography of Revolution: China, Vietnam, and Thailand." *The Journal of Conflict Resolution* 11 (June 1967), 153-67.

McCormack, William. "Factionalism in a Mysore Village." In *Leadership and Political Institutions in India*, edited by Richard L. Park and Irene Tinker. Princeton, N.J.: Princeton University Press, 1959.

Majumdar, D. N. *Caste and Communication in an Indian Village*. Bombay: Asia Publishing House, 1958.

Malinowski, B. *The Dynamics of Culture Change: An Inquiry into Race Relations in Africa*. New Haven: Yale University Press, 1945.

Malthus, Thomas. "A Summary View of the Principle of Population." In *On Population, Three Essays, Thomas Malthus, Julian Huxley, Frederick Osborn*. A Mentor Book. New York: The New American Library, 1960.

Mamdani, Mahmood. *The Myth of Population Control:*

Family, Caste, and Class in an Indian Village. New York: Monthly Review Press, 1972.

Mangin, William, ed. *Peasants in Cities, Readings in the Anthropology of Urbanization.* Boston: Houghton Mifflin, 1970.

Mao Tse-tung. *Mind the Living Conditions of the Masses and Attend to the Methods of Work.* Peking: Foreign Languages Press, 1953.

————. *Report of an Investigation into the Peasant Movement in Hunan.* Peking: Foreign Languages Press, 1953.

March, James G., and Simon, Herbert A. *Organizations.* New York: Wiley, 1958.

Marriot, McKim. "Technological Change in Overdeveloped Rural Areas." *Economic Development and Cultural Change* 1 (1952-53), 261-72.

Mathiason, John R., and Powell, John D. "Participation and Efficacy: Aspects of Peasant Involvement in Political Mobilization." Revised version of paper presented at the Annual Meeting of the American Political Science Association, September 4, 1969.

Mercier Vega, Luis. *Guerrillas in Latin America, The Technique of the Counter-State.* New York: Frederick A. Praeger, 1969.

Migdal, Joel S. "Peasants in a Shrinking World." Unpublished Ph.D. Dissertation, Harvard University, 1972.

Mintz, Sidney W., and Wolf, Eric R. "An Analysis of Ritual Co-Parenthood (Compadrazgo)." In *Peasant Society, A Reader*, edited by Jack M. Potter, May N. Diaz, and George M. Foster. Boston: Little, Brown, 1966.

Moerman, Michael. *Agricultural Change and Peasant Choice in a Thai Village.* Berkeley: University of California Press, 1968.

Montgomery, John D. "Allocation of Authority in Land Reform Programs: A Comparative Study of Administrative Processes and Outputs." *Administrative Science Quarterly* 17 (March 1972), 62-75.

Moore, Barrington, Jr. *Social Origins of Dictatorship and Democracy, Lord and Peasant in the Making of the Modern World*. Boston: Beacon Press, 1966.

Mosca, Gaetano. *The Ruling Class*. New York: McGraw-Hill, 1939.

Myers, Ramon H. *The Chinese Peasant Economy, Agricultural Development in Hopei and Shantung, 1890-1949*. Cambridge, Mass.: Harvard University Press, 1970.

Myrdal, Jan. *Report from a Chinese Village*. New York: Pantheon, 1965.

Nash, Manning. "Political Relations in Guatemala." *Social and Economic Studies* 7 (March 1958), 65-75.

———. *Primitive and Peasant Economic Systems*. San Francisco: Chandler Publishing, 1966.

Neher, Philip A. "Peasants, Procreation, and Pensions." *American Economic Review* 61 (June 1971), 380-389.

Nicholas, Ralph W. "Factions: A Comparative Analysis." In *Political Systems and the Distribution of Power*, edited by Michael Benton. New York: Barnes and Noble, 1965.

———. "Rules, Resources, and Political Activity." In *Local-Level Politics, Social and Cultural Perspectives*, edited by Marc J. Swartz. Chicago: Aldine, 1968.

Nurge, Ethel. *Life in a Leyte Village*. Seattle: University of Washington Press, 1965.

Nydegger, William F. and Corinne. *Tarong: An Ilocos Barrio in the Philippines*. New York: John Wiley and Sons, 1966.

Nye, Joseph S. "Corruption and Political Development: A Cost-Benefit Analysis." *American Political Science Review* 61 (June 1967), 417-27.

Olson, Mancur, Jr. *The Logic of Collective Action: Public Goods and the Theory of Groups*. Cambridge, Mass.: Harvard University Press, 1965.

Orenstein, Henry. *Gaon, Conflict and Cohesion in an Indian Village*. Princeton, N.J.: Princeton University Press, 1965.

Patai, Raphael. "On Culture Contact and its Working in Modern Palestine." *American Anthropologist*, new ser. 49

289

(October 1947). No. 67 of the Titles in the Memoir Series of the American Anthropological Association.

Pearse, Andrew. "Agrarian Change Trends in Latin America." *Latin American Research Review* 1 (Summer 1966), 45-69.

Pearse, Andrew. "Metropolis and Peasant: The Expansion of the Urban-Industrial Complex and the Changing Rural Structure." In *Peasants and Peasant Societies*, edited by Teodor Shanin. Baltimore, Penguin Books, 1971.

———. "Peasants and Revolution: The Case of Bolivia: Part II." *Economy and Society* 1 (August 1972), 399-424.

The Peasant: A Symposium Concerning the Peasant Way and View of Life, edited by F. G. Friedmann. Mimeo.

Peter, Hollis W., ed. *Comparative Theories of Social Change*. Ann Arbor, Mich.: Foundation for Research on Human Behavior, 1966.

Pierce, Joe E. *Life in a Turkish Village*. New York: Holt, Rinehart and Winston, 1964.

Pike, Douglas. *Viet Cong, The Organization and Techniques of the National Liberation Front of South Vietnam*. Cambridge, Mass.: The M.I.T. Press, 1966.

Popkin, Samuel L. "South Vietnam." In *Conflict in World Politics*, edited by Steven L. Spiegel and Kenneth N. Waltz. Cambridge, Mass.: Winthrop, 1971.

Potter, Jack M. *Capitalism and the Chinese Peasant, Social and Economic Change in a Hong Kong Village*. Berkeley: University of California Press, 1968.

Powell, John Duncan. "Peasant Society and Clientilist Politics." *American Political Science Review* 64 (June 1970), 411-25.

———. *Political Mobilization of the Venezuelan Peasant*. Cambridge, Mass.: Harvard University Press, 1971.

———. "Venezuelan Agrarian Problems in Comparative Perspective." *Comparative Studies in Society and History* 13 (July 1971), 282-300.

———. "Venezuela: The Peasant Union Movement." In *Latin American Peasant Movements*, edited by Henry

A. Landsberger. Ithaca, N.Y.: Cornell University Press, 1969.

Power, Eileen. *The Wool Trade in English Medieval History.* New York: Oxford University Press, 1941.

Presthus, Robert. *The Organizational Society, An Analysis and a Theory.* New York: Alfred A. Knopf, 1962.

Pye, Lucian W. *Politics, Personality, and Nation Building, Burma's Search for Identity.* New Haven: Yale University Press, 1962.

Race, Jeffrey. *War Comes to Long An, Revolutionary Conflict in a Vietnamese Province.* Berkeley: University of California Press, 1972.

Ranga, N. G. *Credo of World Peasantry.* Andhra, India: Indian Peasants' Institute, 1957.

Redfield, Robert. *A Village That Chose Progress.* Phoenix Books. Chicago: The University of Chicago Press, 1962.

————. *Peasant Society and Culture. Phoenix Books.* Chicago: The University of Chicago Press, 1960.

————. "The Social Organization of Tradition." *The Far Eastern Quarterly* 15 (November 1955), 13-21.

————, and Villa Rojas, Alfonso. *Chan Kom, A Maya Village.* Phoenix Books. Chicago: University of Chicago Press, 1962.

Reichel-Dolmatoff, Gerardo and Alicia. *The People of Aritama, The Cultural Personality of a Colombian Mestizo Village.* London: Routledge and Kegan Paul, 1961.

Rhodes, Robert I. "The Disguised Conservatism in Evolutionary Development Theory." *Science and Society* 32 (Fall 1969), 383-412.

Robinson, Warren C. "The Economies of Work Sharing in Peasant Agriculture." *Economic Development and Cultural Change* 20 (October 1971), 131-41.

Rogers, Everett M. *Modernization Among Peasants: The Impact of Communication.* New York: Holt, Rinehart, 1969.

Rojas Gonzalez, Francisco. "La Institución del Compadrazgo entre los Indios de México." *Revista Mexicara de Sociología* 5 (1943), 201-13 (Spanish).

291

Rotberg, Robert I. *Haiti, The Politics of Squalor*. Boston: Houghton Mifflin, 1971.

Ryan, Bryce. *Sinhalese Village*. Coral Gables, Fla.: University of Miami Press, 1958.

Saenz, Carlos Joaquim. "Population Growth, Economic Progress and Opportunities on the Land: The Case of Costa Rica." Madison: The Land Tenure Center, University of Wisconsin, R.P. no. 47, June 1972.

Sansom, Robert L. *The Economics of Insurgency in the Mekong Delta of Vietnam*. Cambridge, Mass.: The M.I.T. Press, 1970.

Schultz, Theodor W. *The Economic Organization of Agriculture*. New York: McGraw-Hill, 1953.

―――. *Transforming Traditional Agriculture*. New Haven: Yale University Press, 1964.

Scobie, James R. *Revolution on the Pampas, A Social History of Argentine Wheat, 1860-1910*. Austin: University of Texas Press, 1964.

Scott, James C. "Corruption, Machine Politics, and Political Change." *American Political Science Review* 63 (December 1969), 1142-58.

―――. "Patron-Client Politics and Political Change." Paper presented at the American Political Science Association meetings, Los Angeles, Calif., September 8-12, 1970.

Selden, Mark. "Revolution and Third World Development, People's War and the Transformation of Peasant Society." In *National Liberation, Revolution in the Third World*, edited by Norman Miller and Roderick Aya. New York: The Free Press, 1971.

―――. "The Yenan Legacy: The Mass Line." In *Chinese Communist Politics in Action*, edited by A. Doak Barnett. Seattle: University of Washington Press, 1969.

Shanin, Teodor. "Peasantry as a Political Factor." In *Peasants and Peasant Societies*, edited by Shanin. Baltimore: Penguin Books, 1971.

Sharp, Lauriston; Hauck, Hazel M.; Janlekha, Kamol; and Textor, Robert B. *Siamese Rice Village, A Preliminary*

Study of Bang Chan 1948-1949. Bangkok, Thailand: Cornell Research Center, 1953.

Silverman, Sydel F. "Agricultural Organization, Social Structure, and Values in Italy: Amoral Familism Reconsidered." *American Anthropologist* 70 (February 1968), 1-20.

————. " 'Exploitation' in Rural Central Italy: Structure and Ideology in Stratification Study." *Comparative Studies in Society and History* 12 (July 1970), 327-39.

Silvert, Kalman H. *Man's Power, A Biased Guide to Political Thought and Action*. New York: The Viking Press, 1970.

Sivertsen, Dagfinn. *When Caste Barriers Fall, A Study of Social and Economic Change in a South Indian Village*. Norway: George Allen and Unwin, 1963.

Skinner, G. William. "Chinese Peasants and the Closed Community: An Open and Shut Case." *Comparative Studies in Society and History* 13 (July 1971), 270-81.

————. "Marketing and Social Structure in Rural China." *The Journal of Asian Studies* 24. Part I (November 1964), 3-43; Part II (February 1965), 195-228; Part III (May 1965), 363-99.

Smelser, Neil J. *Theory of Collective Behavior*. New York: The Free Press, 1962.

Snyder, Joan. "The Changing Context of an Andean Community." In *Cultural Stability and Cultural Change*, edited by Verne F. Ray. Proceedings of the 1957 Annual Spring Meeting of the American Ethnological Society. Seattle, Wash.: American Ethnological Society, 1957.

Srinivas, M. N. "The Social System of a Mysore Village." In *Village India, Studies in the Little Community*, edited by McKim Marriott. Chicago: University of Chicago Press, 1955.

Stein, William W. *Hualcan: Life in the Highlands of Peru*. Ithaca, N.Y.: Cornell University Press, 1961.

————. "Outside Contact and Cultural Stability in a Peruvian Highland Village." In *Cultural Stability and Cultural*

293

Change, edited by Verne F. Ray. Proceedings of the 1957 Annual Spring Meeting of the American Ethnological Society. Seattle, Wash.: American Ethnological Society, 1957.

Stinchcombe, Arthur L. "Agricultural Enterprise and Rural Class Relations," *The American Journal of Sociology* 67 (September 1961), 165-176.

Stirling, Paul. *Turkish Village*. London: Weidenfeld and Nicolson, 1965.

Stone, Lawrence. *The Crisis of the Aristocracy, 1558-1641*. Oxford: Clarendon Press, 1965.

Tannenbaum, Frank. *Ten Keys to Latin America*. New York: Alfred A. Knopf, 1962.

Tanter, Raymond, and Midlarsky, Manus. "A Theory of Revolution." *The Journal of Conflict Resolution* 11 (September 1967), 264-80.

Tax, Sol. *Penny Capitalism, A Guatemalan Indian Economy*. Chicago: University of Chicago Press, 1963.

Tilly, Charles. *The Vendée*. Science Editions. New York: John Wiley and Sons, 1967.

Tullis, F. Lamond. *Lord and Peasant in Peru, A Paradigm of Political and Social Change*. Cambridge, Mass.: Harvard University Press, 1970.

Tumin, Melvin M. *Caste in a Peasant Society: A Case Study in the Dynamics of Caste*. Princeton, N.J.: Princeton University Press, 1952.

United Nations. *Statistical Yearbook, 1971*. New York: 1972.

Wagley, Charles. "The Peasant." In *Continuity and Change in Latin America*, edited by John J. Johnson. Stanford: Stanford University Press, 1964.

Warriner, Doreen. *Economics of Peasant Farming*. 2d ed. London: Frank Cass, 1964.

Whitaker, C. S. "A Dysrhythmic Process of Political Change." *World Politics* 19 (January 1967), 190-217.

White, Robert A., S.J. "Mexico: The Zapata Movement and the Revolution." In *Latin American Peasant Movements*, edited by Henry A. Landsberger. Ithaca, N.Y.: Cornell University Press, 1969.

Whittlesey, Derwett. "Major Agricultural Regions of the Earth." In *Readings in Cultural Geography*, edited by Philip L. Wagner and Marvin W. Mikesell. Chicago: University of Chicago Press, 1962.

Whyte, William F., and Williams, Lawrence K. *Towards an Integrated Theory of Development: Economic and Noneconomic Variables in Rural Development*. Ithaca, N.Y.: New York State School of Industrial and Labor Relations, Cornell University, 1968.

Willems, Emilio. *Buzios Island, A Caiçara Community in Southern Brazil*. Locust Valley, N.Y.: J. J. Augustin, 1952.

Williams, Eric. *Capitalism and Slavery*. London: Andre Deutsch, 1964.

Wilson, Peter J. *A Malay Village and Malaysia, Social Values and Rural Development*. New Haven: HRAF Press, 1967.

Wiser, William H. and Charlotte Viall. *Behind Mud Walls, 1930-1960*. Berkeley: University of California Press, 1964.

Wolf, Charles, Jr. "Insurgency and Counterinsurgency: New Myths and Old Realities." *Yale Review* 56 (Winter 1967), 225-41.

―――. "United States Interests in Asia." Rand Collection, January 1966.

―――. *United States Policy and the Third World*. Boston: Little, Brown, 1967.

Wolf, Eric R. "Aspects of Group Relations in a Complex Society: Mexico." *American Anthropologist* 58 (December 1956), 1065-78.

―――. "Closed Corporate Communities in Mesoamerica and Central Java." *Southwestern Journal of Anthropology* 13 (Spring 1957), 1-18.

―――. "Peasant Rebellion and Revolution." In *National Liberation, Revolution in the Third World*, edited by Norman Miller and Roderick Aya. New York: The Free Press, 1971.

Wolf, Eric R. *Peasants*. Englewood Cliffs, N.J.: Prentince-Hall, 1966.

———. *Peasant Wars of the Twentieth Century*. New York: Harper and Row, 1969.

———. "The Social Organization of Mecca and the Origins of Islam." *Southwestern Journal of Anthropology* 7 (Winter 1951), 329-56.

———. "Types of Latin American Peasantry: A Preliminary Analysis." *American Anthropologist* 57 (June 1955), 452-71.

Womack, John, Jr. *Zapata and the Mexican Revolution*. New York: Alfred A. Knopf, 1969.

Wyon, John B., and Gordon, John E. *The Khanna Study, Population Problems in the Rural Punjab*. Cambridge, Mass.: Harvard University Press, 1971.

Yang, Ch'ing-K'un. *A Chinese Village and its Early Change Under Communism*. Cambridge, Mass.: Massachusetts Institute of Technology Center for International Studies, 1945.

Yang, Martin C. *A Chinese Village: Taitou, Shantung Province*. New York: Columbia University Press, 1945.

Yasa, Ibrahim. *Hasanoğlan, Socio-Economic Structure of a Turkish Village*. Ankara, Turkey: Yeni Matbaa, Public Administration Institute for Turkey and the Middle East, 1957.

Young, Frank W. and Ruth C. "Two Determinants of Community Reaction to Industrialization in Rural Mexico." *Economic Development and Cultural Change* 8 (April 1960), 257-64.

Zeitlin, Maurice. *Revolutionary Politics and the Cuban Working Class*. Princeton, N.J.: Princeton University Press, 1967.

Library of Congress Cataloging in Publication Data

Migdal, Joel S
  Peasants, politics, and revolution.

  Bibliography: p.
  1. Underdeveloped areas—Peasantry. 2. Underdeveloped areas
—Political participation. I. Title.
HN980.M43   301.44'43   74-2972
ISBN 0-691-07567-0